Pro Wicket

■ ■ ■

Karthik Gurumurthy

Apress®

Pro Wicket

Copyright © 2006 by Karthik Gurumurthy

ISBN 978-1-4842-2096-2   ISBN 978-1-4302-0228-8   (eBook)

DOI 10.1007/978-1-4302-0228-8

9 8 7 6 5 4 3 2 1

Library of Congress Cataloging-in-Publication data is available upon request.

Lead Editor: Steve Anglin
Technical Reviewers: David Heffelfinger, Igor Vaynberg
Editorial Board: Steve Anglin, Ewan Buckingham, Gary Cornell, Jason Gilmore, Jonathan Gennick,
    Jonathan Hassell, James Huddleston, Chris Mills, Matthew Moodie, Dominic Shakeshaft,
    Jim Sumser, Keir Thomas, Matt Wade
Project Manager: Kylie Johnston
Copy Edit Manager: Nicole LeClerc
Copy Editor: Ami Knox
Assistant Production Director: Kari Brooks-Copony
Production Editor: Laura Esterman
Compositor: Dina Quan
Proofreader: Lori Bring
Indexers: Toma Mulligan, Carol Burbo
Cover Designer: Kurt Krames
Manufacturing Director: Tom Debolski

Distributed to the book trade worldwide by Springer-Verlag New York, Inc., 233 Spring Street, 6th Floor, New York, NY 10013. Phone 1-800-SPRINGER, fax 201-348-4505, e-mail orders-ny@springer-sbm.com, or visit http://www.springeronline.com.

For information on translations, please contact Apress directly at 2560 Ninth Street, Suite 219, Berkeley, CA 94710. Phone 510-549-5930, fax 510-549-5939, e-mail info@apress.com, or visit http://www.apress.com.

The source code for this book is available to readers at http://www.apress.com in the Source Code section.

To Amma and Appa for everything!
And to my wonderful wife, Gayathri

Contents at a Glance

Contents

About the Author

 **KARTHIK GURUMURTHY** has been associated with the IT industry for more than six years now and has employed several open-source libraries to address business problems. Karthik's involvement with open source also includes contribution to a popular open-source project: XDoclet2. He has been having a great time with Wicket since day one of adoption and would like to let others know how Wicket succeeds in bringing back the fun that has been missing in the Java web development space. He also contributed to the Wicket project through the Wicket-Spring integration module using Jakarta Commons attributes and testing out the beta releases and reporting any bugs in the process.

About the Technical Reviewers

■**DAVID HEFFELFINGER** has been developing software professionally since 1995, and he has been using Java as his primary programming language since 1996. He has worked on many large-scale projects for several clients including Freddie Mac, Fannie Mae, and the US Department of Defense. He has a master's degree in software engineering from Southern Methodist University. David is editor in chief of Ensode.net (http://www.ensode.net), a web site about Java, Linux, and other technology topics.

 ■**IGOR VAYNBERG** is a senior software engineer at TeachScape, Inc., residing in Sacramento, California. His liking for computers was sparked when he received a Sinclair Z80 for his birthday at the age of ten. Since then he has worked with companies both large and small building modular multitiered web applications. Igor's main interest is finding ways to simplify development of complex user interfaces for the web tier. Igor is a committer for the Wicket framework, the aim of which is to simplify the programming model as well as reintroduce OOP to the web UI tier. In his AFK time, Igor enjoys spending time with his beautiful wife and children. You can reach him at igor.vaynberg@gmail.com.

Acknowledgments

Authoring a book, like any other project, is a team effort. I'm indebted to everyone who was involved in this project. First and foremost, I would like to thank Steve Anglin at Apress for providing me with the opportunity to write this book. Ami Knox deserves special mention for her stupendous work during the copy editing process and so does Senior Project Manager Kylie Johnston for coordinating the efforts. My heartfelt thanks to Laura Esterman and all others who were involved during the production.

My utmost thanks to the reviewers David Heffelfinger and Wicket developer Igor Vaynberg for their invaluable inputs. Anybody who is a part of the Wicket mailing list knows what Igor means to the Wicket community. I can say without any hesitation that this book would not exist without Igor's encouragement and expert advice. Thank you Igor! Many thanks to all the core Wicket developers for creating, maintaining, and adding new features to this wonderful framework and for patiently answering all the questions thrown at you on the mailing list.

I always used to wonder why authors make it a point to thank their better half on finishing a book. Now I know! Gayathri, your belief in this project never ceases to amaze me despite your vastly different "management" background. It's probably your faith and unflinching support that kept me afloat through the pain and joy of the book writing process. I would also like to thank my in-laws and other well-wishers.

And then I'm really not sure how I can express my gratitude to the two souls who not only brought me into this world, but also taught me, in addition to other things, that perseverance can go a long way in realizing your dreams. I'm indebted to you forever—Amma and Appa!

Introduction

Welcome to Wicket, an open source, lightweight, component-based Java web framework that brings the Java Swing event-based programming model to web development. Component-based web frameworks are being touted as the future of Java web development, and Wicket is easily one of the leading implementations in this area. Wicket strives for a clean separation of the roles of HTML page designer and Java developer by supporting plain-vanilla HTML templates that can be mocked up, previewed, and later revised using standard WYSIWYG HTML design tools.

Wicket counters the statelessness of HTTP by providing stateful components, thereby improving productivity. If you are looking to hone your object-oriented programming skills, Wicket fits like a glove in that respect as well, since it has an architecture and rich component suite that encourages clean object-oriented design.

Pro Wicket aims to get you up and running quickly with this framework. You will learn how to configure Wicket and then gradually gain exposure to the "Wicket way" of addressing web development requirements. You will learn about important techniques of working with Wicket through simple examples. People have come to expect a few things from a modern web framework—Spring Framework integration and baked-in Ajax support are probably at the top of that list. I have taken care to address these aspects of Wicket in the book. You will learn to integrate Wicket and EJB 3 API using the services of Spring 2.0, for example. Also included is a separate chapter dedicated to Wicket's integration with Ajax.

I have been having a great time with Wicket since day one of my adoption of this technology. I wrote this book to let you know how Wicket, in addition to being a robust web application framework, succeeds in bringing back the fun that has been missing in the Java web development space.

Who This Book Is For

This book is for anyone who wants to learn how to develop J2EE-based web applications using Wicket. This book assumes that the reader understands the Java language constructs and its APIs and has a basic knowledge of HTML and CSS. The book does not assume any prior knowledge of the Wicket framework. Even though Wicket does not require Java 5, a basic understanding of the Java 5 Annotation feature would also help in understanding some of the nifty framework features. That said, there are a couple of chapters that deal with Wicket's integration with other frameworks and technologies like Spring, Velocity, Ajax, and EJB 3. A quick introduction to these topics has been included in the related chapters. If that does not suffice, you could easily acquire the required familiarity with the aforementioned subjects by reading some basic introductory articles that are available on the Internet. References are provided as appropriate throughout the book.

If you are curious how Wicket stacks up against other component-based web development frameworks, this book will certainly help you determine that.

This book should also serve as a good guide to understanding the Wicket way of addressing various aspects of J2EE web development.

How This Book Is Structured

Pro Wicket gradually builds upon the concepts and examples introduced in preceding chapters, and therefore, in order to derive the most out of this book, it is better read cover to cover. Use this chapter outline for a quick overview of what you will find inside.

- Chapter 1, "Wicket: The First Steps," helps you to quickly get started with Wicket development. You will develop your first web page using Wicket and then build a few more to get introduced to some of the core Wicket concepts like Wicket models.

- Chapter 2, "Validation with Wicket," shows how you can apply Wicket's built-in validation support to your application pages. Here you will also learn about Wicket's converters.

- Chapter 3, "Developing a Simple Application," introduces several important Wicket concepts like the global application object, session, etc., through development of a simple application. You cannot afford to skip this, as all the remaining chapters use the sample application that you will be developing in this chapter. It discusses several important concepts central to Wicket such as behaviors, different flavors of Wicket models, and support for authorization and authentication.

- Chapter 4, "Providing a Common Layout to Wicket Pages," goes into details of the page layout support in Wicket. In this chapter, you will learn to use Wicket's Border components and markup inheritance to provide a consistent layout to your application pages.

- Chapter 5, "Integration with Other Frameworks," first discusses how Wicket integrates with view technologies like Velocity and FreeMarker. Then it deals with a topic I'm sure you must be really curious about: Wicket's integration with the Spring Framework. Such a chapter cannot be complete without a discussion on EJB 3—you will learn how to specifically integrate Hibernate's EJB 3 implementation with Wicket using Spring 2.0.

- Chapter 6, "Localization Support," outlines and explains Wicket's support for localization. Localized text can be specified in resources external to the pages, and this chapter also explains the search mechanism employed by Wicket when looking for localized content. You will also learn about a couple of model classes that offer help with localization.

- Chapter 7, "Custom Wicket Components and Wicket Extensions," introduces readers to an area where Wicket really shines—writing custom components. You will also put to use some of the existing Wicket-Extensions components in this chapter.

- Chapter 8, "Wicket and Ajax," discusses Wicket's integration with Ajax. You will learn that, to a great extent, you could Ajax-ify Wicket web applications without writing a single line of JavaScript code. Wicket models Ajax support through a concept of behaviors, and you will be introduced to several flavors of built-in Ajax behavior in this chapter.

- Chapter 9, "Additional Wicket Topics," starts off with a discussion on Wicket's built-in support for unit testing. Next, you will get a sneak peek into the features that will be part of the next version of Wicket that is currently under development.

Prerequisites

This book does not assume any prior knowledge of Wicket. The book covers Wicket integration with frameworks like Spring, EJB 3, Velocity, and FreeMarker. A basic introduction to these third-party libraries and appropriate references are included as necessary. The book also includes a chapter on Wicket's support for Ajax. A basic idea of Ajax is enough to understand the chapter, as Wicket abstracts most of the JavaScript code from the users of the framework. The required third-party libraries are also packaged along with the source code to make it easier for you to play around with the examples. A basic knowledge of the Java 5 Annotation feature would help you in understanding a couple of nifty Wicket features.

Downloading the Code

The source code for this book is available to readers at http://www.apress.com in the Source Code section. Please feel free to visit the Apress web site and download all the code there. You can also check for errata and find related titles from Apress.

Contacting the Author

Karthik Gurumurthy can be contacted at karthik.guru@gmail.com. The author also maintains a blog at http://www.jroller.com/page/karthikg.

CHAPTER 1

■ ■ ■

Wicket: The First Steps

In this chapter, after a quick introduction to Wicket, you will learn to obtain and set up the requisite software for Wicket-based web development. Then you will learn to develop interactive web pages using Wicket. Along the way, you will be introduced to some key Wicket concepts.

What Is Wicket?

Wicket is a *component-oriented* Java web application framework. It's very different from *action-/request-based* frameworks like Struts, WebWork, or Spring MVC where form submission ultimately translates to a single action. In Wicket, a user action typically triggers an event on one of the form components, which in turn responds to the event through strongly typed event listeners. Some of the other frameworks that fall in this category are Tapestry, JSF, and ASP.NET. Essentially, frameworks like Struts gave birth to a concept of web-MVC that comprises coarse-grained actions—in contrast to the fine-grained actions we developers are so used to when programming desktop applications. Component-oriented frameworks such as Wicket bring this more familiar programming experience to the Web.

Obtaining and Setting Up Wicket

Wicket relies on the Java servlet specification and accordingly requires a servlet container that implements the specification (servlet specification 2.3 and above) in order to run Wicket-based web applications. Jetty (http://jetty.mortbay.org) is a popular, open-source implementation of the servlet specification and is a good fit for developing Wicket applications.

The Wicket core classes have minimal dependencies on external libraries. But downloading the jar files and setting up a development environment on your own does require some time. In order to get you quickly started, Wicket provides for a "Quick Start" project. The details can be found here: http://wicket.sourceforge.net/wicket-quickstart/. Download the latest project files through the "Download" link provided on the page. Having obtained the project file, extract it to a folder on the file system. Rename the folder to which you extracted the distribution to your required project name. As you can see in Figure 1-1, I've renamed the directory on my system to Beginning Wicket.

Figure 1-1. *Extract the contents of the Wicket Quick Start distribution to a file system folder.*

Setting up Wicket Quick Start to work with an IDE like Eclipse is quite straightforward. It is assumed that you have Eclipse (3.0 and above) and Java (1.4 and above) installed on your machine.

Eclipse Development Environment Setup Using Quick Start

The steps for setting up Eclipse with Wicket Quick Start are as follows:

1. Copy the files `eclipse-classpath.xml` and `.project` over to the project folder that you just created. These files are available in the directory `src\main\resources` under your project folder.

2. Create an Eclipse Java project, specifying you want it created from an existing source with the directory pointing to the one that you created earlier (the `Beginning Wicket` folder in this example, as shown in Figure 1-2). Accept the default values for other options and click Finish. This is all you require to start working with Wicket.

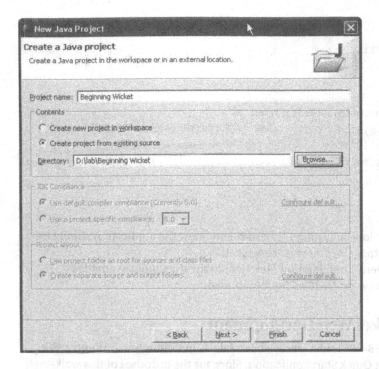

Figure 1-2. *An Eclipse Java project pointing to the folder previously created*

Running the Application

The Quick Start application ships with an embedded Jetty server. You can start the server by right-clicking the src/main/java directory in the project and selecting the menu commands Run as ➤ Java application. If Eclipse prompts you for a main class, browse to the class named Start. This is all that is needed to kick-start Wicket development.

You can access your first Wicket application by pointing the browser to http://localhost:8081/quickstart.

How to Alter the Jetty Configuration

The Jetty configuration file is located in the project directory src/main/resources/jetty-config.xml.

Notice from the file that Jetty, by default, is configured to start on port 8081. If you want to override the default Jetty settings, this is the file you need to be editing. Next, you will change the default web application context from quickstart to wicket, as demonstrated in Listing 1-1. You will also change the default port from 8081 to 8080.

Listing 1-1. *The Modified jetty-config.xml*

```
    <!--rest snipped for clarity -->

  <Call name="addListener">
    <Arg>
      <New class="org.mortbay.http.SocketListener">
          <Set name="Port"><SystemProperty name="jetty.port" default="8081"/></Set>
    <!--rest snipped for clarity -->
  <Call name="addWebApplication">
    <Arg>/wicket</Arg>
    <Arg>src/webapp</Arg>
  </Call>
```

After making the modifications in Listing 1-1, restart Jetty. Now the application should be accessible through the URL http://localhost:8080/wicket.

For more information on Jetty configuration files, refer to the document available at http://jetty.mortbay.org/jetty/tut/XmlConfiguration.html.

The web.xml for Wicket Web Development

You will find the src/webapp/WEB-INF folder already has a fully functioning web.xml entry. But that corresponds to the default Quick Start application. Since for the purposes of this walk-through you will develop a Wicket application from scratch, replace the existing web.xml content with the one shown in Listing 1-2. This registers the Wicket servlet and maps it to the /helloworld URL pattern.

Listing 1-2. *web.xml*

```
<?xml version="1.0" encoding="UTF-8"?>
<!DOCTYPE web-app PUBLIC "-//Sun Microsystems, Inc.//DTD
Web Application 2.3//EN"
"http://java.sun.com/dtd/web-app_2_3.dtd">
<web-app>
  <display-name>Wicket Shop</display-name>
    <servlet>
        <servlet-name>HelloWorldApplication</servlet-name>
        <servlet-class>wicket.protocol.http.WicketServlet</servlet-class>
        <load-on-startup>1</load-on-startup>
    </servlet>

    <servlet-mapping>
        <servlet-name>HelloWorldApplication</servlet-name>
        <url-pattern>/helloworld/*</url-pattern>
    </servlet-mapping>

</web-app>
```

The URL to access the application would be http://localhost:8080/wicket/helloworld.

Now that you are done with initial configuration, you'll develop a simple application that emulates a basic login use case.

Developing a Simple Sign-in Application

The sign-in application requires a login page that allows you to enter your credentials and then log in. Listing 1-3 represents the template file for one such page.

Listing 1-3. *Login.html*

```html
<html>
  <title>Hello World</title>
  <body>
    <form wicket:id="loginForm">
      User Name  <input type="text" wicket:id="userId"/><br/>
      Password   <input type="password" wicket:id="password"/><br/><hr>
      <input type="submit" value="Login"/>
    </form>
  </body>
</html>
```

Figure 1-3 shows how this looks in the browser.

Figure 1-3. *Login page when previewed on the browser*

Double-click the file, and it will open in your favorite browser. Depending upon where you come from (JSP-based frameworks/Tapestry), it could come as a surprise to be able to open your template in a browser and see it render just fine. It must have been a dream sometime back with JSP-based frameworks, but luckily, it's a reality with Wicket. You would be forced to start a web server at minimum when using a JSP-based framework/JSF for that matter. Note that the template has a few instances of a Wicket-specific attribute named *wicket:id* interspersed here and there (ignored by the browser), but otherwise it is plain vanilla HTML.

Wicket mandates that every HTML template be backed by a corresponding Page class of the same name. This tells you that you need to have Login.java. This is often referred to as a *page-centric* approach to web development. Tapestry falls under the same category as well.

The HTML template needs to be in the same package as the corresponding Page class. An internal Wicket component that is entrusted with the job of locating the HTML markup corresponding to a Page looks for the markup in the same place as the Page class. Wicket allows you to easily customize this default behavior though. All user pages typically extend Wicket's WebPage—a subclass of Wicket's Page class. There needs to be a one-to-one correspondence between the HTML elements with a *wicket:id* attribute and the Page components. The HTML template could in fact be termed as a *view* with the actual component hierarchy being described in the Page class. Wicket components need to be supplied with an id parameter and an IModel implementation during construction (some exceptions will be discussed in the section "How to Specify a CompoundPropertyModel for a Page." The component's id value must match the *wicket:id* attribute value of the template's corresponding HTML element. Essentially, if the template contains an HTML text element with a *wicket:id* value of name, then the corresponding wicket's TextField instance with an id of name needs to be added to the Page class. Wicket supplies components that correspond to basic HTML elements concerned with user interaction. Examples of such elements are HTML input fields of type text, HTML select, HTML link, etc. The corresponding Wicket components would be TextField, DropDownChoice, and Link, respectively.

Wicket Models

Components are closely tied to another important Wicket concept called *models*. In Wicket, a model (an object implementing the IModel interface) acts as the source of data for a component. It needs to be specified when constructing the component (doing a new); some exceptions will be discussed in the section "How to Specify a CompoundPropertyModel for a Page" later. Actually, IModel is a bit of a misnomer: it helps to think about Wicket's IModel hierarchy as model locators. These classes exist to help the components locate your actual model object; i.e., they act as another level of indirection between Wicket components and the "actual" model object. This indirection is of great help when the actual object is not available at the time of component construction and instead needs to be retrieved from somewhere else at runtime. Wicket extracts the value from the model while rendering the corresponding component and sets its value when the containing HTML form is submitted. This is the essence of the Wicket way of doing things. You need to inform a Wicket component of the object it is to read and update.

Wicket could also be classified as an event-driven framework. Wicket HTML components register themselves as listeners (defined through several Wicket listener interfaces) for requests originating from the client browser. For example, Wicket's Form component registers itself as an IFormSubmitListener, while a DropDownChoice implements the IOnChangeListener interface. When a client activity results in some kind of request on a component, Wicket calls the corresponding listener method. For example, on an HTML page submit, a Form component's onSubmit() method gets called, while a change in a drop-down selection results in a call to DropDownChoice.onSelectionChanged. (Actually, whether a change in a drop-down selection should result in a server-side event or not is configurable. We will discuss this in Chapter 3.)

If you want to do something meaningful during Form submit, then you need to override that onSubmit() method in your class. On the click of the Login button, the code in Listing 1-4 prints the user name and the password that was entered.

Listing 1-4. *Login.java*

```
package com.apress.wicketbook.forms;

import wicket.markup.html.WebPage;
import wicket.markup.html.form.Form;
import wicket.markup.html.form.PasswordTextField;
import wicket.markup.html.form.TextField;

public class Login extends WebPage {

    /**
     * Login page constituents are the same as Login.html except that
     * it is made up of equivalent Wicket components
     */

    private TextField userIdField;
    private PasswordTextField passField;
    private Form form;

    public Login(){

        /**
         * The first parameter to all Wicket component constructors is
         * the same as the ID that is used in the template
         */

        userIdField = new TextField("userId", new Model(""));
        passField = new PasswordTextField("password",new Model(""));

        /* Make sure that password field shows up during page re-render **/

        passField.setResetPassword(false);

        form = new LoginForm("loginForm");
        form.add(userIdField);
        form.add(passField);
        add(form);
    }

    // Define your LoginForm and override onSubmit
    class LoginForm extends Form {
        public LoginForm(String id) {
            super(id);
        }
```

```
    @Override
    public void onSubmit() {
        String userId = Login.this.getUserId();
        String password = Login.this.getPassword();
        System.out.println("You entered User id "+  userId +
                " and Password  " + password);
    }
}


/** Helper methods to retrieve the userId and the password **/

protected String getUserId() {
    return userIdField.getModelObjectAsString();
}


protected String getPassword() {
    return passField.getModelObjectAsString();
}

}
```

All Wicket pages extend the WebPage class. There is a one-to-one correspondence between the HTML widgets with a *wicket:id* attribute and the Page components. The HTML template could in fact be termed a *view* with the actual component hierarchy being described in the Page class. Wicket components need to be supplied with an id parameter and an IModel implementation during construction (some exceptions will be discussed in the section "How to Specify a CompoundPropertyModel for a Page"). The model object acts as the source of data for the component. The component's id value must match the wicket:id attribute of the template's corresponding HTML component. Essentially, if the wicket:id of an HTML text element is name, the corresponding Wicket's TextField class with an ID of name needs to be added to the Page class. When a page is requested, Wicket knows the HTML template it maps to (it looks for a template whose name is the same as the Page class with an .html extension in a folder location that mimics the Page class package). During the page render phase, Wicket does the following:

1. It kicks off the page rendering process by calling the Page.render() method.

2. The Page locates the corresponding markup template and begins iterating over the HTML tags, converting them into an internal Java representation in the process.

3. If a tag without *wicket:id* is found, it is rendered as is.

4. If a tag with *wicket:id* is found, the corresponding Wicket component in the Page is located, and the rendering is delegated to the component.

5. The Page instance is then stored in an internal store called PageMap. Wicket maintains one PageMap per user session.

The following illustrates this HTML widgets–Page components correspondence:

```
Login.html                          <=>        Login.java
<html>                              <=>        wicket.markup.html.WebPage
 |                                               |
 |_<form wicket:id="loginForm">     <=>          |_ LoginForm("loginForm")
   |                                              |
   |_ <input type="text"            <=>          |_ TextField("userId")
   |     wicket:id="userId"/>                     |
   |                                              |
   |_ <input type="password"        <=>          |_ PasswordTextField("password")
         wicket:id="password"/>
```

EXPLICIT COMPONENT HIERARCHY SPECIFICATION

In Wicket, the component hierarchy is specified explicitly through Java code—which allows you to modularize code and reuse components via all the standard abstraction features of a modern object-oriented language. This is quite different from other frameworks like Tapestry, wherein the page components are typically specified in an XML page specification file listing the components used in the page. (Tapestry 4 makes even this page specification optional.)

It's always good to have the application pages extend from a base page class. One of the reasons to do so is that functionality common to all actions can be placed in the base class. Let's define an AppBasePage that all pages will extend, as shown in Listing 1-5. It currently does nothing. Set AppBasePage as Login page's superclass.

Listing 1-5. *AppBasePage.java*

```java
public class AppBasePage extends WebPage {
  public AppBasePage(){
    super();
  }
}
```

You can liken Wicket development to Swing development. A Swing application will typically have a main class that kicks off the application. Wicket also has one. A class that extends WebApplication informs Wicket of the home page that users first see when they access the application. The Application class may specify other Wicket page classes that have special meaning to an application (e.g., error display pages). The Application class in Listing 1-6 identifies the home page.

Listing 1-6. *HelloWorldApplication.java*

```java
package com.apress.wicketbook.forms;

import wicket.protocol.http.WebApplication;

public class HelloWorldApplication extends WebApplication {

    public HelloWorldApplication(){}

    public Class getHomePage(){
      return Login.class;
    }

}
```

Now that you are done registering the web application main class, start Tomcat and see whether the application starts up:

Jetty/Eclipse Console on Startup

```
wicket.WicketRuntimeException: servlet init param [applicationClassName]
is missing. If you are trying to use your own
implementation of IWebApplicationFactory and get this message then the
servlet init param [applicationFactoryClassName] is missing
  at wicket.protocol.http.ContextParamWebApplicationFactory.createApplication
(ContextParamWebApplicationFactory.java:44)
  at wicket.protocol.http.WicketServlet.init(WicketServlet.java:269)
  at javax.servlet.GenericServlet.init(GenericServlet.java:168)
```

The Eclipse console seems to suggest otherwise and for a good reason. The stack trace seems to reveal that a Wicket class named ContextParamWebApplicationFactory failed to create the WebApplication class in the first place! Note that the factory class implements the IWebApplicationFactory interface.

SPECIFYING IWEBAPPLICATIONFACTORY IMPLEMENTATION

WicketServlet expects to be supplied with an IWebApplicationFactory implementation in order to delegate the responsibility of creating the WebApplication class. A factory implementation could be specified as a servlet initialization parameter in web.xml against the key application➡ FactoryClassName. In the absence of such an entry, WicketServlet uses ContextParamWeb➡ ApplicationFactory by default. As the name suggests, this class looks up a servlet context parameter to determine the WebApplication class name. The expected web.xml param-name in this case is applicationClassName. ContextParamWebApplicationFactory works perfectly for majority of the cases. But there is at least one scenario that requires a different implementation be specified, and we will discuss that in Chapter 5.

Let's specify this important piece of information in the web.xml file as an initial parameter to WicketServlet. Listing 1-7 presents the modified web.xml.

Listing 1-7. *web.xml Modified to Specify the Application Class Name*

```xml
<?xml version="1.0" encoding="UTF-8"?>
<!DOCTYPE web-app PUBLIC "-//Sun Microsystems, Inc.
  //DTD Web Application 2.3//EN"
  "http://java.sun.com/dtd/web-app_2_3.dtd">
<web-app>
  <display-name>Wicket Shop</display-name>
    <servlet>
        <servlet-name>HelloWorldApplication</servlet-name>
        <servlet-class>wicket.protocol.http.WicketServlet</servlet-class>

        <!-- HelloWorldApplication is the WebApplication class -->
        <init-param>
          <param-name>applicationClassName</param-name>
            <param-value>com.apress.wicketbook.forms.HelloWorldApplication
          </param-value>
        </init-param>

        <load-on-startup>1</load-on-startup>
    </servlet>

    <servlet-mapping>
        <servlet-name>HelloWorldApplication</servlet-name>
        <url-pattern>/helloworld/*</url-pattern>
    </servlet-mapping>

</web-app>
```

Now start Tomcat and verify that things are OK:

Jetty/Eclipse Console After Specifying the applicationClassName Parameter

```
01:49:29.140 INFO
[main] wicket.protocol.http.WicketServlet
.init(WicketServlet.java:280)
>13> WicketServlet
loaded application HelloWorldApplication via
wicket.protocol.http.ContextParamWebApplicationFactory
factory
01:49:29.140 INFO   [main] wicket.Application.configure
(Application.java:326) >17>
You are in DEVELOPMENT mode
```

```
INFO  - Container                - Started WebApplicationContext[/wicket,/wicket]
INFO  - SocketListener           - Started SocketListener on 0.0.0.0:7000
INFO  - Container                - Started org.mortbay.jetty.Server@1c0ec97
```

Congratulations! Your first Wicket web application is up and running!

Enter the URL http://localhost:8080/wicket/helloworld in your browser and the login page should show up. Since you have already informed Wicket that the login page is your home page, it will render it by default.

Just to make sure that you aren't celebrating too soon, enter **wicket-user** as both user name and password on the login page and click Login. You should see the login and the password you typed in getting printed to the console.

But how did Wicket manage to get to the correct Page class instance to the Form component and then invoke the onSubmit() listener method? You will find out next.

What Happened on Form Submit?

Right-click the login page and select View Source. The actual HTML rendered on the browser looks like this:

```
<html>
  <title>Hello World</title>

  <head>
    <script type="text/javascript"
src="/wicket/helloworld/resources/wicket.markup.html.
WebPage/cookies.js;
jsessionid=15o9ti4t9rn59"></script>
    <script type="text/javascript">
      var pagemapcookie = getWicketCookie('pm-null/wicketHelloWorldApplication');
      if(!pagemapcookie && pagemapcookie != '1')
{setWicketCookie('pm-null/wicketHelloWorldApplication',1);}
      else {document.location.href = '/wicket/helloworld;
jsessionid=15o9ti4t9rn59?wicket:bookmarkablePage=wicket-
0:com.apress.wicketbook.forms.Login';}
    </script>
  </head>

  <body onUnLoad="deleteWicketCookie('pm-null/wicketHelloWorldApplication');">

    <form action="/wicket/helloworld;jsessionid=15o9ti4t9rn59?wicket:interface=:0:
loginForm::IFormSubmitListener" wicket:id="loginForm" method="post"
id="loginForm">
```

```
        <input type="hidden" name="loginForm:hf:0" id="loginForm:hf:0"/>
        User Name   <input value="" type="text" wicket:id="userId" name="userId"/><br/>
        Password    <input value="" type="password" wicket:id="password"
          name="password"/><br/><hr>
        <input type="submit" value="Login"/>
      </form>
    </body>
  </html>
```

The Form's action value is of interest:

- /wicket/helloworld: This ensures the request makes it to the WicketServlet. (Ignore the jsessionid for now.) Then Wicket takes over.

- wicket:interface: See the last entry in this list.

- :0: In the PageMap, this looks for a page instance with ID 0. This is the Login page instance that got instantiated on first access to the Page.

- :loginForm: In the Page in question, find the component with ID loginForm.

- ::IFormSubmitListener: Invoke the callback method specified in the IFormSubmitListener interface (specified by wicket:interface) on that component.

loginForm is a Form instance that indeed implements the IFormSubmitListener interface. Hence this results in a call to the Form.onFormSubmitted() method. onFormSubmitted, in addition to other things, does the following:

1. It converts the request parameters to the appropriate type as indicated by the backing model. We will take a detailed look at Wicket converters in Chapter 2.

2. It validates the Form components that in turn validate its child components.

3. When the child components are found to be valid, it pushes the data from request into the component model.

4. Finally, it calls onSubmit().

Thus, by the time your onSubmit() is called, Wicket makes sure that the model object corresponding to all the nested form components are appropriately updated, and that is when you print out the updated model values. For now, ignore the component validation step. You will get a detailed look at Wicket's validation support in the next chapter.

This is often referred to as a *postback* mechanism, in which the page that renders a form or view also handles user interactions with the rendered screen.

Depending upon your preference, you might not like the fact that Wicket's components are being held as instance variables in the Login class. (In fact, keeping references to components just to get to their request values is considered an *antipattern* in Wicket. It was used only to demonstrate one of the several ways of handling input data in Wicket.) Wouldn't it be good if you could just have the user name and password strings as instance variables and somehow get Wicket to update those variables on form submit? Let's quickly see how that can be achieved through Wicket's PropertyModel, as Listing 1-8 demonstrates.

Listing 1-8. *Login.java*

```java
import wicket.markup.html.WebPage;
import wicket.markup.html.form.Form;
import wicket.markup.html.form.PasswordTextField;
import wicket.markup.html.form.TextField;
import wicket.model.PropertyModel;

public class Login extends AppBasePage {

  private String userId;
  private String password;

  public Login(){

    TextField userIdField = new TextField("userId",
                new PropertyModel(this,"userId"));

    PasswordTextField passField = new PasswordTextField("password",
          new PropertyModel(this, "password"));

    Form form = new LoginForm("loginForm");
    form.add(userIdField);
    form.add(passField);
    add(form);
  }

  class LoginForm extends Form {
    public LoginForm(String id) {
       super(id);
    }

    @Override
    public void onSubmit() {
       String userId = getUserId();
       String password = getPassword();
       System.out.println("You entered User id "+  userId +
                 " and Password  " + password);
    }
  }

  public String getUserId() {
    return userId;
  }
```

```
public String getPassword() {
  return password
}

public void setUserId(String userId) {
  this.userId = userId;
}

public void setPassword(String password) {
  this.password= password;
}
}
```

Make the preceding change to Login.java, access the login page, enter values for the User Name and Password fields, and click Login. You should see the same effect as earlier. Some radical changes have been made to the code though that require some explanation.

This time around, note that you don't retain Wicket components as the properties of the page. You have string variables to capture the form inputs instead. But there is something else that demands attention; take a look at Listing 1-9.

Listing 1-9. *Login Constructor*

```
TextField userIdField = new TextField("userId", new PropertyModel(this,"userId"));
```

You still specify the ID of the component as userId (first argument to the TextField component) as earlier. But instead of a model object, you supply another implementation of Wicket's IModel interface—PropertyModel.

How Does PropertyModel Work?

When you include new PropertyModel(this,"userId"), you inform the TextField component that it needs to use the Login instance (this) as its model (source of data) and that it should access the property userId of the Login instance for *rendering* and *setting* purposes. Wicket employs a mechanism that is very similar to the OGNL expression language (http://www.ognl.org). OGNL expects the presence of getProperty and setProperty methods for expression evaluation, and so does Wicket's implementation. For example, you can access subproperties via reflection using a dotted path notation, which means the property expression loginForm.userId is equivalent to calling getLoginForm().getUserId() on the given model object (loginForm). Also, loginForm.userId=<something> translates to getLoginForm().setUserId(something). (loginForm is an instance of the Login class). In fact, prior to the 1.2 release, Wicket used to employ the services of OGNL, until it was discovered that the latter resulted in limiting Wicket's performance to a considerable extent and was subsequently replaced with an internal implementation.

I like this page-centric approach, but then I like cricket (http://www.cricinfo.com), too. I guess it's a good idea to let you know of some of the "modeling" options that I'm aware of, as I believe that the user is the best judge in such circumstances. Wicket allows you to model your model object as a plain Java object, also known as POJO. (POJO actually stands for Plain Old Java Object.) You can specify a POJO as the backing model for the entire page. Such a model is referred to as a CompoundPropertyModel in Wicket. A Wicket Page class is derived from the Component class and models are applicable to all components. Let's develop another page that allows one to specify personal user details to demonstrate that.

How to Specify a CompoundPropertyModel for a Page

Figure 1-4 shows another not-so-good-looking page that allows the user to enter his or her profile. Remember, the majority of us are Java developers who don't understand HTML! We will leave the job of beautifying the template to the people who do it best—HTML designers. Therein lies the beauty of Wicket. Its design encourages a clean separation of roles of the designer and the back-end developer with a very minimal overlap.

Figure 1-4 shows a simple page that captures user-related information.

Figure 1-4. *UserProfilePage for capturing user-related information*

See Listing 1-10 for the corresponding HTML template code.

Listing 1-10. *UserProfilePage.html*

```html
<html>
  <title>User Profile</title>
  <body>
    <form wicket:id="userProfile">
      User Name <input type="text" wicket:id="name"/><br/>
      Address<input type="text" wicket:id="address"/><br/>
      City <input type="text" wicket:id="city"/><br/>
      Country <select wicket:id="country">
      <!--The markup here is for preview purposes only. Wicket
      replaces this with actual data when rendering the page -->
        <option>India</option>
        <option>USA</option>
        <option>UK</option>
      </select><br/>
      Pin <input type="text" wicket:id="pin"/><br/>
      <hr/>
      <input type="submit" value="Save"/>
    </form>
  </body>
</html>
```

In this case, the POJO UserProfile class (see Listing 1-11) has been designed to hold onto the information supplied in the HTML template.

Listing 1-11. *UserProfile.java*

```java
package com.apress.wicketbook.common;
import java.io.Serializable;

public class UserProfile implements Serializable {

  private String name;
  private String address;
  private String city;
  private String country;
  private int pin;

  public String getAddress() {
    return address;
  }
```

```java
  public void setAddress(String address) {
    this.address = address;
  }

  public String getCity() {
    return city;
  }

  public void setCity(String city) {
    this.city = city;
  }

  public String getCountry() {
    return country;
  }

  public void setCountry(String country) {
    this.country = country;
  }

  public String getName() {
    return name;
  }

  public void setName(String name) {
    this.name = name;
  }

  /*
  * You can return an int!
  */

  public int getPin() {
    return pin;
  }


  public void setPin(int pin) {
    this.pin = pin;
  }

  /* Returns a friendly representation of the UserProfile object */
```

```
public String toString(){
  String result = " Mr " + getName();
  result+= "\n resides at " + getAddress();
  result+= "\n in the city " + getCity();
  result+= "\n having Pin Code " + getPin();
  result+= "\n in the country " + getCountry();
  return result;
}


private static final long serialVersionUID = 1L;
}
```

There is a one-to-one mapping between the HTML page *wicket:id* attributes and the properties of the UserProfile Java bean. The Wicket components corresponding to the HTML elements identified by *wicket:id* need not map to the same model class. It's been designed that way in this example in order to demonstrate the workings of one of the Wicket's model classes. You also aren't required to create a new POJO for every Wicket page. You can reuse one if it already exists. For example, information like a user profile is stored in the back-end repository store and is typically modeled in Java through *Data Transfer Objects* (DTOs). If you already have a DTO that maps to the information captured in the UserProfilePage template, you could use that as the backing model class for the page, for instance. (Please refer to http://www.corej2eepatterns.com/Patterns2ndEd/TransferObject.htm if you need more information on DTOs.) Wicket, being a component-oriented framework, encourages very high levels of reuse.

You just specified the UserProfile model class, but you need the corresponding Page class, too (see Listing 1-12).

Listing 1-12. *UserProfilePage.java*

```
import java.util.Arrays;

import wicket.markup.html.WebPage;
import wicket.markup.html.form.DropDownChoice;
import wicket.markup.html.form.Form;
import wicket.markup.html.form.TextField;
import wicket.model.CompoundPropertyModel;
import com.wicketdev.app.model.UserProfile;

public class UserProfilePage extends AppBasePage{

  public UserProfilePage() {

    UserProfile userProfile = new UserProfile();
    CompoundPropertyModel userProfileModel = new CompoundPropertyModel(userProfile);
```

```
    Form form = new UserProfileForm("userProfile",userProfileModel);

    add(form);

    TextField userNameComp = new TextField("name");
    TextField addressComp = new TextField("address");
    TextField cityComp = new TextField("city");

    /*
    * Corresponding to HTML Select, we have a DropDownChoice component in Wicket.
    * The constructor passes in the component ID "country" (that maps to wicket:id
    * in the HTML template) as usual and along with it a list for the
    * DropDownChoice component to render
    */

    DropDownChoice countriesComp = new DropDownChoice("country",
       Arrays.asList(new String[] {"India", "US", "UK" }));

    TextField pinComp = new TextField("pin");

    form.add(userNameComp);
    form.add(addressComp);
    form.add(cityComp);
    form.add(countriesComp);
    form.add(pinComp);

}

class UserProfileForm extends Form {

    // PropertyModel is an IModel implementation
    public UserProfileForm (String id,IModel model) {
        super(id,model);
    }

    @Override
    public void onSubmit() {
      /* Print the contents of its own model object */
      System.out.println(getModelObject());
    }
  }
}
```

Note that none of the Wicket components are associated with a model! The question "Where would it source its data from while rendering or update the data back on submit?" still remains unaddressed. The answer lies in the UserProfilePage constructor:

```
public class UserProfilePage....{

  /** Content omitted for clarity **/
  public UserProfilePage(){

    /* Create an instance of the UserProfile class */
    UserProfile userProfile = new UserProfile();

    /*
    * Configure that as the model in a CompoundPropertyModel object.
    * You will see next that it allows you
    * to share the same model object between parent and its child components.
    */

    CompoundPropertyModel userProfileModel = new CompoundPropertyModel(userProfile);

    /*
    * Register the CompoundPropertyModel instance with the parent component,
    * Form in this case, for the children to inherit from. So all the
    * remaining components will then use the UserProfile instance
    * as its model, using OGNL like 'setters' and 'getters'
    */

    Form form = new UserProfileForm("userProfile",userProfileModel);
      //...

      /*
      * The following code ensures that rest of the components are Form's
      * children, enabling them to share Form's model.
      */

      form.add(userNameComp);
      form.add(addressComp);
      form.add(cityComp);
      form.add(countriesComp);
      form.add(pinComp);
      //...
}
```

Wicket's CompoundPropertyModel allows you to use each component's ID as a property-path expression to the parent component's model. Notice that the form's text field components do not have a model associated with them. When a component does not have a model, it will try to search up its hierarchy to find any parent's model that implements the ICompoundModel interface, and it will use the first one it finds, along with its own component ID to identify its model. Actually, the CompoundPropertyModel can be set up in such a way that it uses the component ID as a property expression to identify its model.

You do not have to worry about this now. We will take a look at some concrete examples in later chapters that will make it clear.

So in essence every child component added to the form will use part of the form's CompoundPropertyModel as its own because the containing Form object is the first component in the upwards hierarchy whose model implements ICompoundModel.

Fill in the form values and click Save. You should see something similar to the following on the Eclipse console:

Eclipse Console Displaying the Input Values

```
02:09:47.265 INFO   [ModificationWatcher Task]
wicket.markup.MarkupCache$1.onChange(MarkupCache.java:309) >
06> Remove markup from cache:
file:/D:/software/lab/eclipse-workspace/WicketRevealedSource/
context/WEB-INF/classes/com/apress/wicketbook/forms/UserProfilePage.html
 Mr Karthik
 resides at Brooke Fields
 in the city Bangalore
 having Pin Code 569900
 in the country India
02:09:50.546 INFO   [SocketListener0-1]
wicket.markup.MarkupCache.loadMarkupAndWatchForChanges
(MarkupCache.java:319) >
```

Struts users can probably relate to this way of using models as they are somewhat similar to Struts ActionForms. For JSF users, it should suffice to say that it's not too different from a JSF-managed bean. Using distinct POJOs as model objects probably makes it easier to move things around while refactoring. The good thing is that Wicket doesn't dictate anything and will work like a charm irrespective of which "modeling" option you choose.

Development vs. Deployment Mode

Modify the label User Name to User Name1 in Login.html and refresh the page; you will notice the template now displays User Name1. Essentially, any change to the template is reflected in the subsequent page access. Wicket checks for any changes to a template file and loads the new one if it indeed has been modified. This is of great help during the development phase. But you probably wouldn't be looking for this default "feature" when deploying in production, as it may lead to the application performing slowly. Wicket easily allows you to change this behavior through the wicket.Application.configure("*deployment*") method (see Listing 1-13). Note that the default value is development.

Listing 1-13. *HelloWorldApplication.java*

```java
import wicket.protocol.http.WebApplication;
import wicket..Application;

public class HelloWorldApplication extends WebApplication {
    public HelloWorldApplication() {
        configure(Application.DEVELOPMENT);
    }

    public Class getHomePage() {
        return Login.class;
    }
}
```

This looks more like a configuration parameter, and hence you should specify it as one in web.xml. The WebApplication class that you configured in web.xml allows access to wicket. protocol.http.WicketServlet (see Listing 1-14).

Listing 1-14. *web.xml*

```xml
<?xml version="1.0" encoding="UTF-8"?>
<!DOCTYPE web-app PUBLIC "-//Sun Microsystems, Inc
.//DTD Web Application 2.3//EN"
"http://java.sun.com/dtd/web-app_2_3.dtd">
<web-app>
 <display-name>Wicket Shop</display-name>
  <servlet>
   <servlet-name>HelloWorldApplication</servlet-name>
   <servlet-class>wicket.protocol.http.WicketServlet</servlet-class>
   <init-param>
     <param-name>applicationClassName</param-name>
     <param-value>com.wicketdev.app.HelloWorldApplication</param-value>
   </init-param>
   <init-param>
     <param-name>configuration</param-name>
     <param-value>development</param-value>
   </init-param>
   <load-on-startup>1</load-on-startup>
  </servlet>

  <servlet-mapping>
    <servlet-name>HelloWorldApplication</servlet-name>
    <url-pattern>/helloworld/*</url-pattern>
  </servlet-mapping>

</web-app>
```

Now that you are done specifying the init-param, the only thing you are left with is accessing the same and setting it on Wicket's ApplicationSettings object. Change the HelloWorldApplication class like this:

```
public class HelloWorldApplication extends WebApplication {

    public HelloWorldApplication(){
        String deploymentMode = getWicketServlet().getInitParameter("configuration");
        configure(deploymentMode);
    }

    public Class getHomePage() {
        return Login.class;
    }

}
```

Alas, Wicket doesn't seem to be too happy with the modifications that you made:

```
02:13:31.046 INFO    [main] wicket.Application.configure
(Application.java:326) >17> You are in DEVELOPMENT mode
java.lang.IllegalStateException: wicketServlet is not
set yet. Any code in your Application object that uses
the wicketServlet instance should be put in the init()
method instead of your constructor
at wicket.protocol.http.WebApplication.getWicketServlet(
WebApplication.java:169) at
com.apress.wicketbook.forms.HelloWorldApplication.<init>(
HelloWorldApplication.java:8){note}
```

But you've got to appreciate the fact that it informs you of the corrective action that it expects you to take (see Listing 1-15).

Listing 1-15. *HelloWorldApplication.java*

```
public class HelloWorldApplication extends WebApplication {

    public void init(){
        String deploymentMode =
            getWicketServlet().getInitParameter(
                        Application.CONFIGURATION);
        configure(deploymentMode);
    }
```

```
    public HelloWorldApplication(){}

    public Class getHomePage() {
        return Login.class;
    }

}
```

Actually, you are not required to set the deployment mode in the init as in Listing 1-15. Just setting the servlet initialization parameter against the key configuration should be sufficient. Wicket takes care of setting the deployment mode internally.

SPECIFYING THE CONFIGURATION PARAMETER

Wicket looks for the presence of a system property called `wicket.configuration` first. If it doesn't find one, it looks for the value corresponding to a servlet initialization parameter named `configuration`. In the absence of the preceding settings, it looks for an identical servlet context parameter setting. If none of the preceding listed lookups succeed, Wicket configures the application in development mode by default. Note that the value for `configuration` has to be either `development` or `deployment` identified by fields `wicket.Application.DEVELOPMENT` and `wicket.Application.DEPLOYMENT`, respectively.

Instead of refreshing the same page on every request, you'll next provide a personalized greeting in the form of a Welcome page once the user has logged in.

Displaying the Welcome Page

Listing 1-16 represents a simple Welcome page that has a placeholder for displaying a personalized greeting.

Listing 1-16. *Welcome.html*

```
<html>
  <title>Welcome to Wicket Application</title>
  <body>
    Welcome To Wicket Mr <span wicket:id="message">Message goes here</span>
  </body>
</html>
```

Welcome.html has a span tag marked as a Wicket component. This corresponds to Wicket's Label component. The Welcome page provides a personalized greeting to the user and accordingly accepts the userId/name as the label content (see Listing 1-17).

Listing 1-17. *Welcome.java*

```java
import wicket.markup.html.WebPage;
import wicket.markup.html.basic.Label;

public class Welcome extends WebPage {

    private String userId;

    public Welcome(){
     add(new Label("message",new PropertyModel(this,"userId")));
    }

    public String getUserId() {
      return userId;
    }

    public void setUserId(String userId) {
      this.userId = userId;
    }
}
```

Rendering a different page in response to the user input is as simple as setting it as the response page as shown in Listing 1-18.

Listing 1-18. *Login.java*

```java
public class Login extends WebPage {
 //..
 public Login(){
    form = new LoginForm("loginForm");
    //..
 }

  class LoginForm extends Form {
    public LoginForm(String id) {
       super(id);
    }

    @Override
    public void onSubmit() {
        String userId = Login.this.getUserId();
        String password = Login.this.getPassword();

        /* Instantiate the result page and set it as the response page */
```

```
        Welcome welcomePage = new Welcome();
        welcomePage.setUserId(userId);
        setResponsePage(welcomePage);
    }
  }

}
```

You can directly access the Welcome page by typing the URL on the browser and passing in the value for userId as a page parameter. The only change required would be that the Welcome constructor needs to be modified to accept the page parameter being passed into it. You will add another constructor that accepts an argument of type PageParameters (see Listing 1-19).

Listing 1-19. *Welcome Page That Accepts PageParameters in the Constructor*

```
import wicket.PageParameters;
public class Welcome extends WebPage {
    //..
    public Welcome(){
      //..
    }

    public Welcome(PageParameters params){
      this();

      /*
       * PageParameters class has methods to get to the parameter value
       * when supplied with the key.
       */

      setUserid(params.getString("userId"));
    }
    //..
}
```

and the URL to access the same would be http://localhost:7000/wicket/helloworld?wicket: bookmarkablePage=:com.apress.wicketbook.forms.Welcome&userId=wicket.

Currently, you don't have any authentication built into your application and therefore any user ID/password combination is acceptable. Go ahead and enter the values and click the Login button. This will take you to a primitive-looking Welcome page, shown in Figure 1-5, that displays a personalized greeting. If you are looking to navigate to the other sample pages developed sometime back, one option is to access them directly by typing in the URL on the browser, and the other could be to get to them through HTML links. Let's try getting the latter to work.

Figure 1-5. *Accessing the Welcome page through the URL passing in PageParameters*

BOOKMARKABLE PAGE

You must be curious about the parameter bookmarkablePage in the URL. Actually, there is nothing special that makes the page bookmarkable. Any page is considered bookmarkable if it has a public default constructor and/ or a public constructor with a PageParameters argument. A bookmarkable page URL can be cached by the browser and can be used to access the page at a later point in time, while a non-bookmarkable page cannot be accessed this way. A non-bookmarkable page URL makes sense only in the context it was generated. If the page wants to be bookmarkable and accept parameters off the URL, it needs to implement the Page(PageParameters params) constructor.

Adding a Link to the Welcome Page

Add a link named "Login" that is intended to take you back to the Login page, as shown in Listing 1-20. (Normally, there is no reason why somebody would want to do this, but this will let you quickly cover some ground with Wicket development.)

Listing 1-20. *Welcome.html*

```
<html>
  <title>Welcome to Wicket Application</title>
  <body>
    Welcome To Wicket Mr <span wicket:id="message">Message goes here</span>
    <a href="#" wicket:id='linkToUserProfile'>User Profile</a><br/>
    <a href="#" wicket:id='linkToLogin'>Login</a><br/></body>
</html>
```

Now you will see how a click on an HTML link translates to an onClick event on the corresponding server-side component.

Modify the Page class in order to accommodate the links and set the target page in the onClick method of wicket's Link class (see Listing 1-21).

Listing 1-21. *Welcome.java*

```java
import wicket.markup.html.link.Link;

class Welcome ..

  public Welcome(){
    //..
    //..
    Link linkToUserProfile = new Link("linkToUserProfile"){
       public void onClick(){
         // Set the response page
         setResponsePage(UserProfilePage.class);
       }
    };

    Link linkToLogin = new Link("linkToLogin"){
       public void onClick(){
         setResponsePage(Login.class);
       }
    };

    // Don't forget to add them to the Form
    form.add(linkToUserProfile);
    form.add(linkToLogin);
  }
}
```

PAGE INSTANCE CACHING

After the page is rendered, it is put into a PageMap. The PageMap instance lives in session and keeps the last *n* pages (this number is configurable through Wicket's ApplicationSettings object). When a form is submitted, the page is brought back from PageMap and the form handler is executed on it. The PageMap uses a Least Recently Used (LRU) algorithm by default to evict pages—to reduce space taken up in session. You can configure Wicket with your own implementation of the eviction strategy. Wicket specifies the strategy through the interface wicket.session.pagemap.IPageMapEvictionStrategy. You can configure your implementation by invoking getSessionSettings().setPageMapEvictionStrategy (yourPageMapEvicationStrategyInstance) in the WebApplication.init() method. This could prove to be extremely crucial when tuning Wicket to suit your application needs.

Go back to the login page, enter values for user ID and password, and click the Login button. You should see something like what appears in Figure 1-6.

Figure 1-6. *Welcome page with links to other pages*

The rendered URL for the "Login" link looks like this:

```
<a href="/wicket/helloworld?wicket:interface=:0:form:linkToLogin::
ILinkListener" wicket:id="linkToLogin">Login</a><br/>
```

This URL has a reference to a particular page instance in the PageMap (denoted by parameter :0) at this point in time and hence is not bookmarkable. You will see later how you can have bookmarkable links that can be cached in the browser for use at a later point in time.

Click the "Login" link and you should be taken to the login screen again (see Figure 1-7).

Figure 1-7. *Clicking the "Login" link displays the login page with blank fields.*

The User Name and Password fields turn out to be blank. This was because you specified the response page class—Login.class—on onClick. Wicket accordingly created a new instance of the Login page and rendered that on the browser. Since the Login constructor initializes the TextField and PasswordTextField widgets to empty strings, the corresponding HTML widgets turn out blank on the browser. Note that you could have passed the original Login page instance to the Welcome page and specified that as the argument to setResponsePage on onClick. That way you would have gotten back the "original" Login page with the user input intact. This scenario is indicated in Listing 1-22.

Listing 1-22. *Welcome Page Modified to Accept the Previous Page During Construction*

```
public class Welcome extends WebPage {
    String userId;
    Page prevPage;

    public Welcome(String userId, Page prevPage){
        this.userId;
        this.prevPage = prevPage;
        //..
    }

    Link linkToLogin = new Link("linkToLogin"){
        public void onClick(){
            setResponsePage(prevPage==null?new Login():prevPage);
        }
    };
}
```

Listing 1-23 shows the modifications needed to the Login page.

Listing 1-23. *Login Page Modified to Pass Itself As the Argument*

```
public class Login extends WebPage {
  //..
  class LoginForm extends Form {
    public LoginForm(String id) {
      super(id);
    }

    @Override
    public void onSubmit() {
      String userId = getUserId();
      String password = getPassword();
      /* Instantiate the result page and set it as the response page */
      Welcome welcomePage = new Welcome(userId,Login.this);
      setResponsePage(welcomePage);
    }
  }
}
```

Now click the "Login" link, and it should take you back to the login page with the previously entered input intact.

This tells us that Wicket is an *unmanaged* framework. You can instantiate pages or components anywhere in the application, and the framework doesn't restrict you in any fashion. It is in fact a widely followed practice when developing applications with Wicket. In this respect, it's quite different from *managed* frameworks, like Tapestry, which don't allow you to instantiate pages at any arbitrary point in your code.

In this example, you set out to develop a login use case, and not having an authentication feature, however trivial it may be, just doesn't cut it. Let's quickly put one in place.

Adding Basic Authentication to the Login Page

Let's add a basic authentication mechanism to the login page (see Listing 1-24). For now, you will support "wicket"/"wicket" as the only valid user ID/password combination.

Listing 1-24. *Login.java*

```java
public class Login extends WebPage
  //..
  public Login() {

    Form form = new LoginForm("loginForm");
    //...
  }

  class LoginForm extends Form {
    public LoginForm(String id) {
        super(id);
    }

    @Override
    public void onSubmit() {
        String password = getPassword();
        String userId  = getUserId();
        if (authenticate(userId,password)){
            Welcome welcomePage = new Welcome();
            welcomePage.setUserId(userId);
            setResponsePage(welcomePage);
        }else{
            System.out.println("The user id/ password
                combination is incorrect!\n");
        }
    }
  }

  public final boolean authenticate(final String username,
          final String password){
      if ("wicket".equalsIgnoreCase(username) &&
         "wicket".equalsIgnoreCase(password))
        return true;
      else
        return false;
  }
}
```

If you supply an invalid user ID/password combination, you will not see the Welcome page in response. Since you didn't specify a response page for this scenario, Wicket will redisplay the current page, i.e., the login page instead (via postback mechanism). One glaring issue with this example is that the user doesn't really get to know what actually went wrong, as the failed login information is logged to the console. Relax—you will find out how to address this and much more by the end of the next chapter.

Summary

In this chapter, you learned how to set up Wicket, Eclipse, and the Jetty Launcher Plug-in for Wicket-based web development. You also learned that Wicket Form and TextField components help in user interaction. Every HTML widget has an equivalent Wicket component. These components, in turn, rely on the model object to get and set data during template rendering and submission. You learned to use two of Wicket's IModel implementations—PropertyModel and CompoundPropertyModel. You also saw that there are various ways of configuring the model objects and briefly explored the "Tapestry way" and "Struts/JSF way" of writing model objects. The Form component's onSubmit() method should be overridden to process user inputs. Wicket caches pages in a PageMap for a given session and follows the LRU algorithm to evict pages from the cache. Wicket allows you to configure a custom implementation of the page-eviction strategy as well. Later, you learned that the Component.setResponsePage method can be used to direct the user to a different page after page submit. You also used Wicket's Link component, which maps to an HTML link, to direct users to a different page. Through the Welcome page that has links, you also learned that Wicket is an *unmanaged* framework that allows you to instantiate pages or components anywhere in the application, and this framework doesn't restrict you in any fashion.

CHAPTER 2

■■■

Validation with Wicket

Validating input data assumes prime importance in a web application, as invalid data is undesirable in any kind of system. It's essential for a web framework to have some kind of built-in validation support for the developers to rely on; examples might be ease of configuration of field validation, feedback on what has gone wrong, ease of configuration of error messages, etc., and luckily Wicket has a lot to offer on this front. In this chapter, you will learn how to provide user feedback and set up form field validations in Wicket. You will also learn to use some of the built-in validators that ship with Wicket. Data validation and type conversion are somewhat related to each other. We will take a look at some of the existing Wicket type converters, and to get a feel for the Wicket Converter API, I will show you how to develop a type converter of your own. It's quite possible that you might want to customize the feedback message display. This requires a little bit of insight into the way Wicket handles feedback messages, and later you will build your own feedback component using Wicket's built-in ListView component.

Providing User Feedback

Let's revisit the login page to which you added some basic authentication feature. Enter a user name/password combination different from "wicket"/"wicket" and click Login. You will see that the same page is returned to you, as it fails the security check. What is missing here is some form of feedback to the user indicating what has actually gone wrong. We will look at the Wicket way of resolving this issue.

Wicket has a FeedbackPanel component that can display all types of messages associated with components nested within a page, and it knows how to render them in a predefined HTML format. Messages are typically attached to a component. (They are actually stored somewhere else, and we will take a look at this shortly.) You specifically need access to messages of type error. Let's add the component to the template first (see Listing 2-1).

Listing 2-1. *Login.html*

```
<html>
 <title>Sample Wicket Application</title>
 <body>
```

```
<!-- Added a span to display feedback -->
<span wicket:id = "feedback">
  Feedback messages will be here
</span>

  <form wicket:id="loginForm">
    User Name  <input type="text" wicket:id="userId"/><br/>
    Password<input type="password" wicket:id="password"/><br/>
    <hr>
    <input type="submit" value="Login"/>
  </form>
</body>
</html>
```

If you are developing an application that targets an international audience, it makes sense to localize the error messages. Wicket ships with a Localizer class that has methods to retrieve locale-specific messages. At present, you are just interested in externalizing the error messages so that they can be changed without requiring modifications to the Java code, and Localizer is the component that lets you retrieve the message.

The modified Login page that reflects the changes that we just discussed is shown in Listing 2-2.

Listing 2-2. *Login.java*

```
// Other imports
import wicket.markup.html.panel.FeedbackPanel;

public class Login extends WebPage

    //...
    public Login() {

        // Create the panel that will display feedback messages
        FeedbackPanel feedback = new FeedbackPanel("feedback");
        Form form = new LoginForm("loginForm");
        //...
        // Add the FeedbackPanel to the page
        add(feedback);
        add(form);
    };

    class LoginForm extends Form {

        public LoginForm(String id) {
            super(id);
        }
```

```
@Override
public void onSubmit() {
  String userId = Login.this.getUserId();
  String password = Login.this.getPassword();
  if (authenticate(userId, password)) {
    Welcome welcomePage = new Welcome();
    welcomePage.setUserId(userId);
    setResponsePage(welcomePage);
  } else {
    String errMsg = getLocalizer().getString(
      "login.errors.invalidCredentials ", Login.this,
        "Unable to sign you in");

    // Register this error message with the form component.
    error(errMsg);
  }
 }
 }
 }
}
```

Everything about the code snippet in Listing 2-2 should be quite familiar except probably for this:

```
String errMsg = getLocalizer().getString(
          "login.errors.invalidCredentials", Login.this,
          "Unable to sign you in");
```

In general, all Wicket components can access the Localizer class through the getLocalizer( ) method. This method call instructs Wicket's Localizer class to look for a message mapped to the key "login.errors.invalidCredentials" in a properties file having the same name as the second argument to the method call—Login.this. Since you haven't specified a locale-specific message yet, the default value—"Unable to sign you in"—is used on entering an invalid user name/password combination as input (see Figure 2-1).

Figure 2-1. *Feedback error message on supplying invalid credentials*

In order to provide locale-specific messages, you need a way for the application to find the messages specific to a given locale. In Java, this is typically done through the `java.util.PropertyResourceBundle` class. These properties files should contain a set of key=value pairs, mapping the keys you want to use to look up the texts to find the correct text for that locale. Java's `ResourceBundle` support typically takes into consideration the locale information when looking for resource bundles, while Wicket supports a concept of style and variation in addition to locale. We will discuss this in greater detail in Chapter 6. In this case, since the `Localizer` will look for a properties file having the same name as the `Page` class in the same location by convention, create a file `Login.properties` in the same folder location as the `Page` class with the content shown in Listing 2-3.

Listing 2-3. *Login.properties*

```
login.errors.invalidCredentials =Try wicket/wicket as the
user name/password combination
```

Refresh the page. On entering invalid credentials, you will notice that the error message is being retrieved from the properties files instead, as shown in Figure 2-2. If the preceding key is not found in `Login.properties`, Wicket will look for the message in other files as well, but the message search order is the topic of another chapter (specifically, Chapter 6).

Figure 2-2. *Sourcing the feedback message from Login.properties*

`Localizer` will display the default message "Unable to sign you in" in the absence of the key `"login.errors.invalidCredentials"` in the `Login.properties` file. Had you used the other overloaded `Localizer.getString(String key, Component comp)` method (which doesn't accept the default value), and if the key were not to be found in the properties file, the framework would have thrown a `MissingResourceException`.

If you find this default behavior a little too extreme for your taste, you can turn it off through a getExceptionSettings().setThrowExceptionOnMissingResource(false) call in your WebApplication class.

Now check whether this setting makes any difference to the way Wicket handles missing resources.

```
String errmsg = getLocalizer().getString("login.errors.invalidCredentials ", this);
```

In Login.properties, comment out the entry by placing a # in front of the entry to simulate absence of a resource key.

```
# login.errors.invalidCredentials =Try wicket/wicket as the user
name/password combination
```

Click your browser's Refresh button, and you should see the message that appears in Figure 2-3.

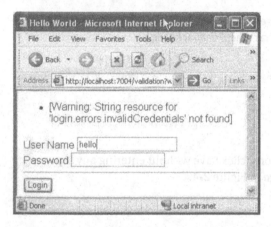

Figure 2-3. *A warning message is displayed in the absence of the message key in the properties file, depending upon the exception settings.*

Now that you have some idea of how page validation works in Wicket, let's delve deeper into the validation framework.

More Validation

Next you will revisit the UserProfilePage that you developed in the first chapter. Let's add the FeedbackPanel component to the Page, as shown in Listing 2-4. Earlier, on form submission, you were printing the model object to the console, which probably doesn't make much sense in a web application. So this time you'll add it as an "info" message to the page. As discussed earlier, the FeedbackPanel component will display the "info" message as well.

Listing 2-4. *UserProfilePage with an Attached Feedback Component*

```
public class UserProfilePage extends...

  public UserProfilePage(){
    // Add the FeedbackPanel to the Page for displaying error messages
    add(new FeedbackPanel("feedback"));
    //...
  }

  class UserProfileForm extends Form {

    public UserProfileForm(String id, IModel model) {
      super(id, model);
    }
    public void onSubmit() {
      // Add the String representation of UserProfile object as
      // an "info" message to the page so that the FeedbackPanel
      // can display it

      info(getModelObjectAsString());
    }
  }
}
```

After incorporating the preceding modifications, click Save without entering any input values. You should see something like the message in Figure 2-4.

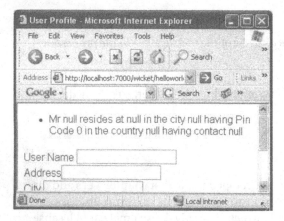

Figure 2-4. *The UserProfilePage allows "blank" input values in the absence of a validation check.*

This of course is unacceptable. This page begs for some kind of field-level validation to be put in place before the `Form.onSubmit()` method is called. For now, assume that User Name and Pin input fields are required. Additionally, the PIN needs to be in the range 0–5000.

Now let's modify `UserProfilePage` to accommodate the preceding validation as shown in Listing 2-5. You can use Wicket's `Base` component's method, `error()`, to log validation error messages.

Listing 2-5. *UserProfilePage with Validation*

```
public class UserProfilePage extendsBasePage

    //..
  class UserProfileForm extends Form {

      public UserProfileForm(String id, IModel model) {
        super(id, model);
      }

      public void onSubmit() {
        UserProfile up = (UserProfile) getModelObject();
        // Retrieve the values from the model object and signal an error
        int pin = up.getPin();
        String name = up.getName();
        // For now let's not worry about localization
        if (name == null) {
          error("User Name is a required field");
        }
        int minPinVal = 0;
        int maxPinVal = 5000;
        if (pin < minPinVal || pin > maxPinVal) {
          error("Please enter pin in the range "
                      + Integer.toString(minPinVal) + " - "
                      + Integer.toString(maxPinVal));
        }

      }
  }
}
```

As shown in Figure 2-5, the result is as you expect.

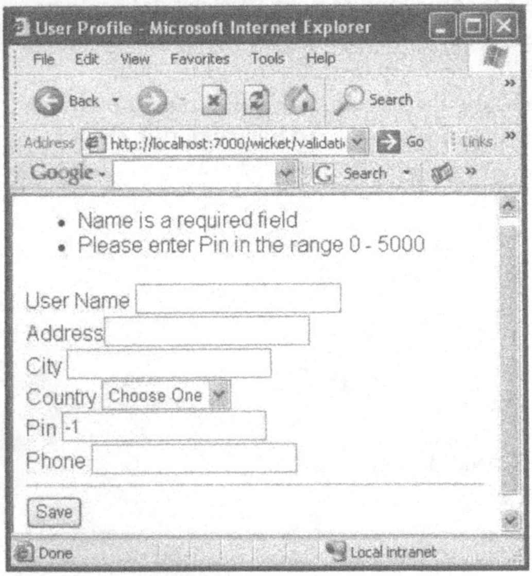

Figure 2-5. *Validation error messages on leaving input fields blank*

Even though you managed to incorporate field-level validation in your application, it still doesn't look right—it would have been better if validation had kicked in before the execution of business logic (onSubmit() in this case); in other words, why even get to the "submit" process when you know up front that certain kinds of inputs are unacceptable?

Wicket offers some help here, and we will discuss that next.

Using Wicket Validators

While handling the request cycle, the Form validates all the contained FormComponents by calling the validator registered with each component. It does this by traversing the component tree and calling validate() on each component. If any of the components fails this validation, the page processing doesn't proceed further, and the response is returned to the user with the error messages intact. Note that Wicket does call validate() on the subsequent components, even if a component featured ahead in the page hierarchy has failed validation, accumulating the error messages on the way. This behavior makes sense—it's better to inform the user up front of all the invalid inputs instead of waiting for him or her to correct them one by one after each submit. They are then typically displayed by the FeedbackPanel component that we discussed earlier.

Validation in Wicket is specified through the IValidator interface. Since you can attach any number of IValidator interface implementations to a Wicket component through the component's overloaded add() method, Wicket developers have made sure that they can be chained as well. The business logic dictates that you do the following:

- Make sure that the Wicket components corresponding to the fields User Name and Pin are marked as required fields.

- Attach a NumberValidator to ensure that the entered PIN value is within the acceptable range.

These business rules translate to Java code as shown in Listing 2-6.

Listing 2-6. *UserProfilePage.java*

```java
import wicket.markup.html.form.validation.NumberValidator;
import wicket.markup.html.panel.FeedbackPanel;

public class UserProfilePage extends AppBasePage{

  public UserProfilePage() {

    UserProfile userProfile = new UserProfile();
    CompoundPropertyModel userProfileModel = new CompoundPropertyModel(userProfile);

    Form form = new UserProfileForm("userProfile",userProfileModel);

    // Add the FeedbackPanel to the Page for displaying error messages
    add(new FeedbackPanel("feedback"));

    add(form);

    TextField userNameComp = new TextField("name");

    // Mark the Name field as required
    userNameComp.setRequired(true);

    TextField addressComp = new TextField("address");
    TextField cityComp = new TextField("city");

    DropDownChoice countriesComp = new DropDownChoice("country",
       Arrays.asList(new String[] {"India", "US", "UK" }));

    TextField pinComp = new TextField("pin");

    // Pin is a required field.

    pinComp.setRequired(true);
    // Validators are thread-safe. It is OK to link the same
    // validator instance with multiple components.

    pinComp.add(NumberValidator.range(1000,5000));

    // NumberValidator deprecates IntegerValdiator, and it
    // needs to be told the type against which it needs to be validated.

    pinComp.setType(int.class);
```

```
      form.add(userNameComp);
      form.add(addressComp);
      form.add(cityComp);
      form.add(countriesComp);
      form.add(pinComp);

  }

  class UserProfileForm extends Form{
    public void onSubmit() {
      info(getModelObjectAsString());
    }
  }
}
```

The error message will be retrieved using the Localizer for the Form component. The Localizer looks for the error message in a string resource bundle (properties file) associated with the page in which this validator is contained. Actually, it searches up the component hierarchy for the key and then in properties files named after the WebApplication subclass and then Application.properties. (Do not worry about the message search algorithm for now. Chapter 6 is dedicated to it.) The key that is used to get the validator messages can be located by either consulting the Javadoc of the validator class or looking at the default Application. properties, which contains localized messages for all validators. You might also want to display the localized name for the Form component that failed the validation check. This can be specified in the properties file as well. In this case, Wicket expects the following pattern:

`<form-name/id>.<component-name/id>`

Actually you could just specify component-id (more on this in Chapter 6). But then you could have more than one component with the same ID falling under a different hierarchy in the Page. Wicket does not prevent you from doing this. By including the form-id as well, you could ensure to a certain extent that the key identifies the component uniquely.

Accordingly, you will need the entries shown in Listing 2-7 in the file.

Listing 2-7. *UserProfilePage.properties*

```
userProfile.name= Name
userProfile.pin = Pin
RequiredValidator=${label} is a required field
NumberValidator.range=Please enter ${label} in the range ${minimum} - ${maximum}
```

If you don't want to specify the component labels in a properties file, you could instead do it in the Java code as well:

```
TextField userNameComp = new TextField("name");
// Set the component Label here
userNameComp.setLabel(new Model("Name"));
```

but the label can no longer be internationalized. Well, you could internationalize it by querying the Localizer to fetch it from a properties file. Instead, you are better off storing it in the properties file itself. If you don't do either of these things, Wicket will use the component-id as its Label by default, which might not be easy on your eyes.

Wicket also allows you to include certain predefined variables in validation message text. They will be substituted at runtime. In the properties file shown in Listing 2-7, minimum and maximum are examples of predefined variables. Wicket will automatically populate it depending upon the range you specify in the Java representation of the Page class. Some of the other available variables for interpolation are as follows:

Variable	Description
${input}	The user's input.
${name}	The name of the component.
${label}	The label of the component; either comes from FormComponent.labelModel or resource key <form-id>.<form-component-id> in that order, but specific validator subclasses may add more values.

Actually, having the page properties file as in Listing 2-7 for declaring error messages is not a must. Wicket will default to the Application.properties file that it ships with if it does not find the error message keys in other properties files based on its search algorithm.

Listing 2-8 shows the content of the default Application.properties file.

Listing 2-8. *wicket.Application.properties*

```
RequiredValidator=field '${label}' is required.
TypeValidator='${input}' is not a valid ${type}.

NumberValidator.range=${input} must be between ${minimum} and ${maximum}.
NumberValidator.minimum='${input}' must be greater than ${minimum}.
NumberValidator.maximum='${input}' must be smaller than ${maximum}.

StringValidator.range='${input}' must be between ${minimum} and ${maximum} chars.
StringValidator.minimum='${input}' must be at least ${mimimum} chars.
StringValidator.maximum='${input}' must be at most ${maximum} chars.

DateValidator.range='${input}' must be between ${minimum} and ${maximum}.
DateValidator.minimum='${input}' must be greater than ${minimum}.
DateValidator.maximum='${input}' must be smaller than ${maximum}.

PatternValidator='${input}' does not match pattern '${pattern}'
EmailAddressPatternValidator='${input}' is not a valid email address.

EqualInputValidator='${input0}' from ${label0} and '${input1}'
from ${label1} must be equal.
EqualPasswordInputValidator=${label0} and ${label1} must be equal.

null=Choose One
nullValid=
```

You can override these messages in your page.properties file only if you aren't fine with the default ones. Note that you can override the messages specified in Application.properties in your WebApplication subclass properties file. But remember that it will be applicable globally to all the pages.

There is something else that requires your attention. HTTP request parameters are plain Strings. In spite of that, Wicket automatically converts the request input value to the appropriate model object type. (The field UserProfile.pin is of type int and still had its value set correctly on form submit.) This works as long as the value that needs to be set on the model object is of a primitive type like int, float, or java.util.Date. Wicket has default converters that handle such conversions. But this conversion will not happen automatically if you have a custom model object type. They can be easily handled through custom Wicket converters, which are discussed next.

Writing Custom Converters

One of Wicket's greatest strengths lies in its ability to shield the developer from the intricacies of the underlying HTTP protocol. It acts as a translation layer between HTTP request parameters and your model class, and the way it does this is through *converters*.

Wicket accesses the converters through a factory class and makes it centrally available through Wicket's ApplicationSettings class.

Wicket's built-in converters are good enough to handle a majority of the requirements. But there are always situations when built-in components aren't sufficient. You might have an "HTML request parameter to custom class" mapping requirement that isn't quite straightforward. In this section, you will learn to build a custom converter that does just that.

As an exercise, try adding an input field to accept a phone number as a part of the user profile. Correspondingly, add another TextField component to the UserProfilePage class and map it to the phoneNumber property in the model class (UserProfile.java).

Let's start by defining a class that represents a phone number first, as shown in Listing 2-9. Assume that the user will enter the phone number in the following format:

[prefix]-[area code]-[number]

That is, [xxx]-[xxx]-[xxxx], all numeric: for example, 123-456-7890.

Listing 2-9. *PhoneNumber.java*

```java
public class PhoneNumber implements Serializable{
    private String areaCode;
    private String prefix;
    private String number;

    public PhoneNumber(String code, String number, String prefix) {
        this.areaCode = code;
        this.number = number;
        this.prefix = prefix;
    }
```

```
    public String getAreaCode() {
      return areaCode;
    }

    public String getNumber() {
      return number;
    }

    public String getPrefix() {
      return prefix;
    }
}
```

Add a text field to the HTML template (see Listing 2-10).

Listing 2-10. *UserProfilePage.html*

```
<html>
  <title>User Profile</title>
  <body>
    <form wicket:id="userProfile">
      User Name <input type="text" wicket:id="name"/><br/>
      Address<input type="text" wicket:id="address"/><br/>
      City <input type="text" wicket:id="city"/><br/>
      Country <select wicket:id="country">
                <option>Country-1</option>
                <option>Country-2</option>
                <option>Country-3</option>
              </select><br/>
      Pin <input type="text" wicket:id="pin"/><br/>
      Phone <input type="text" wicket:id="phoneNumber"/><br/>
      <hr/>
      <input type="submit" value="Save"/>
    </form>
  </body>
</html>
```

All converters are supposed to implement the IConverter interface. It has a single method:

```
public Object convert(Object value, Class c)
```

Argument	Description
value	Argument passed in (HTML string when updating the underlying model OR the model object when rendering)
c	The class the value needs to be converted to (e.g., c might be PhoneNumber during form submit and String.class when rendering)

Listing 2-11 shows one of the ways of implementing the custom converter:
`PhoneNumberConverter`.

Listing 2-11. *UserProfilePage.PhoneNumberConverter*

```java
public class UserProfilePage extends AppBasePage{

  //...
  //...

  public static class PhoneNumberConverter implements IConverter{

    private Locale locale;
    // This is the method that the framework calls
    public Object convert(Object value, Class c) {

      if (value == null){
        return null;
      }

      // If the target type for conversion is String,
      // convert the PhoneNumber to the form xxx-xxx-xxxx

      if (c == String.class){
          PhoneNumber phoneNumber = (PhoneNumber) value;
          return
              phoneNumber.getPrefix() + "-" +
              phoneNumber.getAreaCode() + "-" +
              phoneNumber.getNumber();
      }

      // Assume for now that the input is of the form xxx-xxx-xxxx

      String numericString = stripExtraChars((String)value);
      String areaCode = numericString.substring(0,3);
      String prefix = numericString.substring(3,6);
      String number = numericString.substring(6);
      UserProfile.PhoneNumber phoneNumber =
        new UserProfile.PhoneNumber(areaCode, prefix, number);
      return phoneNumber;
    }

    // Removes all nonnumeric characters from the input.
    // If supplied with 123-456-7890, it returns 1234567890.
```

```
    private String stripExtraChars(String input ) {
      return input.replaceAll("[^0-9]", "");
}

    // Currently you are not doing locale-specific parsing
    public void setLocale(Locale locale) {
        this.locale = locale;
    }

    public Locale getLocale() {
      return this.locale;
    }

}
```

Now that you have seen the meaty part, the only thing left is to let the component know of this Converter class. All components allow you to specify the custom converter through the getConverter() method. So you just override it to return your custom converter class.

Note that the target type (PhoneNumber.class) to which you want the input converted must be specified when constructing the TextField component corresponding to the phone number (see Listing 2-12). If this is not specified, Wicket will not call the custom converter.

Listing 2-12. *UserProfilePage.java*

```
public class UserProfilePage extends AppBasePage{

 public UserProfilePage (){
 //..

  TextField phoneComp = new TextField("phoneNumber",PhoneNumber.class){
     public IConverter getConverter() {
        return new PhoneNumberConverter();
     }
  };

  form.add(phoneComp);
  //..
  //..
 }
}
```

By implementing a custom converter, you ensure that the phone numbers are interpreted correctly. But what if the user does not enter the phone number in the required format, inputting something like "abc-xyz-rst" instead? You need to make sure that by the time actual conversion happens, the input has been run through a thorough validation check. You could employ some parsing logic to make sure that it indeed is in the required format. But that would seem like an old-fashioned way of doing things, especially when Java ships with regular expression support in the form of a java.util.regex package. java.util.regex.Pattern accepts a pattern string that is used to match against the user input. If the supplied user input does not match the pattern, the PhoneNumberConverter registers it as an error with the Page. You just need to throw a ConversionException to ensure this (see Listing 2-13). (Internally it does the same thing as the validation logic you created on your own, except that Wicket does not call the Form's onSubmit() method on validation failure—a feature you really want to include.)

Listing 2-13. *Specifying a "Regex" Pattern to Match Phone Numbers*

```
import wicket.util.convert.ConversionException;

public static class PhoneNumberConverter implements IConverter{

    static Pattern pattern = Pattern.compile("\\d{3}-\\d{3}-\\d{4}");

    // This is the method that the framework calls
    public Object convert(Object value, Class c) {
        //
        // Assume for now that the input is of the form xxx-xxx-xxxx
        // Check if the user input matches the required phone nummber
        // pattern.
        // A pattern that matches a string comprising of 3 digits followed
        // by a '-' separator, followed by 3 digits again, followed by a
        //'-' separator and 4 digits after that.


        if (!pattern.matcher((String) value).matches()) {
            // If the pattern does not match, throw ConversionException
            throw new ConversionException("Supplied value " + value
                + " does not match the pattern " + pattern.toString(),
                value, locale);
        }    //..

    }
```

If a component is associated with a type during creation, and if the type conversion fails during form submit, Wicket looks for the error message against the key TypeValdiator. <Type Class name>. Now update UserProfilePage.properties to reflect the feedback that the user gets to see in case of invalid input:

```
TypeValidator.PhoneNumber=${label} must be all numeric
the form xxx-xxx-xxxx (Eg 123-456-7890).${input} does not conform to the format
```

Figure 2-6 shows the result of invalid user input.

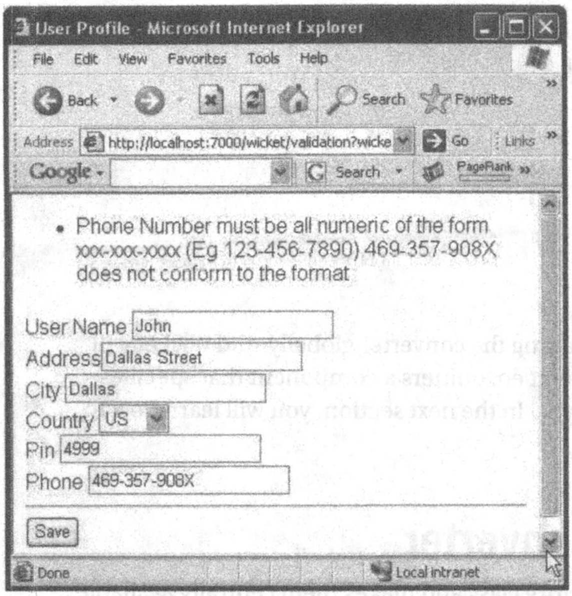

Figure 2-6. *Phone number conversion error when input format is illegal*

The ability to associate a custom converter implementation with a TextField is really useful. But there could be cases where you might be accepting input of the type phone number in multiple pages. Associating each of those TextField components with the custom converter could quickly become tedious. A couple of solutions exist to this problem. You can define a custom PhoneInputField that registers the custom converter and extends Wicket's TextField component. You can avoid the redundant process of registering the converter with the TextField by using PhoneInputField instead (see Listing 2-14).

Listing 2-14. *PhoneInputField.java*

```
public class PhoneInputField extends TextField{
   public PhoneInputField(String id, Model model){
      super(id,model,PhoneNumber.class);
   }

   public PhoneInputField(String id){
      super(id,PhoneNumber.class);
   }

   public IConverter getConverter() {
      return new PhoneNumberConverter();
   }
}
```

And in the page class:

```java
public class UserProfilePage extends WebPage{
  public UserProfilePage(){
    //..
    //..
    add(new PhoneInputField("phoneNumber"));
  }

}
```

A similar effect can be achieved by registering the converter globally, and Wicket will make sure that it calls this converter whenever it encounters a component that specifies PhoneNumber as its underlying model object type. In the next section, you will learn how to make a converter globally available.

Globally Registering a Converter

Wicket accesses the converters through a factory class and makes them centrally available through Wicket's ApplicationSettings class. Wicket has quite a few globally available built-in converters, and it allows you to register one through well-defined abstractions. The IConverterFactory implementation, as the name suggests, acts as a factory for an IConverter implementation. Wicket uses the built-in Converter class as the default IConverter implementation. This class in turn maintains a set of ITypeConverter implementations that handle conversion for a given type. When registering your converter, you need to make sure that the existing converter behavior remains unaltered, and luckily the default Converter class allows you to register custom ITypeConverter implementations.

The PhoneNumberConverter in Listing 2-15 implements ITypeConverter through AbstractConverter. It does the same thing as the earlier version except that it adapts to the ITypeConverter specifications.

Listing 2-15. *PhoneNumberConverter.java*

```java
import javax.util.regex.Pattern;

public static class PhoneNumberConverter extends AbstractConverter {

    Pattern pattern = Pattern.compile("\\d{3}-\\d{3}-\\d{4}");

    /**
    * The singleton instance for a phone number converter
    */
```

```
public static final ITypeConverter INSTANCE = new PhoneNumberConverter();
@Override
protected Class getTargetType() {
    return UserProfile.PhoneNumber.class;
}

public Object convert(Object value, Locale locale) {

    // Before converting the value, make sure that it matches the pattern.
    // If it doesn't, Wicket expects you to throw the built-in
    // runtime exception - ConversionException.

    if (!pattern.matcher((String) value).matches()) {
        throw newConversionException("Supplied value " + value
        + " does not match the pattern " + pattern.toString(),
        value, locale);
    }

    String numericString = stripExtraChars((String) value);
    String areaCode = numericString.substring(0, 3);
    String prefix = numericString.substring(3, 6);
    String number = numericString.substring(6);
    UserProfile.PhoneNumber phoneNumber = new UserProfile.PhoneNumber(
        areaCode, prefix, number);
    return phoneNumber;
}

private String stripExtraChars(String input) {
    return input.replaceAll("[^0-9]", "");
}
}
```

Define a custom converter that registers the PhoneNumberConverter with the default converter (see Listing 2-16).

Listing 2-16. *CustomConverter.java*

```
class CustomConverter extends Converter {
    CustomConverter(Locale locale) {
        super();
        setLocale(locale);
        // Register the custom ITypeConverter. Now it will be globally available.
        set(PhoneNumber.class,PhoneNumberConverter.INSTANCE);
    }
}
```

And then register the custom converter as shown in Listing 2-17.

Listing 2-17. *ValidationApplication.java*

```
class ValidationApplication.java extends WebApplication{

    public void init() {
        super.init();
        getApplicationSettings().setConverterFactory(new IConverterFactory() {
            public IConverter newConverter(final Locale locale) {
                return new CustomConverter(locale);
            }
        });
        //..
    }
}
```

Henceforth, you can use Wicket's TextField component even when accepting input of type phone number as follows:

```
form.add(new TextField("phoneNumber",PhoneNumber.class))
```

Note that you just have to specify the type of the underlying model. You don't have to explicitly specify the converter. Wicket will determine that based on the type specified in the constructor.

Registering String Converters Globally

If you play around with the input field that accepts a phone number, you would observe something really strange. Every time you enter a phone number in a valid format, you would see something like what appears in Figure 2-7.

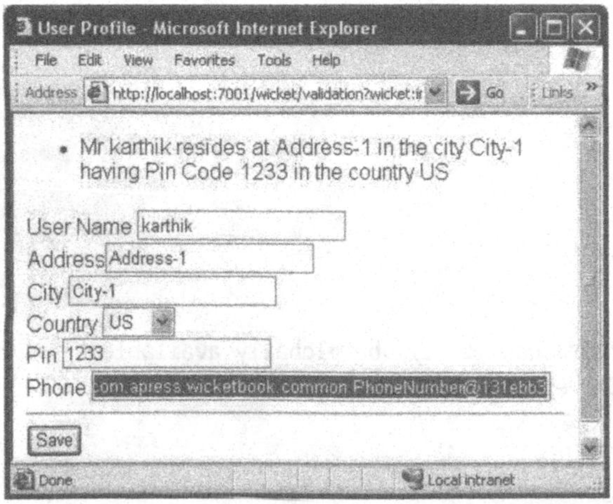

Figure 2-7. *Phone field incorrectly displaying the fully qualified class name of PhoneNumber instead of the user input*

The text that is displayed in the input field after refresh is actually the fully qualified name of the PhoneNumber class. Wicket defaults to this behavior since it doesn't know that the phone number needs to be displayed in the format *xxx-xxx-xxxx*. Wicket actually does a two-way conversion: once when converting HTTP parameters to the "backing model" type and then when the model object needs to be displayed on the browser.

So even though you took care of the first case, you really didn't address the next. PhoneNumberToStringConverter class solves this problem (see Listings 2-18 and 2-19).

Listing 2-18. *A Custom Converter for Obtaining the String Representation of PhoneNumber*

```
package com.apress.wicketbook.validation;

import java.util.Locale;
import com.apress.wicketbook.common.PhoneNumber;
import wicket.util.convert.converters.AbstractConverter;
public class PhoneNumberToStringConverter extends AbstractConverter {

  public static ITypeConverter INSTANCE = new PhoneNumberToStringConverter();

  @Override
  protected Class getTargetType() {
    return String.class;
  }
  public Object convert(Object value, Locale locale) {
    if (value == null) return null;
    PhoneNumber phoneNumber = (PhoneNumber) value;
    return phoneNumber.getPrefix() + "-" + phoneNumber.getAreaCode() + "-"
      + phoneNumber.getNumber();
  }
}
```

Listing 2-19. *Registering Both PhoneNumberConverter and PhoneNumberToStringConverter with Wicket*

```
class CustomConverter extends Converter {
    CustomConverter(Locale locale) {
        super();
        setLocale(locale);
        // Register the custom ITypeConverter. Now it will be globally available.
        set(PhoneNumber.class,PhoneNumberConverter.INSTANCE);

        // Get the converter Wicket uses to convert model objects to String.
        StringConverter sConverter = (StringConverter) get(String.class);
        // Register the custom ITypeConverter to convert PhoneNumber to its String
        // representation.
        sConverter.set(PhoneNumber.class, PhoneNumberToStringConverter.INSTANCE);
    }
}
```

If you are finding all of the preceding a little discomforting for your taste, you can get away from all the complexity of developing a PhoneNumberToStringConverter by just overriding the java.lang.Object's toString() method in PhoneNumber that returns the string that you want displayed on the browser:

```
public class PhoneNumber implements Serializable{
  //..
  public String toString(){
   return getPrefix() + "-" + getAreaCode() + "-"
     + getNumber();
  }
}
```

In the absence of a string converter for a type, Wicket calls the model object's toString() method as a last resort. The fully qualified PhoneNumber class name that was getting displayed earlier should not come across as a surprise given this behavior.

How Wicket's FormValidator Works

In the previous sections, you saw quite a few of the validators that ship with Wicket. While being extremely useful, it's important to note that they work at a field level and do not satisfy validation requirements at a global or form level. A Wicket Form is essentially composed of FormComponents, and even though the individual FormComponents might have passed the validation checks (depending upon the configured validators), you might still want to validate the Form in its entirety. You might want to make sure that all components together satisfy some global validation requirement. Let's look at an example to illustrate this.

When you sign up for a Yahoo! e-mail account, you are required to input the password in two distinct password fields. In addition to being mandatory fields, you are also required to make sure that the inputs are identical. Figure 2-8 shows one such trivial registration page.

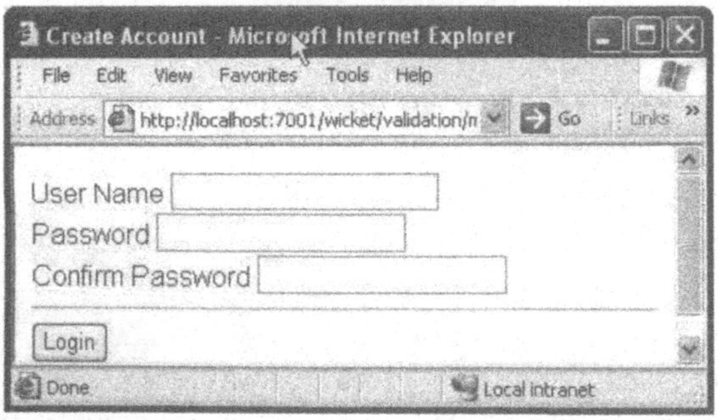

Figure 2-8. *A simple account signup page*

Listing 2-20 shows the underlying template for this simple signup page.

Listing 2-20. *A Signup Page*

```
<html>
  <title>Create Account</title>
  <body>
    <span wicket:id="feedback">[feedback panel]</span>
    <form wicket:id="createAccountForm">
    User Name <input type="text" wicket:id="userId"/><br/>
    Password    <input type="password" wicket:id="password"/><br/>
    Confirm Password    <input type="password" wicket:id="confirmPassword"/><br/>
    <hr>
    <input type="submit" value="Login"/>
    </form>
  </body>
</html>
```

You know that the user needs to supply values for all the FormComponents (hence they need to be marked "required"). Once the TextField components pass the preceding validation check, you need to make sure the inputs for the PassWordTextFields password and confirmPassword are identical. Wicket guarantees this behavior through the wicket. markup.html.form.validation.IFormValidator interface. You are required to specify the FormComponents that need to pass the validation checks before Wicket calls the IFormValidator.validate() method. You do this through the IFormValidator. getDependentFormComponents() method (see Listing 2-21).

Listing 2-21. *Wicket's IFormValidator Interface*

```
package wicket.markup.html.form.validation;

import wicket.markup.html.form.Form;
import wicket.markup.html.form.FormComponent;

public interface IFormValidator{
    /**
    * @return array of FormComponents that this validator depends on
    */
    FormComponent[] getDependentFormComponents();

    /**
    * This method is run if all components returned by
    * getDependentFormComponents()} are valid.
    */
    void validate(Form form);
}
```

You can create your own implementations by extending the helper wicket.markup. html.form.validation.AbstractFormValidator class. In this case specifically, you really don't have to do anything special, as Wicket's EqualPasswordInputValidator addresses your requirement. It takes the PasswordTextField components whose input you want compared and throws a validation error if it doesn't find them to be equal. Let's employ this validator in the CreateAccount page class, shown in Listing 2-22.

Listing 2-22. *The CreateAccount Page Class with FormValidator*

```
package com.apress.wicketbook.validation;

import wicket.markup.html.form.validation.EqualPasswordInputValidator;
// Other imports
public class CreateAccount extends WebPage {
  private String userId;
  private String password;
  private String confirmPassword;

  public CreateAccount() {
    FeedbackPanel feedback = new FeedbackPanel("feedback");
    Form form = new CreateAccountForm("createAccountForm");
    form.add(new TextField("userId", new PropertyModel(this,
            "userId")).setRequired(true));
    PasswordTextField password = (PasswordTextField)new
    PasswordTextField("password",
        new PropertyModel(this, "password"));
    password.setResetPassword(false);
    form.add(password);
    PasswordTextField confirmPassword = (PasswordTextField)new
          PasswordTextField("confirmPassword",
        new PropertyModel(this, "confirmPassword")).setRequired(true);
    confirmPassword.setResetPassword(false);
    form.add(confirmPassword);
    form.add(new EqualPasswordInputValidator(password, confirmPassword));
    add(form);
    add(feedback);
  }

  public String getUserId() {
    return userId;
  }

  public String getPassword() {
    return password;
  }
```

```
class CreateAccountForm extends Form {
  public CreateAccountForm(String id) {
    super(id);
  }
}

public void setPassword(String password) {
  this.password = password;
}

public void setUserId(String userId) {
  this.userId = userId;
}

public String getConfirmPassword() {
  return confirmPassword;
}

public void setConfirmPassword(String confirmPassword) {
  this.confirmPassword = confirmPassword;
}
}
```

If you input different values for the Password and Confirm Password fields, you should see an error message as shown in Figure 2-9.

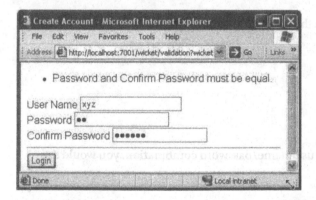

Figure 2-9. *EqualPasswordInputValidator validation failure on entering different values for the Password and Confirm Password fields*

The error message specified in the Application.properties file (see Listing 2-8) is being used. Of course, you can override the message at different levels as discussed earlier.

How to Set Session-Level Feedback Messages

You already know that feedback messages can be associated with a Page. But there is another way of specifying feedback messages as well: you can associate them with the Session.

Note that Session-level feedback messages are cleaned up once they are rendered. In that sense, the messages do not last the entire session, in case your thoughts wandered in that direction. Let's look at an example that demonstrates how Session-level messages are specified.

```
package com.apress.wicketbook.validation;

public class Login extends WebPage{
  //..
  class LoginForm extends Form {
  //..
  @Override
  public void onSubmit() {
    if (authenticate(userId, password)) {
      Session.get().info("You have logged in successfully");
      Welcome welcomePage = new Welcome(userId);
      setResponsePage(welcomePage);
    }else{
    //..
    }
  }
 }
}
```

You need to add the FeedbackPanel in the Welcome page:

```
public class Welcome extends WebPage{
  public Welcome(){
    add(new FeedbackPanel());
    //..
  }
}
```

On entering "wicket"/"wicket" as the user name/password combination, you would see the message that appears in Figure 2-10.

Figure 2-10. *Session-level feedback message display on successful login*

Note that the FeedbackPanel combines both Page- and Session-level messages by default for display.

Now that you have seen different ways of associating feedback messages, in the upcoming section you will learn how to change the manner in which they are being displayed. The feedback error messages are currently being displayed one by one through HTML <li> elements by Wicket's FeedbackPanel component. As you might have noticed, the page template just carries a <span> element, and you could substitute the FeedbackPanel with something else, too. We'll explore this next.

Changing Feedback Display

FeedbackPanel sources the feedback messages from the Page it is attached to, and they are represented by a class with the same name—FeedbackMessages. Getting to that object is as simple as calling pageInstance.getFeedbackMessages(). FeedbackMessages acts as a container for messages logged at any level, namely debug, info, error, warn. You can access messages specified at a particular log level in the form of a list (java.util.List) by supplying a filter of the type IFeedbackMessageFilter to FeedbackMessages. The filter implementation specifies the kind of messages to display; ErrorLevelFeedbackMessageFilter is one such filter that accepts the log level at which you want to filter the messages. There is a ContainerFeedbackMessage→ Filter that can get you messages logged at the specified component level. Let's try displaying the messages in a tabular format with the message description and the associated log levels (in addition to error(), note that Wicket's Component class provides other log methods like debug(), info(), etc.). Wicket makes it easy to work with such lists by providing Loop and ListView components. In this exercise, you will use the ListView component. Before that, set up the feedback panel template for the modified display style. It needs to display the message and its log level inside an HTML table (see Listing 2-23).

Listing 2-23. *UserProfilePage.html Modified for Feedback Message Display*

```
<html>
<head>
  <title>User Profile</title>
</head>
  <body>
    <table border="1">
    <tr wicket:id="feedback">
        <td><span wicket:id="message">Message goes here</span></td>
        <td><span wicket:id="level">Message log level</span></td>
    </tr>
    </table>

    <!-- everything beyond this remains unchanged -->
    <form wicket:id="userProfile">
```

How the ListView Components Work

Your requirement is to render a list of messages. As shown in Listing 2-23, an HTML table element is used to render these messages, with each message represented within a <tr> (table row) element. Each <tr> in turn holds on to the actual feedback message and the associated level. Wicket models this requirement through a ListView component. When constructing the ListView component, you are required to supply the list of objects that you want to iterate through and render. In this case, it happens to be a list of FeedbackMessages.

The ListView component creates a basic WebMarkupContainer called ListItem for every item in the list. This frees you from the responsibility of creating one by yourself. You could treat ListItem as the component corresponding to the <tr> element. But the ListItem still does not know about the child components that it needs to render. However, you are aware of the components you want rendered within the <tr> element—they are the <span> elements that carry the *wicket:ids* message and level. ListView allows you to specify this information through the callback method ListView.populateItem(ListItem listItem), passing in the enclosing WebMarkupContainer (ListItem) that it created on your behalf. This allows you to add the Label components to the ListItem.

But for the Label to render any meaningful information, it needs to be supplied with a backing model object. The model object has to be one of the FeedbackMessage objects contained within the list so that the label can use that to extract the information it wants displayed. So it relies on the ListView component to supply that information. Before calling populateItem, ListView configures the ListItem component with an item from the original list as its model object. In this case, it will be a FeedbackMessage object from a FeedbackMessages list. As you would expect, this object can be accessed within the populateItem method through the ListItem.getModelObject() method call. You can then use this object to supply the model information to other components nested within the enclosing ListView component.

It's perfectly normal for a Wicket newbie to forget to add the components to the ListItem. Remember that ListItem represents the outer markup container (<tr>), and so in order to respect the template hierarchy, you have to add the contained components to the ListItem. This is Wicket's ListView way of working. In fact, all Wicket "repeater" components like Loop work in a similar manner.

You now know that the ListView component accepts a list and renders the list as per instructions. But you have a problem—you do not directly populate the message list instance as such (the Page does), and you do not have access to the list at the time of the ListView component construction (errors result because of incorrect user input, which is likely to happen at a later point in time). What you do have access to is the "list source" through FeedbackMessages. Remember that this is not a list, whereas ListView expects some form of a list to iterate through. You shall instead configure the ListView with a Wicket model that returns the list when accessed. You will see more examples that make use of this additional level of indirection offered by Wicket models in later chapters as well. You need to ensure that when the ListView component is called upon to render data, it pulls the actual list of messages from the FeedbackMessages class, which in turn is accessible to all components through the enclosing Page.

```
import wicket.model.AbstractReadOnlyModel;

IModel messagesModel=new AbstractReadOnlyModel() {
        // Wicket calls this method to get the actual "model object"
        // at runtime
        Object getObject(Component component) {
            return component.getPage().getFeedbackMessages(new
                ErrorLevelFeedabackMessageFilter(FeedbackMessage.ERROR));
        }
};
```

Just to reiterate what we discussed earlier—ListView renders the list supplied to it by calling the populateItem() method, supplying the ListItem for every item in the List.

ListItem should contain the data for one round of iteration—i.e., a <tr> element in this case. It still doesn't have data for the message and level span child elements though. So you will add the corresponding component (a Label corresponding to a span in this case) to the object in the populateItem method. ListView makes sure that each of the list constituents is set as the model for the corresponding ListItem.

```
ListView feedback = new ListView("feedback",messagesModel){
        public void populateItem(ListItem listItem){
            // Access the item from the the FeedbackMessages list that
            // you supplied earlier.
            FeedbackMessage message = (FeedbackMessage)item.getModelObject();
            listItem.add(new Label("message",new
                PropertyModel(message,"message")));
            listItem.add(new Label("level",new PropertyModel(message,"level")));
        }
};
add(feedback);
```

On leaving the input fields blank and clicking the Save button, you should see the error messages being displayed in a format shown in Figure 2-11.

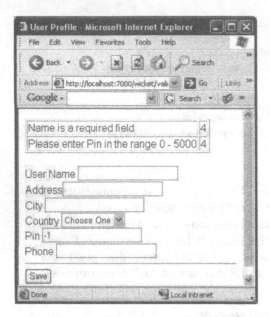

Figure 2-11. *Changing the feedback message display format using the ListView component*

The display style doesn't look intuitive, but you now know how Wicket handles feedback and the inner workings of the ListView component.

Summary

Input validation is very significant to all web applications, and you saw that Wicket has a nice subframework dedicated just for that. User feedback is typically provided using Wicket's FeedbackPanel component. All components allow you to associate an error with them through the error() method, which takes a string error message as an argument. These errors are ultimately accumulated by the encompassing Page class and are finally displayed by the FeedbackPanel component. In fact, you also have the option of associating feedback messages with a Wicket session.

You also saw that wicket.Localizer encapsulates all of the localization-related functionality in a way that can be accessed by all areas of the framework in a consistent manner. All localized messages can be specified in a properties file whose name is the same as the Page class. By default, Wicket looks for Page_Class_Name.properties and, depending upon the locale, looks for the properties file named accordingly. For example, the locale for Page_Class_Name_fr.properties is French. In the absence of such a properties file, Wicket will use the default properties file Page_Class_Name.properties. If the page.properties file or the message key is missing, Wicket looks up Application.properties. Application.properties acts as a repository of all globally accessible messages.

You learned how to put Wicket's built-in validators, namely RequiredValidator and NumberValidator, to use. Wicket does not call the form processing logic (e.g., onSubmit() in the case of the chapter example) if any of the validators signal failure. It displays the same page again instead, retaining the invalid inputs that caused the error in the first place. You also learned that you could validate multiple FormComponents at the same time by implementing Wicket's IFormValidator interface. Wicket ships some default IFormValidator implementations like the EqualPasswordInputValidator class

You also learned that Wicket converters act as bridges between HTTP parameters and the model classes. Even though the built-in converters are sufficient for majority of cases, I showed you a case where a custom converter was required. I walked you through the creation of one such converter—PhoneNumberConverter. Toward the end, you put the ListView component to use in order to render data in a tabular format.

■ ■ ■

CHAPTER 3

Developing a Simple Application

In this chapter, you will first learn about the Wicket way of handling Session. You will also learn to configure "nice" URLs for accessing Wicket pages. You will then see how to develop a shopping cart application that will provide you with ample opportunities to explore key Wicket areas. There's a lot of ground to cover, and it's extremely important that you understand the concepts explained in this chapter. The sample application that you will develop will also serve as the base for the rest of the chapters to follow.

Securing Wicket Pages

Just as a recap, let's make sure that the pages you developed in the last couple of chapters show up just fine. This should serve as a general-purpose template for the URL to access the pages you developed in the last chapter:

```
http://<host>:<port>/webapp_context/wicket_servlet_mapping?
wicket:bookmarkablePage=fully_qualfied_name of the_page_class
```

The URL to access the login page, for example, looks like this:

```
http://localhost:8080/helloworld/app?wicket:bookmarkablePage=:com.apress.wicketbook.
forms.Login
```

Even though it's somewhat clear that Wicket manages to decode the preceding URL based on the specified package name, the URL still has a cryptic feel to it. Wicket provides a nice way of overriding this though, and we shall discuss that next.

Nice Wicket URLs and Mounted Pages

In order to enable "nice" URLs for your application, you need to configure a few things in your application's init() method, as shown in Listing 3-1. For example, if you want to access the Login and UserProfilePage through a URL pattern such as /login and /userprofile, you need to instruct Wicket to map calls to Login and UserProfilePage pages to the paths /login and /userprofile, respectively.

Listing 3-1. *HelloWorldApplication Configured for Nice URLs*

```
// Imports same as earlier
public class HelloWorldApplication extends WebApplication {

    public void init(){
        // Map Login page to the path /login and
        // UserProfilePage to /userprofile.
        mountBookmarkablePage("/login", Login.class);
        mountBookmarkablePage("/userprofile", UserProfilePage.class);
    }
}
```

Now you just need to enter the URL http://localhost:8080/helloworld/app/login to access the login page. Depending upon the number of pages in your application, registering them as shown previously through repeated calls to WebApplication.mountBookmarkablePage() could become tedious. Most programmers are lazy when it comes to such things, and Wicket recognizes this: if you have "packaged" your pages such that the URLs are mapped the way you want, and if you are fine with addressing pages by their class name, you can use the code in Listing 3-2 in your application class.

Listing 3-2. *Nice URLs Configured for All Pages Within a Package*

```
import wicket.util.lang.PackageName;

public class HelloWorldApplication extends WebApplication {
    public void init() {
        super.init();
            // All pages that reside in the same package as the
            // the home page - the Login class can be addressed through the
            // URL /pages/PageClassName.
        mount("/pages", PackageName.forPackage(Login.class.getPackage()));
    }

    public Class getHomePage(){
        return com.apress.wicketbook.forms.Login.class;
    }
}
```

Now you can enter the various URLs to access the different pages:

- http://localhost:8080/helloworld/app/pages/Login to access the login page.

- http://localhost:8080/helloworld/app/pages/UserProfilePage to access the user profile page.

- http://localhost:8080/helloworld/app/pages/Welcome/userId/Igor to access the Welcome page, passing in the page parameter corresponding to userId. Of course, for this to work, the Welcome page should have a constructor that accepts page parameters, and you did accommodate this requirement in the first chapter.

All of the pages should render just fine, but the worrying aspect is that none of them are secured. You did accommodate a trivial authentication mechanism in the login page toward the end of the first chapter, but you didn't bother to pass on this context to other pages. Let's fix that problem this time around to avoid any security breaches. This context is typically passed on to other pages through a *web* or *user* session. HTTP by nature is a stateless protocol. *Session* enables you to establish that state and track a user activity over multiple web pages. A session is defined as a series of related browser requests that come from the same client during a certain time period. During every page access, you need to make sure that user is logged in. Let's get all pages to check for the presence of a valid User object in the session, its presence indicating a valid user session and its absence indicating otherwise. You also need to redirect the user to the login page on illegal access.

The User object needs to be stored in the session first. You already have a login screen and authentication routine in place. Once the user provides valid credentials, you'll store the information in the user session in the form of a User object.

The class in Listing 3-3 represents a logged-in user.

Listing 3-3. *User.java*

```java
public class User implements Serializable {
  private String userId;
    public User(String userId){
      if (userId == null || user.trim().length() == 0)
        throw new IllegalArgumentException("A user needs to have an associated Id");
      this.userId = userId;
    }
    public String getUserId() {
      return userId;
    }
}
```

You would be required to change the Login page as shown in Listing 3-4.

Listing 3-4. *Login.java*

```java
public class Login...
  //...
    public Login() {
      Form form = new Form("loginForm") {
        public void onSubmit() {
          String password = Login.this.getPassword();
          String userId  = Login.this.getUserId();
          if (authenticate(userId,password)){
            User loggedInUser = new User(userId);

            // Somehow access the session object and store the loggedInUser
```

```
            // Set Welcome page as response as earlier.
            Welcome welcomePage = new Welcome();
            welcomePage.setUserId(userId);
            setResponsePage(welcomePage);
        }
    }
    };

    //..
}
```

Before we move on to bigger things, there is a basic question that hasn't been addressed yet: how do you access session in Wicket? We will discuss that next.

Accessing Wicket Application Session

A quick look at the Wicket API Javadocs reveals that there are a couple of session-related classes—an abstract Session class and its concrete implementation, WebSession. All Wicket components and therefore Pages have access to the current user session through the getSession() method. It's probably a good idea to retrieve the Session and set the User object on it. Even though you have access to the Wicket Session object from a Page, it hides the underlying javax.servlet.http.HttpSession from the developers and, more significantly, it blocks access to the HttpSession.setAttribute() method by specifying the access specifier as "protected" in the base class. This is quite different from other frameworks that allow you uninhibited access to HttpSession. Since storing the User object directly in HttpSession is not an option, the only way to implement this is by having a custom Session class that extends from Wicket's WebSession class and then storing the User object as a session attribute. You can have a getter/setter combination to access it. The WebSession along with the instance variables stored within it end up in the HttpSession.

A browser request is first intercepted by the WicketServlet (more specifically the servlet's doGet method) that in turn asks the configured WebApplication for an ISessionFactory implementation. ISessionFactory, as the name suggests, is entrusted with the job of returning a Wicket Session or more specifically its subclass—WebSession. Let's provide both the implementations—a class that extends WebSession and allows you to set/retrieve the User object (see Listing 3-5).

Listing 3-5. *HelloWorldSession.java*

```
public class HelloWorldSession extends WebSession {

    private User user;

    /** WebSession needs a reference to the Application class. **/
    public HelloWorldSession(WebApplication application){
        super(application);
    }
```

```
  public void setUser(User user){
    this.user = user;
  }

  public User getUser(){
    return this.user;
  }

  // A helper to determine whether the user is logged in
  public boolean isUserLoggedIn(){
    return (user != null);
  }
}
```

Listing 3-6 shows an ISessionFactory that returns the newly instituted Session class.

Listing 3-6. *HelloWorldApplication.java*

```
public class HelloWorldApplication extends WebApplication {
  //..
  public ISessionFactory getSessionFactory(){
    return new ISessionFactory(){
      public Session newSession(){
        return new HelloWorldSession(HelloWorldApplication.this);
      }
    };
  }
}
```

Note that if you don't return your own ISessionFactory implementation, Wicket will use WebSession as its Session class instead. Now that you know how to access the Session class, let's get the Login page to store the User object in the session after authentication, as shown in Listing 3-7.

Listing 3-7. *Login.java*

```
public class Login extends WebPage
  ...
  ...

  public Login() {
    Form form = new Form("loginForm") {
      public void onSubmit() {
        String password = Login.this.getPassword();
        String userId   = Login.this.getUserId();
        if (authenticate(userId,password)){
          User loggedInUser = new User(userId);
            // Components can access the Session through getSession().
          HelloWorldSession session = (HelloWorldSession)getSession();
```

```
            session.setUser(loggedInUser);
            Welcome welcomePage = new Welcome();
            welcomePage.setUserId(userId);
            setResponsePage(welcomePage);
        }
      }
    };


  public final boolean authenticate(final String username, final String password){
      if ("wicket".equalsIgnoreCase(username) &&
                "wicket".equalsIgnoreCase(password))
        return true;
      else
        return false;
  }
}
```

By forcing developers to extend WebSession to accommodate application-specific state management, Wicket encourages an interaction that involves strongly typed objects. In other frameworks like Struts, you could get away with setting any arbitrary object in HttpSession (through setAttribute calls), sometimes polluting the session on the way. HTTP is a stateless protocol, and Wicket takes it on by providing stateful components, thereby alleviating developer pain considerably. Note that you definitely can access HttpSession through the protected setAttribute() method in your custom WebSession. But then remember that Wicket is already managing the page state for you—the page along with the nested components and associated models are held in a PageMap that is in turn stored in the HttpSession. Make sure that you have a really compelling reason to expose HttpSession.setAttribute() in case you choose to.

Once the preceding change is incorporated, the check for the presence of a user-session object and subsequent redirect to the login page needs to be added as a part of the page construction process. Since the routine that does the preceding needs to be called during every page construction, let's move the code some place common—SecuredBasePage (see Listing 3-8). You can get other application pages to extend it. Don't use this as the base class for the Login page, though, for obvious reasons.

Listing 3-8. *SecuredBasePage Checking for the Presence of a Valid User Session*

```
public abstract class SecuredBasePage extends WebPage {
  public AppBasePage() {
   super();
   verifyAccess();
  }

  protected void verifyAccess(){
   // Redirect to Login page on invalid access.
   if (!isUserLoggedIn()){
     throw new
     RestartResponseAtInterceptPageException(Login.class);
```

```
    }
  }

  protected boolean isUserLoggedIn(){
    return ((HelloWorldSession)getSession()).isUserLoggedIn();
  }
}
```

WHAT IS SO SPECIAL ABOUT RESTARTRESPONSEATINTERCEPTPAGEEXCEPTION?

Throwing `RestartResponseAtInterceptPageException` (interceptPage) tells Wicket that the current request has been intercepted and that there is every chance that the user might be redirected to the current page once the user gets past the intercept page (on successful login). Accordingly, Wicket stores the current request in the `PageMap` before redirecting the request to the intercept page. The intercept page can later revive the request that was originally made, by calling `continueToOriginalDestination()` (see Listing 3-9). You might be required to build your own logic if `setResponsePage()` were to be used instead.

Listing 3-9. *Login.LoginForm Can Continue to the Original Destination*

```
class Login extends ..
//..
class LoginForm extends Form {
  public LoginForm(String id) {
    super(id);
  }

  public void onSubmit() {
    String userId = Login.this.getUserId();
    String password = Login.this.getPassword();
    if (authenticate(userId, password)) {
      User loggedInUser = new User(userId);
      HelloWorldSession session = (HelloWorldSession) getSession();
      session.setUser(loggedInUser);
        // Continue to original request if present. Else display
        // Welcome page.
      if (!continueToOriginalDestination()) {
        Welcome welcomePage = new Welcome();
        welcomePage.setUserId(userId);
        setResponsePage(welcomePage);
      }
    }
  }
}
```

```
}
//..
}
```

Now that you have familiarized yourself with some Wicket concepts, let's put them to practical use by developing a shopping cart application for an online bookstore. (A shopping cart application was chosen here so that we need not spend too much time discussing the problem domain. It allows you to concentrate on honing your Wicket application development skills.)

Developing an Online Bookstore

In the following sections, you will develop an online bookstore that allows you to perform basic operations like browse books based on selected category, add books to the shopping cart, and complete the subsequent book checkout. First things first. You need a class to represent the Book entity (see Listing 3-10).

Listing 3-10. *Book.java*

```java
import java.io.Serializable;

public class Book implements Serializable {

    // Internal counter to determine book ID
    private static int counter;
    private int id;
    private String title;
    private String author;
    private float price;
    private String publisher;
    private String category;

    public Book(String author, String category, String title, float price,
        String publisher) {
        super();
        // Generate internal book ID.
        id = ++counter;
        this.author = author;
        this.category = category;
        this.title = title;
        this.price = price;
        this.publisher = publisher;
    }

    // Define Java bean style getters for all the properties.

}
```

Define a helper class that holds onto and allows you to query the book (in-memory) database as shown in Listing 3-11.

Listing 3-11. *BookDao.java*

```java
public class BookDao implements Serializable {

    /* Some publishers */
    private static String APRESS = "Apress";
    private static String MANNING = "Manning";
    private static String OREILLY = "Oreilly";

    /* Some categories */
    private static String CATEGORY_J2EE = "J2EE";
    private static String CATEGORY_SCRIPTING = "Scripting";
    private static String CATEGORY_ALL = "All";

    private List books = new ArrayList();

    private String[] categories = new String[] { CATEGORY_J2EE,
        CATEGORY_SCRIPTING, CATEGORY_ALL };

    // Add a few books to the book database.
    public BookDao() {
        addBook(new Book("Rob Harrop", CATEGORY_J2EE, "Pro Spring", 30.00f,
            APRESS));
        addBook(new Book("Damian Conway", CATEGORY_SCRIPTING,
            "Object Oriented Perl", 40.00f, MANNING));
        addBook(new Book("Ted Husted", CATEGORY_J2EE, "Struts In Action",
            40.00f, MANNING));
        addBook(new Book("Alex Martelli", CATEGORY_SCRIPTING,
             "Python in a Nutshell", 35.00f, OREILLY));
        addBook(new Book("Alex Martelli", CATEGORY_SCRIPTING,
             "Python Cookbook", 35.00f, OREILLY));
    }

    public void addBook(Book book) {
        books.add(book);
    }

    /** Retrieve a book given its ID. **/

    public Book getBook(int id) {
        for (int i = 0; i < books.size(); i++) {
            Book book = (Book) books.get(i);
            if (book.getId() == id) {
                return book;
            }
```

```java
    }
    throw new RuntimeException("Book with id " + id + " not found ");
}

/* Get the number of books belonging to a category. */

public int getBookCount(String category){
    if (CATEGORY_ALL.equals(category)){
        return findAllBooks().size();
    }
    int count=0;
    for (int i = 0; i < books.size(); i++) {
        Book book = (Book) books.get(i);
        if (book.getCategory().equals(category)) {
            count++;
        }
    }
    return count;
}

/** Get books that belong to a particular category. **/

public List findBooksForCategory(String category) {
    if (CATEGORY_ALL.equals(category)) {
        return findAllBooks();
    }
    List result = new ArrayList();
    for (int i = 0; i < books.size(); i++) {
        Book book = (Book) books.get(i);
        if (book.getCategory().equals(category)) {
            result.add(book);
        }
    }
    return result;
}

public List findAllBooks() {
    return books;
}

/* Get the supported book categories. */

public List getSupportedCategories() {
    return Arrays.asList(categories);
}

/* You will see why you need this later. */
```

```
public List getBooksForCategory(String category,int start,int count) {
    return findBooksForCategory(category).subList(start,start+count);
}

}
```

The next step would be to define the required WebApplication class. Also, the BookDao class, which lets you access the data store, needs to be accessible globally, and you shouldn't really be needing more than one instance of this class.

Where to Store Global Objects?

If you have global objects that are not tied to any particular session, it's a good idea to tie them to your application-specific WebApplication class. Only one instance of WebApplication exists for a deployed Wicket application and could very well function as a registry for global objects. Instantiating BookDao within the WebApplication's constructor will ensure that only one instance of the former exists (see Listing 3-12).

Listing 3-12. *BookStoreApplication.java*

```
public class BookStoreApplication extends WebApplication implements Serializable{

    private BookDao bookDao;

    public BookStoreApplication(){

      // Instantiate the only instance of BookDao.

      bookDao = new BookDao();
    }

    public BookDao getBookDao(){
        return bookDao;
    }

    public ISessionFactory getSessionFactory(){
        return new ISessionFactory(){
         public Session newSession(){
          return new BookStoreSession(BookStoreApplication.this);
         }
        };
    }

    public Class getHomePage() {
        return ViewBooks.class;
    }

}
```

Books on Display at the Online Bookstore

Essentially the Browse Books screen, shown in Figure 3-1, allows you to browse books belonging to a particular category and select books that need to go into the shopping cart. This isn't too bad to start with. The underlying markup is shown in Listing 3-13.

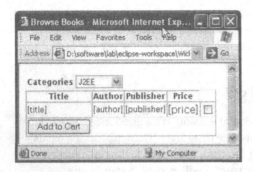

Figure 3-1. *The page that allows you to browse books when previewed on a browser*

Listing 3-13. *ViewBooks.html*

```
<html>
<head><title>Browse Books</title></head>
<body>
<form name="viewBookForm" wicket:id="bookForm">
  <table>
    <tr>
      <td><b>Categories</b></td>
      <td>
        <!-- The corresponding Wicket component is
        wicket.markup.html.form.DropDownChoice.
        The "select" content will be replaced at
        runtime -->
        <select wicket:id="categories">
         <option>category-1</option>
         <option>category-2</option>
         <option>category-3</option>
        </select>
      </td>
    </table>
    <table cellspacing="0" class="dataview" border="1">
      <tr>
        <th align="center">Title</th>
        <th align="center">Author</th>
        <th align="center">Publisher</th>
        <th align="center">Price</th>
      </tr>
```

```
<!-- This data will be dynamically generated -->
<tr wicket:id="books">
   <td><span wicket:id="title">[title]</span></td>
   <td><span wicket:id="author">[author]</span> </td>
   <td><span wicket:id="publisher">[publisher]</span></td>
   <td align="right"><span wicket:id="price">[price]</span></td>
   <td align="right"><input type="checkbox" wicket:id="selected" /></td>
</tr>
<tr>
   <td><input type="submit" value="Add to Cart" wicket:id="addToCart"/></td>
</tr>
   </table>
</form>
</body>
</html>
```

The template indicates that the books need to be listed in a tabular format. You used Wicket's ListView component for displaying tabular data earlier (refer to Chapter 2). But one of the issues with the ListView component is that it expects the entire "list" of data to be available up front. Actually, it has another constructor that doesn't necessarily need a List at the time of construction, as you discovered in Chapter 2. You could still use the ListView component as long as the amount of data that needs to be displayed is minimal. But imagine fetching data all at once from a database table that has a large amount of data. ListView does not offer an elegant solution for such real-world situations. Wicket ships components that address such a requirement through the Wicket-Extensions subproject. The core framework concentrates on working with default Java constructs, while the extensions focus on adapting Wicket components for commonly used real-world situations.

You will make use of one such extension component called DataView—a close cousin of ListView, but superior to the latter in many ways. One of the nice improvements over its predecessor is that it works with an implementation of Wicket's IDataProvider interface that in turn takes into consideration the fact that not all information can be displayed at once and allows for pagination of data.

How IDataProvider Allows for Pagination of Data

All Wicket-Extensions "repeater" components like DataView work with an IDataProvider implementation. The IDataProvider interface allows the implementers to return an iterator over a subset of data. The components like DataView in turn specify that subset (data bounds) and keep track of the paging for you. In order to manage paging, these components also need to know the total number of data rows they are dealing with. The method IDataProvider.size() exists just for that.

Since IDataProvider works with the standard java.util.Iterator, it integrates well with any kind of data store or persistence frameworks like Hibernate, IBatis, or EJB 3. Listing 3-14 shows one such implementation that works with the BookDao in Listing 3-10.

Listing 3-14. *BookDataProvider.java—An IDataProvider Implementation*

```java
import wicket.extensions.markup.html.repeater.data.IDataProvider;

public class BookDataProvider implements IDataProvider{

  // Holds on to the current user-selected category
  //('ALL'/'J2EE'/'Scripting')

  private String category;

  public BookDataProvider(String category){
    this.category = category;
  }

  // By default display all books.
  public BookDataProvider(){
    this(BookDao.CATEGORY_ALL);
  }

  /** @see Iterator IDataProvider.iterator(
  final int first, final int count) **/
  // The data for the "current" page

  public Iterator iterator(final int first, final int count){
    return getBookDao().getBooksForCategory(
      category,first,count).iterator();
  }

  /** @see int IDataProvider.size() **/
  // This is required to determine the total number of
  // Pages the DataView or an equivalent "repeater"
  // component is working with.
  public int size(){
    return getBookDao().getBookCount(category);
  }

  /** @see IModel IDataProvider.model(Object object) **/

  public IModel model(Object object){
      // You will see shortly what you need to be
      // returning from this method.

  }
```

```
// The BookDao has to be looked up when required.
private BookDao getBookDao(){
  return ((BookStoreApplication)Application.get())
    .getBookDao();
}

public String getCategory() {
  return category;
}

public void setCategory(String category) {
  this.category = category;
}
}
```

Note that BookDataProvider simply delegates the method calls to the BookDao instance to implement all data store–related logic, and it's pretty obvious too. This might tempt you to hold onto the BookDao object as an instance variable instead of doing repeated lookups in the getBookDao() method. Even though there isn't anything wrong with that in pure object-oriented (OO) terms, it might turn out to be extremely dangerous in a Wicket scenario.

You know that Wicket stores the component along with its model in the Session, and the last thing you would want is to hog the server memory by storing heavy objects that might, in the worst-case scenario, crash the system. There is also the Wicket Session replication that you have to deal with in a clustered environment. An object that abstracts and encapsulates all access to the persistence store is called a *Data Access Object* (DAO). The BookDao that you developed is one such example. You can refer to http://corej2eepatterns.com/ Patterns2ndEd/DataAccessObject.htm for more information on DAOs. Depending upon your implementation, storing references to DAOs as instance variables in a Wicket model or IDataProvider implementation, for that matter, might result in the entire object graph getting serialized—a situation that you should avoid at any cost. A static lookup mechanism as shown in Listing 3-14 pretty much takes care of this issue.

But this is just one aspect of the problem: remember that the list returned by the IDataProvider.iterator() method is also pushed into the session. However, the good thing is that the interface specifies another method, model(), to let you address this problem as well! The method essentially is a callback that allows the interface implementer to wrap each of the objects retrieved from the iterator() with another lightweight model. The objective is to keep the memory footprint to a minimum (and you have already looked at one way of achieving this through static lookups), and you will see how this objective is met in the next section.

What Is AbstractDetachableModel?

The Wicket's model class, which by now you are familiar with, wraps a Serializable model object that you supply on construction. These objects are stored in the Session along with the related component and the containing Page class, thereby resulting in some form of increased memory consumption. Also, these model objects are serialized during replication in a clustered environment. If you think that your model objects are heavy and you don't want to store them in the Session and replicate them, you need to be looking at one of Wicket's wicket.model.IDetachable implementations.

A *detachable model* in Wicket is a model that can get rid of a large portion of its state to reduce the amount of memory it takes up and to make it cheaper to serialize when replicating it in a clustered environment. When an object is in the detached state, it contains only some very minimal nontransient state such as an object ID that can be used to reconstitute the object from a persistent data store. When a detached object is attached, some logic in the object uses this minimal state to reconstruct the full state of the object. This typically involves restoring fields from persistent storage using a database persistence technology such as JDO or EJB 3, or in this case through the BookDao class.

All model classes in Wicket that are detachable extend the base class wicket.model. AbstractDetachableModel, which encapsulates the logic for attaching and detaching models. The onAttach() abstract method will be called at the first access to the model within a request and, if the model was attached earlier, onDetach() will be called at the end of the request. In effect, attachment and detachment are only done when they are actually needed.

To make implementation of detachable models easy, AbstractDetachableModel provides some basic inheritable logic for attaching and detaching models (see Listing 3-15). You are expected to provide implementation for the methods marked @Override.

Listing 3-15. *A Lightweight DetachableBookModel Class*

```
package com.apress.wicketbook.shop.model;
// Other imports
import wicket.model.AbstractReadOnlyDetachableModel;

public class DetachableBookModel extends AbstractReadOnlyDetachableModel {
  // Required minimal information to look up the book later
  private final int id;
  // Adds "transient" modifier to prevent serialization
  private transient Book book;

  public DetachableBookModel(Book book) {
    this(book.getId());
    this.book = book;
  }

  public DetachableBookModel(int id) {
    if (id == 0) {
      throw new IllegalArgumentException();
    }
    this.id = id;
  }

  /**
   * Returns null to indicate there is no nested model
   */
```

```java
  @Override
  public IModel getNestedModel() {
    return null;
  }

  /**
   * Uses the DAO to load the required Book object when the
   * model is attached to the request
   */
  @Override
  protected void onAttach() {
    book = getBookDao().getBook(id);
  }

  /**
   * Clear the reference to the contact when the model is
   * detached.
   */
  @Override
  protected void onDetach() {
    book = null;
  }

  /**
   * Called after onAttach to return the detachable object.
   * @param component
   *      The component asking for the object
   * @return The detachable object.
   */
  @Override
  protected Object onGetObject(Component component) {
    return book;
  }

  private BookDao getBookDao() {
    return ((BookStoreApplication) Application.get()).getBookDao();
  }
}
```

Now that you have the detachable Book model in place, return it from the
BookDataProvider.model() method that you didn't implement earlier, as shown in
Listing 3-16.

Listing 3-16. *Use the DetachableBookModel Class to Wrap the Object Returned by the DAO*

```
public class BookDataProvider implements IDataProvider{
  //..
  /** @see IModel IDataProvider.model(Object object) **/
  // This method will be called for every Book object
  // returned by the iterator() method.
  public IModel model(Object object){
    return new DetachableBookModel((Book)object);
  }
}
```

What Is LoadableDetachableModel?

Wicket's AbstractReadOnlyDetachableModel, although very powerful, requires you to know quite a bit about the inner workings of Wicket's request cycle to put it to use. You would probably concur that the DetachableBookModel class you developed in the preceding section is a little code heavy. Luckily, the built-in wicket.model.LoadableDetachableModel abstracts out the knowledge of Wicket's request cycle and allows you to concentrate on the "load-mode object-on-demand" feature that you are particularly interested in. It expresses this through its abstract load() method (see Listing 3-17).

Listing 3-17. *A Simpler LoadableDetachableModel Class That Makes Working with Detachable Objects a Breeze*

```
public class LoadableBookModel extends LoadableDetachableModel {

  private final int id;

  public LoadableBookModel(Book book) {
    this(book,book.getId());
  }

  public LoadableBookModel(Book book, int id) {
    // The book instance passed to the LoadableDetachableModel
    // constructor is marked as a transient object. This
    // takes care of the serialization issue.
    super(book);
    if (id == 0) {
      throw new IllegalArgumentException();
    }
    this.id = id;
  }

  private BookDao getBookDao() {
    return ((BookStoreApplication) Application.get()).getBookDao();
  }
```

```
  // You are expected to return the model object.
  @Override
  protected Object load() {
    return getBookDao().getBook(id);
  }
}
```

The new model class is a lot simpler to code and is more compact compared to DetachableBookModel. You could now use LoadableBookModel in place of DetachableBookModel in BookDataProvider.

By now, it should be quite obvious that detachable models could prove to be life-savers in real-world applications. You now know about at least one area that you need to be looking at if your application memory consumption crosses acceptable limits. That said, Wicket actively discourages premature optimization but at the same time provides for all the required hooks to keep it running smoothly under stressful conditions.

Now that you have learned some important Wicket tips, it's time that you address other common use cases related to the fictitious online bookstore.

WICKET SERIALIZATION AND THE LOG4J SETTING

When a new Page is constructed, Wicket pushes the Page instance to the PageMap that is pushed to the HTTP session. If you add the entry log4j.logger.wicket.protocol.http.HttpSessionStoree=➡ DEBUG to the log4j.properties file, Wicket will try to serialize the Page and the associated components and models at the time it pushes the Page to the session. Remember that the serialization process would kick in eventually during replication. Simulating this behavior up front during development could help you iron out the java.io.NotSerializableException that could occur in production. Wicket would inform you of the classes that are not serializable during the development phase itself.

How to Display Books Belonging to a Category When the User Selection Changes

When the user switches to a different category (J2EE, Scripting, etc.) from the one being currently displayed, the underlying table data needs to refresh to display books belonging to the changed category. But a DropDownChoice component, when rendered as an HTML select dropdown, does not trigger a server-side event by default when the selection is changed by the user. DropDownChoice implements Wicket's IOnChangeListener, which in turn maps to such events. You can get Wicket to trigger the IOnChangeListener by returning a boolean value, true, from DropDownChoice.wantOnSelectionChangedNotifications().

As you might have guessed by now, this method returns false by default. Also keep in mind that you need to make sure that the DropDownChoice is a child of a Form component to get this behavior working.

The Page class corresponding to ViewBooks.html is shown in Listing 3-18.

Listing 3-18. *ViewBooks.java*

```java
import wicket.extensions.markup.html.repeater.data.DataView;
import wicket.extensions.markup.html.repeater.refreshing.Item;
import wicket.markup.html.form.DropDownChoice;

public class ViewBooks extends WebPage {

  // Fetches the supported categories from the BookDao that is registered
  // with the BookStoreApplication. Note that a Page (in fact all Wicket
  // components) has access to the
  // application object through getApplication().

  public List getBookCategories(){
    BookStoreApplication application = (BookStoreApplication) getApplication();
    return application.getBookDao().getSupportedCategories();
  }

  public ViewBooks() {

    final Form form = new Form("bookForm");
    final BookDataProvider dataProvider = new BookDataProvider();

    DropDownChoice categories = new CategoryDropDownChoice("categories",
        new PropertyModel(dataProvider, "category"),
            getBookCategories(),books);
    // The drop-down should show a valid value selected.
    categories.setNullValid(false);
    final DataView books = new BookDataView("books", dataProvider);
    form.add(categories);
    form.add(books);
    form.add(new Button("addToCart") {
      public void onSubmit() {
        System.out.println("Need to implement add to cart!!");
      }
    });
    add(form);

  }

// DataView class for tabular data display.
// It works similarly to the ListView component discussed in
// Chapter 2.
```

```
class BookDataView extends DataView{

    public BookDataView(String id, IDataProvider dataProvider) {
        super(id, dataProvider);
    }

    // DataView calls this method for populating the table rows.
    // Refer to Chapter 2 for a detailed discussion on
    // this callback method.

    protected void populateItem(final Item item) {
        Book book = (Book) item.getModelObject();
        // Use the Book object as the compound model for the
        // DataView components. The enclosed components can use
        // the Book object as their own model class.

        item.setModel(new CompoundPropertyModel(book));
        item.add(new Label("title"));
        item.add(new Label("author"));
        item.add(new Label("publisher"));
        item.add(new Label("price"));

        // For now return a blank model just to get it to render.
        item.add(new CheckBox("selected",new Model("")));
    }
}


// A DropDownChoice that represents the displayed categories
class CategoryDropDownChoice extends DropDownChoice{

    DataView bookDataView;

    public CategoryDropDownChoice(String id, IModel model, List
        displayData,DataView bookDataView) {
            super(id,model,displayData);
            this.bookDataView = bookDataView;
    }

    // Indicate that you want a server-side notification
    // when the user changes the drop-down selection.

    public boolean wantOnSelectionChangedNotifications() {
        return true;
    }
```

```
    public void onSelectionChanged(java.lang.Object newSelection) {
        /*
         * Note that you are not required to explicitly update the category -
         * dataProvider.setCategory(newSelection.toString());
         *
         * BookDataProvider's category field is set as the model
         * for DropdownChoice and hence will be automatically updated
         * when the form submits. But the DataView model that displays the
         * books belonging to a particular category needs to reset
         * its current page. You do that through the following method call.
         */
        bookDataView.setCurrentPage(0);
    }
  }

}
```

If you view the generated HTML source, you will find that the HTML select drop-down
has its onChange JavaScript event set up for form submit (see Figure 3-2).

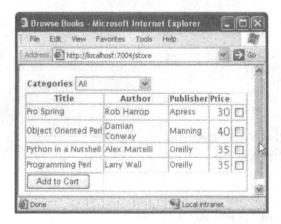

Figure 3-2. *The Wicket-enabled page that fetches book-related data from the server*

Adding Pagination to the ViewBooks Page

Even though the books are being listed just fine, there are still too many items per page, and
this could only get worse as the number of books in the back-end store increases. Maybe you
could do with a little bit of a paging feature built into the application. Adding pagination to
DataView is quite trivial, as you will soon find out. You just need to inform the DataView component about the number of items you want displayed per page and then add to the form a
paging navigator that knows the DataView to which it is attached (see Listing 3-19).

Listing 3-19. *ViewBooks.java*

```
import wicket.markup.html.navigation.paging.PagingNavigator;
  ...
  public class ViewBooks extends WebPage
    public ViewBooks(){
      //..

      /* As the method call indicates,
       * this will ensure that only two items are displayed per page.
       */
      books.setItemsPerPage(2);

      /* But a navigator needs to be associated with
       * the DataView to achieve paging.
       */
      form.add(new PagingNavigator("navigator", books));
  }
}
```

And of course you need to specify the place holder for the navigator in the template (see Listing 3-20).

Listing 3-20. *ViewBooks.html*

```
<!-- Rest of the content snipped for clarity -->
<span wicket:id="navigator">[dataview navigator]</span>
<table cellspacing="0" class="dataview" border="1">
<tr>
<!-- Rest of the content snipped for clarity -->
```

Figure 3-3 shows the resulting changes to the ViewBooks page. Now you can easily navigate through the pages by clicking the paging links.

Figure 3-3. *ViewBooks page with a paging navigator component*

There is still an issue with the check boxes that has not been addressed yet. Now that all the table elements are sourcing their data from the Book model (note the use of CompoundPropertyModel), you need to get the check box also to do the same (see Listing 3-21).

Listing 3-21. *ViewBooks.java*

```
public class ViewBooks extends WebPage
   //..
   class BookDataView extends DataView{
     //..
    protected void populateItem(final Item item) {
      // Rest of the code is same as Listing 3-18


      item.add(new CheckBox("selected"));
    }
   }

 }
```

Add a boolean attribute to Book.java that obeys the Java bean coding conventions (see Listing 3-22).

Listing 3-22. *Add a boolean Attribute to Identify Whether a User Has Selected a Book*

```
class Book{
 //..
 private boolean selected;

 public void setSelected(boolean selected){
   this.selected = selected;
 }

 public boolean isSelected(){
   return selected;
 }

 }
```

Now refresh the page, wait for the modifications to take effect, and try selecting a few books. Try navigating across pages and selecting books from other pages as well. If you repeat this process a couple of times, you will notice that your selections are not being retained as you travel back and forth by clicking the navigator links. On viewing the generated HTML, you will find that the paging links are just that—HTML links—and they do not result in a form submit, and hence the updates are not propagated to the check box model. What you need is a link that results in form submission (more importantly model update), and not surprisingly, Wicket provides one through the SubmitLink component.

But this also means that you will be required to roll out your own navigator scheme that works with SubmitLink, and this involves some effort. The crux of the problem is that the check box is unable to maintain its state—checked/otherwise—during navigation. One solution could be to update the underlying model whenever the user checks/unchecks the check box. The default CheckBox component behavior is the same as that of the DropDownChoice component when the user selection changes—i.e., they both do not propagate the event to the server-side component. Luckily, the Wicket way of providing this behavior is also the same— you are expected to return true by overriding the CheckBox.wantOnSelectionChanged➧ Notifications() method (see Listing 3-23). Live with this solution for now; you will have the opportunity to improve upon it in later chapters.

Listing 3-23. *Add a Custom Check Box That Actively Reacts to User Selections*

```
public class ViewBooks extends WebPage

    //..
    class BookDataView extends DataView{
        //..
        protected void populateItem(final Item item) {

        // Rest of the code is same as Listing 3-18
            item.add(new MyCheckBox("selected"));
        }
        // A custom CheckBox that will result in Form submit
        // when checked/unchecked
        class MyCheckBox extends CheckBox{
            public MyCheckBox(String id) {
                super(id);
            }
            protected boolean wantOnSelectionChangedNotifications() {
                return true;
            }
        }
    }

}
```

After accommodating these changes, the page should render fine, but you still need to verify whether the check box model update problem has been taken care of. Test the links and it should work fine now. Not too bad, given that you had to make minimal modifications to the existing components to get the job done!

Wicket Pages and User Threads

If you think that you are done, then try this—select a book from the first page, move over to the second, and navigate back to the first. Now open another browser and you will see a screen similar to the one marked User Session 2 in Figure 3-4.

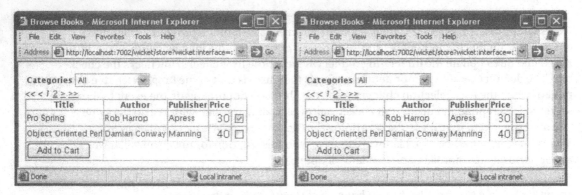

User Session 1   User Session 2

Figure 3-4. *Issues with sharing data across sessions*

Something seems to be going wrong here. Accessing the page in a different browser is equivalent to a new user session (depending upon the browser you use), and for some strange reason the two user sessions are seeing identical selections! This tells you that associating the state of the check box (whether it has been selected or not) with the Book model is not an option. A Book object is a shared resource that is visible across sessions.

WICKET PAGES AND THREAD SAFETY

Wicket maintains a PageMap instance *per user session*. Wicket stores the Page, the contained components, and models in this PageMap. Wicket ensures that access to the Page class is *thread-safe*. This allows you to program without worrying about ConcurrentModificationException when iterating through lists in a Page, for example, in Wicket. Of course, it is assumed that the List instance is not shared globally.

In that respect, Wicket Pages are very different from, say, Struts Action classes that are not inherently thread-safe. It is also quite different from the pooled Tapestry pages. Even though Tapestry pages are thread-safe, there is every possibility that you might be working with Page instance variables that actually belong to a prior request unless you take care of it explicitly. Essentially, Wicket's innate ability to maintain state *per page per user session* is its biggest differentiator. Thread-safe Wicket Pages and components are side effects of this.

You will try a novel way of putting models to work in order to fix this problem. Incorporate the modifications shown in Listing 3-24 to the Page.

Listing 3-24. *ViewBooks.java*

```
public class ViewBooks extends WebPage{

    /* Rest of the content same as previous version */
    // Holds on to the current user selection
```

```
private List booksMarkedForCheckout = new ArrayList();

private class CheckBoxModel implements IModel, Serializable {

  // Book ID the model represents
  private final Integer bookId;

  public CheckBoxModel(int bookId) {
   this.bookId = new Integer(bookId);
  }

  public IModel getNestedModel() {
   return null;
  }

  /*
   * Wicket calls this method when rendering the check box.
   * CheckBox needs to show up selected if the
   * corresponding book has already been selected.
   */

  public Object getObject(Component component) {
     return isBookAlreadyMarkedForCheckout();
  }

  private Boolean isBookAlreadyMarkedForCheckout() {
    if (booksMarkedForCheckout.contains(bookId))
      return Boolean.TRUE;
    else
      return Boolean.FALSE;
  }

  /*
   * Wicket calls this method when pushing the
   * user selection back to the model. If the user has
   * selected a book, the method adds it to the back-end store
   * after making sure that it has not been selected before.
   * If the user has unchecked the check box, the method
   * removes it from the back-end store if present.
   */

  public void setObject(Component component, Object object) {
    boolean selected = ((Boolean) object).booleanValue();
    boolean previouslySelected =
      isBookAlreadyMarkedForCheckout().booleanValue();
    if (selected) {
      if (!previouslySelected) {
        booksMarkedForCheckout.add(bookId);
```

```
        }
      } else {
        if (previouslySelected) {
          booksMarkedForCheckout.remove(bookId);
        }
      }
    }

    public void detach() {}

}

//..
class BookDataView extends DataView{
    //..
    protected void populateItem(final Item item) {

    // Rest of the code is same as Listing 3-18.

      // Use the newly instituted CheckBoxModel.
      item.add(new MyCheckBox("selected",
            new CheckBoxModel(book.getId())));
    }
    // MyCheckBox that accepts a model
    class MyCheckBox extends CheckBox{
      public MyCheckBox(String id,IModel model){
        super(id, model);
      }
      protected boolean wantOnSelectionChangedNotifications() {
        return true;
      }
    }
  }
  //..
}
```

You already know that the Page class, along with its constituent components and models, is held in a PageMap that in turn is held in the user session. That's the reason why the instance variable booksMarkedForCheckout will reflect the current user selection every time there is a Form submit (only as long as you refrain from creating a new instance of the Page class, of course). It's good to be reminded once in a while how Wicket counters the statelessness of HTTP transparently to the user. It's probably time to relax now that you have handled all the glaring issues. Let's perform a sanity check to make sure that it's all fine. Try to do so by performing the following steps:

1. Start a fresh session. It will display books belonging to all categories by default.

2. Select a book from the first page.

3. Change the category in the drop-down to Scripting. Now `DataView` will display the books belonging to that category.

4. Change the category back to ALL.

Guess we celebrated too soon, as Figure 3-5 illustrates.

Browser After Steps 1 and 2

Browser After Step 3

Browser After Step 4

Figure 3-5. *User selection not being retained across page navigation*

It's probably a little discouraging to note that you lost your initial selection again. Isn't Wicket supposed to update form component models during Form submission? Didn't you make sure that when you changed the category, it resulted in form submission? Then why didn't the check box model get updated? Well, as it turns out, what you want here is a behavior Wicket developers intentionally got away from because users didn't want it. Wicket just calls DropDownChoice.onSelectionChanged when the user changes the selection, avoiding Form component model update in the process. But all is not lost; you can still programmatically push updates to the model. Wicket doesn't when you change the DropDownChoice category, but you sure can.

Form exposes a method that updates the underlying models (In fact, Form.process() does more than just update the models. It validates the input, among other things.) In the case of this example, it's about calling this method when the drop-down choice selection changes. Incorporate the changes in Listing 3-25, and that should fix the problem.

Listing 3-25. *ViewBooks.java*

```
public class ViewBooks extends WebPage
    //..
    // Modify the existing DropDownChoice to invoke the form-processing code
    // on onSelectionChanged.

    class CategoryDropDownChoice extends DropDownChoice{
      //
      public void onSelectionChanged(java.lang.Object newSelection) {
        // When selection changes, update the Form component model.
        getForm().process();
        bookDataView.setCurrentPage(0);
      }
    }
    //..
}
```

Using Wicket Behaviors to Add HTML Attributes to the Table Rows

Wicket allows you to modify or add attributes to HTML elements on the fly through the wicket.AttributeModifier class. But before you put that to use, it's of utmost importance that you understand the concept of *behaviors* in Wicket. Wicket models behaviors through the wicket.behavior.IBehavior interface. Components can exhibit different behaviors, and they can be associated with the component at runtime (by simply calling wicket.Component.add (IBehavior)). In addition to other tasks, a behavior gets an opportunity to modify the component tag attributes through the IBehavior.onComponentTag() method. Say you want to add an HTML attribute called class to the rows to indicate whether they are even or odd. Listing 3-26 demonstrates how you would do it.

Listing 3-26. *Existing BooksDataView.java Modified to Add HTML Attributes to Table Rows*

```java
import wicket.AttributeModifier;
import wicket.model.AbstractReadOnlyModel;

    class BookDataView extends DataView{
        //..
        protected void populateItem(final Item item) {

            // Rest of the code is same as the BookDataView class in
            // Listing 3-24.

            // Add an attribute modifier to toggle the class attribute value between
            // "even" and "odd". The argument "true" tells the behavior to overwrite
            // an existing "class" attribute value.

            item.add(new AttributeModifier("class", true, new AbstractReadOnlyModel(){

                // You used this earlier as well with CheckBox model.
                // It is through this method that Wicket adds a level of indirection
                // when fetching the "actual" model object.

                public Object getObject(Component component){
                    return (item.getIndex() % 2 == 1) ? "even" : "odd";
                }
            }));
        }
        //..
    }
```

The piece of code that adds the AttributeModifier requires some explanation. This is what it specifies: add an attribute named class to the HTML <tr> element if it already doesn't exist (indicated through argument true) and use the AbstractReadOnlyModel to retrieve the value for the attribute. Return even/odd based on the index of the current element. AbstractReadOnlyModel, as the name suggests, is read-only. Invoking setObject() on it would result in a runtime exception getting thrown.

If you find the use of AbstractReadOnlyModel a little confusing, you could also use the wicket.behavior.SimpleAttributeModifier class to achieve a similar effect:

```java
String classAttr = (item.getIndex() % 2 == 1) ? "even" : "odd";
item.add(new SimpleAttributeModifier("class",classAttr));
```

While rendering, the attribute value essentially toggles between even and odd, depending upon the index. You could encapsulate this behavior into something reusable as well. The Wicket extension's OddEvenItem class does just that. You saw earlier that Wicket's Item represents one entire row of the DataView class. OddEvenItem extends Item and sets the class attribute of each row to even or odd based on its index in the data provider. But how do you let DataView know that it needs to use OddEvenItem in place of Item? Wicket solves this problem by allowing you to specify the Item object through a factory method. The factory method returns an Item instance by default for every iteration. You just need to override it to return the OddEvenItem instead. Quite a few components that ship with Wicket extensions follow this pattern.

Listing 3-27 shows how it's done.

Listing 3-27. *Returning an Item Subclass Through the Factory Method*

```
import wicket.extensions.markup.html.repeater.refreshing.OddEvenItem;

    class BookDataView extends DataView{
      //..
       protected void populateItem(final Item item) {
       protected void populateItem(final Item item) {
       // Rest of the code is same as the BookDataView class in
       // Listing 3-24.
       }

       @Override
       protected Item newItem(final String id, int index, final IModel model){
          return new OddEvenItem(id, index, model);
       }
       //
    }
```

One important thing to remember here is that OddEvenItem works on a Java-based list index, i.e., it bases its decision on the fact that the index of the first element (in the data provider) is 0 and hence even. Accordingly, the second element in the list will result in the class attribute being set to odd, and so on. So you need to specify your CSS style accordingly.

Modify ViewBooks.html and add inline CSS tags through the <style></style> element as shown in Listing 3-28.

Listing 3-28. *ViewBooks.html Modified with CSS Tags*

```
<html>
 <head><title>Browse Books</title></head>
 <style>
   tr.even{
     background-color: #ffebcd;
   }
   tr.odd{
     background-color: #ffa;
   }
 </style>
 <body>
 <!-- Rest snipped as there are no modifications -->
```

Figure 3-6 shows the results of your changes to ViewBooks.html.

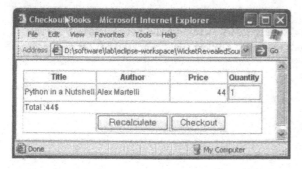

Figure 3-6. *DataView rows acquiring different CSS styles based on their index in the List instance*

Now that you have selected the books you are interested in, the next logical step for you would obviously be to add the books to the shopping cart and subsequently check out. Currently the onSubmit() implementation of the Add to Cart button just prints out a string to the console. Before you redirect the user to the Checkout page, you need to get the Checkout page working first. Once you have the checkout functionality in place, onSubmit() just needs to invoke that page.

Implementing the Checkout Page

Figure 3-7 shows the template you will use to begin with.

Figure 3-7. *The Checkout page preview*

Listing 3-29 presents the HTML that produces the output shown in Figure 3-7.

Listing 3-29. *Checkout.html*

```html
<html>
   <head><title>Checkout Books</title></head>
   <body>
     <form name="checkoutForm" wicket:id="checkoutForm">
       <table cellspacing="0" border="1">
       <tr>
         <th align="center">Title</th>
         <th align="center">Author</th>
         <th align="center">Price</th>
         <th align="center">Quantity</th>
       </tr>
       <tr wicket:id="checkoutBooks">
         <td><span wicket:id="book.title">Python</span></td>
         <td><span wicket:id="book.author">Martelli</span> </td>
         <td align="right"><span wicket:id="book.price">44</span></td>
         <td align="right"><input type="text" value="1" size="4"
           wicket:id="quantity"/></td>
       </tr>
       <tr>
          <td colspan="6">Total :<span wicket:id="priceTotal">44</span>$</td>
       </tr>
       <!-- Add the buttons that you want displayed -->
       <tr>
         <td></td>
         <td><input type="submit" value="Recalculate" wicket:id="recalculate"/></td>
         <td><input type="submit" value="Checkout" wicket:id="checkOut"/></td>
       </tr>
       </table>
   </form>
   </body>
   </html>
```

Figure 3-8 demonstrates how the user is likely to use the recalculate functionality.

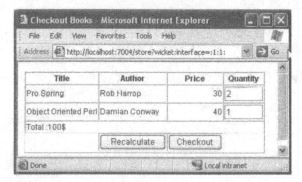

Pro Spring has a quantity of 1.

Enter a quantity of 2 for *Pro Spring* and press Recalculate.

Figure 3-8. *The functioning of the Recalculate button*

A user is likely to buy more than one copy of a book, and you need an attribute in the model to store this information (quantity bought). You saw in the previous exercise that storing this attribute in the shared Book object is not an option. Let's create a view helper object that allows you to store this information. Note that CheckoutBook, shown in Listing 3-30, does not duplicate the attributes of the Book class. Instead, it allows access to the contained Book object.

Listing 3-30. *CheckoutBook.java*

```java
import java.io.Serializable;

public class CheckoutBook implements Serializable {

    private Book book;

    // Set book quantity to 1 by default
    private int quantity=1;

    public CheckoutBook(Book book){
        this.book = book;
    }

    public Book getBook(){
        return book;
    }

    public void setQuantity(int quantity){
        this.quantity = quantity;
    }

    public int getQuantity(){
        return quantity;
    }

    /* Returns the price depending upon the quantity entered */

    public float getTotalPrice(){
        return getBook().getPrice() * getQuantity();
    }

    /*
     * This class is just an extension of the book object.
     * Hence delegate the following method implementation to
     * the original book object.
     */

    public boolean equals(Object obj){
        return book.equals(obj);
    }

    public int hashCode(){
        return book.hashCode();
    }

}
```

Let's have a java representation of the shopping cart as well. The Cart class, shown in Listing 3-31, has methods that allow you to add new books to the cart or query the cart for the existence of a book. Purely from the point of view of economics, it also allows the user to figure out the amount of money he or she owes the bookstore before proceeding with the checkout.

Listing 3-31. *Cart.java*

```java
public class Cart implements Serializable {

    private List checkoutBooks;

    public Cart(){
      checkoutBooks = new ArrayList();
    }

    public void addToCart(CheckoutBook book){
      if (!checkoutBooks.contains(book)){
        checkoutBooks.add(book);
      }
    }

    public boolean containsBook(int bookId){
      for(int i=0; i < checkoutBooks.size(); i++){
        if ((((CheckoutBook)checkoutBooks.get(i)).getBook().getId())== bookId){
          return true;
        }
      }
      return false;
    }

    public List getCheckoutBooks(){
      return checkoutBooks;
    }

    /*
    * Computes the total price of the books in the cart
    */

    public float getTotalPrice(){
      float totalPrice = 0;
      for(int i=0; i < checkoutBooks.size(); i++){
        totalPrice += ((CheckoutBook)checkoutBooks.get(i)).getTotalPrice();
      }
      return totalPrice;
    }

}
```

The user is very likely to add or remove books from the cart during the user session. Hence the cart needs to be made available throughout the entire duration the user is active on the bookstore site. As you might have guessed, the best place for the cart to reside would be in the user session (see Listing 3-32).

Listing 3-32. *BookStoreSession.java*

```java
public class BookStoreSession extends WebSession {

    private Cart cart;

    public BookStoreSession(WebApplication application){
        super(application);
    }

    /* Some users might not be interesting in buying a book.
     * Maybe they are interested in reading a book review, for example.
     * So create the cart on demand and not by default.
     */

    public Cart getCart(){
        if (cart == null)
            cart = new Cart();
        return cart;
    }

}
```

Now that you have the cart and other related infrastructure in place, implement the Checkout page, as shown in Listing 3-33.

Listing 3-33. *Checkout.java*

```java
import wicket.extensions.markup.html.repeater.data.ListDataProvider;

public class Checkout extends WebPage {

    private Cart cart;

    // You might get to this page from another link. So you need a
    // default constructor as well.

    public Checkout() {
        this(Collections.EMPTY_LIST);
    }
```

```java
public Checkout(List checkoutBooksIds) {
    addBooksToCart(checkoutBooksIds);
    cart = ((BookStoreSession)getSession()).getCart();
    Form checkoutForm = new Form("checkoutForm");

    final DataView books = new DataView("checkoutBooks", new ListDataProvider(
        cart.getCheckoutBooks()))) {

        protected void populateItem(final Item item) {

            CheckoutBook cBook  = (CheckoutBook) item.getModelObject();
            final CompoundPropertyModel model = new CompoundPropertyModel(cBook);

            // Model is set at parent level, and child components will look it up.
            item.setModel(model);
             // Evaluates model to cBook.getBook().getTitle()
            item.add(new Label("book.title"));
             // Evaluates model to cBook.getBook().getAuthor()
            item.add(new Label("book.author"));
            // Evaluates model to cBook.getBook().getPrice()
            item.add(new Label("book.price"));
            // Evaluates to cBook.getQuantity() & cBook.setQuantity()
            item.add(new TextField("quantity"));
        }
    };

    checkoutForm.add(books);
    // Get the cart to determine the total price.
    checkoutForm.add(new Label("priceTotal",new
            PropertyModel(this.cart,"totalPrice")));

    /* The book quantity is tied to the CheckoutBook that is present
     * in the cart. The "total price" is also tied to the cart through
     * the use of the PropertyModel class. Hence the new price
     * calculation is automatically taken care of. So "recalculate"
     * comes for free!
     */

    checkoutForm.add(new Button("recalculate"){
        public void onSubmit(){

        }
    });
```

```
          checkoutForm.add(new Button("checkOut")){
              public void onSubmit(){

              }
          });
          add(checkoutForm);

      }

      private void addBooksToCart(List booksMarkedForCheckout) {
          BookDao bookDao = ((BookStoreApplication) getApplication())
              .getBookDao();
          Cart cart = getCart();
          for (Iterator iter = booksMarkedForCheckout.iterator(); iter.hasNext();) {
            int bookId = ((Integer) iter.next()).intValue();
            if (!cart.containsBook(bookId)) {
              Book book = bookDao.getBook(bookId);
              cart.addToCart(new CheckoutBook(book));
            }
          }
      }
  }
```

You know that CompoundPropertyModel allows child components to use the parent's model. But this example demonstrates that you can use the component ID as the property-path expression to evaluate a child component's model as well. This allows you to avoid duplication of Book attributes in the CheckoutBook class. Also note that you could afford to leave the onSubmit() implementation of the Recalculate button blank by virtue of having set the cart as the PropertyModel for displaying the total cost of the books.

We all are prone to mood swings, and therefore there is every chance that the user might choose to either remove a few books from the cart or, worse, empty the cart. Adding these functionalities is trivial. But before we proceed further, make sure that you are directing the user to the Checkout page from the ViewBooks page.

```
class ViewBooks extends WebPage{
  public ViewBooks(){
    //..
    form.add(new Button("addToCart") {
      public void onSubmit() {
          // Set the response as the Checkout page passing in the books selected
          // by the user.
        setResponsePage(new Checkout(ViewBooks.this.booksMarkedForCheckout));
      }
    });
  }
  //..
}
```

Maintaining a Layered Page Hierarchy

As you develop the sample application, you will notice that there is a commonly occurring pattern in the code:

```
BookDao bookDao = ((BookStoreApplication) getApplication())
                .getBookDao();
Cart cart = ((BookStoreSession)getSession()).getCart();
```

These typically have to do with the repeated look-up of your WebApplication and WebSession objects. It's important to realize that such functionality could be layered into a nice Page hierarchy. You could have a BaseApplicationPage along the following lines, for example:

```
Class BaseApplicationPage extends WebPage{

  // Subclasses can then simply call this method to
  // get to the WebApplication class.

  BookStoreApplication getBookStoreApplication(){
    return ((BookStoreApplication) getApplication());
  }

  // Subclasses can then simply call this method to
  // get to the Cart, for example.

  Cart getCart(){
    return ((BookStoreSession)getSession()).getCart();
  }
}
```

You could then get all the application Pages to extend BaseApplicationPage and access the WebApplication and WebSession classes through the superclass methods that you just defined.

Implementing the Remove Book Functionality

Figure 3-9 shows how the Checkout page looks after adding the remove book and empty cart functionality.

Figure 3-9. *Adding the remove book and empty cart functionality to the page*

Listing 3-34 shows the code behind the added functionality.

Listing 3-34. *Adding a Remove Button and a Check Box to Select the Book You Want Removed from the Cart*

```
<-- Rest of the code snipped for clarity -->

<tr wicket:id="checkoutBooks">
 <td><span wicket:id="book.title">Python</span></td>
 <td><span wicket:id="book.author">Martelli</span> </td>
 <td align="right"><span wicket:id="book.price">44</span></td>
 <td align="right"><input type="text" value="1" size="4"
    wicket:id="quantity"/></td>

 <!- Added check box for marking a book for removal -->

 <td align="right"><input type="checkbox" wicket:id="markedForRemoval"/></td>
</tr>
<-- Rest of the code snipped for clarity -->
   <!--Add the buttons that you want displayed -->
   <tr>
     <td></td>
     <td><input type="submit" value="Recalculate" wicket:id="recalculate"/></td>
     <td><input type="submit" value="Checkout" wicket:id="checkOut"/></td>
     <td><input type="submit" value="Remove" wicket:id="removeBooks"/></td>
   </tr>
```

In order to support these functionalities, some changes would be required to some of the classes as follows.

Add an attribute to CheckoutBook to maintain the state of selection of the book in the cart, as shown in Listing 3-35.

Listing 3-35. *CheckoutBook.java*

```java
class CheckoutBook implements Serializable{
  //..
  private boolean markedForRemoval;
  public boolean isMarkedForRemoval() {
     return markedForRemoval;
  }

  public void setMarkedForRemoval(boolean markedForRemoval) {
     this.markedForRemoval = markedForRemoval;
  }
  //..
}
```

Add the server-side components corresponding to the new button you added to the Checkout template. You require a CheckBox component as well to retain the selection of books marked for removal (see Listing 3-36).

Listing 3-36. *Checkout.java*

```java
class Checkout..{
    //..
    public Checkout(){
      //...
      final DataView books =
        new DataView("checkoutBooks", new ListDataProvider(
          cart.getCheckoutBooks())) {
          protected void populateItem(final Item item) {
            CheckoutBook cBook  = (CheckoutBook) item.getModelObject();
            //...
            item.add(new TextField("quantity"));
            /*  CheckoutBook is the model. */
            item.add(new CheckBox("markedForRemoval"));
          }
      };

      checkoutForm.add(new Button("removeBooks"){

        // When asked to remove the books, remove them from the cart.
        public void onSubmit(){
          Cart cart = ((BookStoreSession)getSession()).getCart();
          for(Iterator iter = cart.getCheckoutBooks().iterator();
              iter.hasNext();){
            CheckoutBook book = (CheckoutBook) iter.next();
            if(book.isMarkedForRemoval()){
              iter.remove();
            }
          }
        }
      });
    }
}
```

Checkout Confirmation

Now the only thing that remains is to request the user's billing information and subsequently confirm the purchase. You will not develop these screens now, although you can probably do them as an exercise. But for the sake of completeness, implement the Confirmation page, shown in Listing 3-37.

Listing 3-37. *Confirmation.html*

```
<html>
 <head>
     <title>Book Purchase Confirmation</title>
 </head>
 <body>
   Following books have been shipped to your shipping address
   <br/><br/>
   <table border="1">
     <th>Title</th><th>Quantity</th><th>Price</th>
     <tr wicket:id="booksBought">
       <td><span wicket:id="book.title">Pro Spring</span></td>
       <td><span wicket:id="quantity">1</span></td>
       <td><span wicket:id="totalPrice">1</span></td>
     </tr>
   </table>
   <br>
Total Price : $<span wicket:id="totalPrice">80</span>
 </body>
</html>
```

As shown in Listing 3-38, the Page class just retrieves the books from the session and presents a read-only view using the ListView component.

Listing 3-38. *Confirmation.java*

```
public class Confirmation extends WebPage {
  public Confirmation() {
    add(new ListView("booksBought", getCart().getCheckoutBooks()) {
        protected void populateItem(ListItem item) {
            CheckoutBook book = (CheckoutBook) item.getModelObject();
            item.setModel(new CompoundPropertyModel(book));
            item.add(new Label("book.title"));
            item.add(new Label("quantity"));
            item.add(new Label("totalPrice"));
        }
    });
    add(new Label("totalPrice", new PropertyModel(getCart(),"totalPrice")));
  }
```

```
    private Cart getCart() {
      return ((BookStoreSession) getSession()).getCart();
    }
}
```

Of course, this page needs to be invoked from the Checkout page, as shown in Listing 3-39.

Listing 3-39. *Displaying the Confirmation Page When the Checkout Button Is Clicked*

```
public class Checkout extends WebPage{
    //..
    public Checkout(){
      //..
      checkoutForm.add(new Button("checkOut") {
        public void onSubmit() {
          setResponsePage(new Confirmation());
        }
      });
}
```

One interesting thing here is that until the process of checking books out, the user doesn't really have to be logged in to the system. Yes, you are maintaining a shopping cart for the user, but you really don't require sensitive information like a credit card number until you reach the billing stage. Assuming that the billing-related information like credit card number and billing address have been captured during user account creation, you can get to that information by just asking the user to sign into the system just before confirmation. Essentially access to the Confirmation page needs to be secure.

One way to incorporate this could be to employ some check in the Confirmation page constructor and redirect the user to the login page if the current session didn't have a valid user attached to it. This will work in this scenario, as this is the only page that needs to be secure. Imagine a system with a number of such secured pages; adding this check to every page could quickly become tedious. It also encourages the "copy-paste" style of programming that ultimately leads to defective and unmaintainable code.

One solution could be to alter the code structure, keeping the functionality intact. This is commonly referred to as *code refactoring* in the programming world. Martin Fowler, one of the leading proponents of this "art," maintains a catalog of commonly employed refactorings. After consulting the catalog, it shouldn't be too difficult to infer that "Pull-Up Method" refactoring could be employed here. You could move the code that does the authentication to a superclass and get all pages that require a secure access to extend it. This is a nice, albeit old fashioned, way of doing things, in this case specifically since Wicket has already thought out a comprehensive solution.

IAuthorizationStrategy and Conditional Component Instantiation

Wicket recognizes that you might want to perform custom processing during component instantiation as discussed in the last section and supports it at its core by allowing you to register IComponentInstantiationListener implementations. These listeners are typically registered with the Application class. The listeners then receive messages through the callback method, onInstantiation(Component component), when Wicket components are instantiated.

That's not all. When Wicket runs into an unauthorized access or unauthorized component instantiation, it also allows you to decide the future course of action through the IUnauthorizedComponentInstantiationListener interface. Wicket consults the IAuthorizationStrategy implementation that you provide to determine unauthorized component instantiations.

Wicket's Application class registers a component instantiation listener by default that uses the registered authorization strategy to check component instantiations. On an authorized access, it calls the registered IUnauthorizedComponentInstantiationListener implementation's onUnauthorizedInstantiation(Component component) method.

Essentially you need the following:

- An IAuthorizationStrategy

- An IUnauthorizedComponentInstantiationListener implementation

Before providing the preceding implementations, you need a way to identify a page that needs to be accessed securely. You could get the pages that require authentication to implement a marker interface, or better, get them to use a class-level annotation.

In this case, any page that carries the SecuredWicketPage marker annotation shown in Listing 3-40 is automatically considered secured.

Listing 3-40. *SecuredWicketPage.java*

```java
import java.lang.annotation.ElementType;
import java.lang.annotation.Retention;
import java.lang.annotation.RetentionPolicy;
import java.lang.annotation.Target;

// The annotation should be available for runtime introspection and
// should be specified at the class level.

@Retention(RetentionPolicy.RUNTIME)
@Target(ElementType.TYPE)
public @interface SecuredWicketPage {

}
```

We haven't looked at Wicket's IAuthorizationStrategy contract yet. Here it is, presented in Listing 3-41.

Listing 3-41. *IAuthorizationStrategy.java*

```java
public interface IAuthorizationStrategy{
  /**
  * Checks whether an instance of the given component class may be created.
  */
  boolean isInstantiationAuthorized(Class componentClass);
  boolean isActionAuthorized(Component component, Action action);
}
```

Wicket's AbstractPageAuthorizationStrategy is an IAuthorizationStrategy implementation. It's basically a helper class that checks whether the current request is authorized to instantiate the requested page. It does this by delegating the authorization check to the derived classes through the isPageAuthorized method. Note that you also implement the IUnauthorizedComponentInstantiationListener interface by redirecting the user to the SignOnPage on unauthorized access (see Listing 3-42).

Listing 3-42. *StoreAuthorizationStrategy*

```java
import wicket.RestartResponseAtInterceptPageException;
import wicket.Session;
import wicket.authorization.IUnauthorizedComponentInstantiationListener;
import wicket.authorization.strategies.page.AbstractPageAuthorizationStrategy;

public class StoreAuthorizationStrategy extends
    AbstractPageAuthorizationStrategy implements
  IUnauthorizedComponentInstantiationListener {

  public StoreAuthorizationStrategy() {
  }

  /**
  * @see wicket.authorization.strategies.page.AbstractPageAuthorizationStrategy#
  *      isPageAuthorized(java.lang.Class)
  * If a page has the specified annotation, check for authorization.
  */

  protected boolean isPageAuthorized(final Class pageClass) {
    if (pageClass.isAnnotationPresent(SecuredWicketPage.class)) {
      return isAuthorized();
    }
    // Allow construction by default
    return true;
  }
```

```
/**
 * Gets whether the current user/session is authorized to instantiate a page
 * class that contains the tagging annotation passed to the constructor.
 *
 * @return True if the instantiation should be allowed to proceed, false if
 *         the user should be directed to the application's sign-in page.
 */
protected boolean isAuthorized() {
   BookStoreSession session = ((BookStoreSession) Session.get());
   return session == null ? false : session.isUserLoggedIn();
}


/**
 * On unauthorized access, you redirect the user to the SignOnPage.
 */
public void onUnauthorizedInstantiation(Component component) {
   if (component instanceof Page) {
       throw new RestartResponseAtInterceptPageException(SignOnPage.class);
   }
 }
}
```

You need to register your IAuthorizationStrategy and IUnauthorizedComponent➥
InstantiationListener with the security settings. This can be done in the init method
of your Application class as indicated in Listing 3-43.

Listing 3-43. *Registering the IAuthorizationStrategy Implementation with the WebApplication Subclass*

```
public class BookStoreApplication extends WebApplication
  //..
  public void init(){
    StoreAuthorizationStrategy storeAuthStrategy = new StoreAuthorizationStrategy();
    getSecuritySettings().setAuthorizationStrategy(storeAuthStrategy);
    getSecuritySettings().setUnauthorizedComponentInstantiationListener(
      storeAuthStrategy);
  }
  //..
}
```

Let's quickly look at a typical request cycle flow. When a user requests a page:

1. Wicket invokes the default component instantiation listener (in addition to others).

2. The listener in turn asks the registered authorization strategy (StoreAuthorization➥
   Strategy in this case) if it's okay to instantiate the component (Page in this case).

3. StoreAuthorizationStrategy in turn verifies whether the page is marked secured.

4. If the Page carries the SecuredWicketPage annotation, it checks whether a valid User object is associated with the session. (Note that you do allow unrestricted access to "normal" pages.)

5. If the user session is found to be valid, it allows the current thread to access (or instantiate) the page, and the default request processing cycle executes.

6. But if a User object is not bound to the session, it disallows instantiation of the secured page.

7. Wicket, on realizing this, calls upon the registered IUnauthorizedComponent➥ InstantiationListener(StoreAuthorizationStrategy) to perform its job.

8. The IUnauthorizedComponentInstantiationListener then redirects the user to the SignOnPage.

Summary

We managed to cover lot of ground in this chapter. You first learned to configure nice Wicket URLs through the Application.init() method. Then you saw how Wicket tries to hide the underlying HttpSession in order to encourage a strongly typed interaction with Wicket Session. You later developed a shopping cart application that allowed you to explore quite a few Wicket components like DataView, DropDownChoice, and CheckBox. You saw that DropDownChoice and CheckBox do not by default result in a server-side notification when the user changes the selection on the client. You enabled this behavior though by getting the method wantOnSelectionChangedNotifications to return true. Wicket allows you to add or modify arbitrary attributes to the HTML elements through the wicket.AttributeModifier class, and you used that to apply alternating styles to the table rows generated by the DataView component. You also learned some nice ways of putting Wicket's model to use. Understanding the AbstractDetachableModel and IDataProvider interface is extremely crucial to working with Wicket in real-world scenarios. Wicket allows for configurable authorization strategies through its IAuthorizationStrategy interface. Finally, you saw a detailed implementation of Wicket's IAuthorizationStrategy and conditional component instantiation concept.

CHAPTER 4

■■■

Providing a Common Layout to Wicket Pages

A web site is typically composed of a number of constituent pages. A common requirement is that the pages should carry a consistent look and feel and need to be laid out in a consistent manner, which allows for a smooth user experience. Wicket supports this requirement through *markup inheritance* and *Border components*, thereby providing a functionality similar to Apache Tiles or SiteMesh. You will learn about these two features in this chapter.

Adding "Books," "Promotions," and "Articles" Links to the Bookstore Application

You have made a considerable amount of progress since you started, and apparently so has the fictional bookstore of the examples! Of late, the bookstore has been doing such good business that you have been asked by the investors to overhaul its web site. As a step in that direction, let's offer some form of book promotion and a page that provides links to technology-related articles for the benefit of your customers. Since it should be easy for the users to navigate across pages, the only requirement is that the links must be available at all times. Accordingly, all pages would be required to carry the links to other pages in their template. Figure 4-1 shows how this should look.

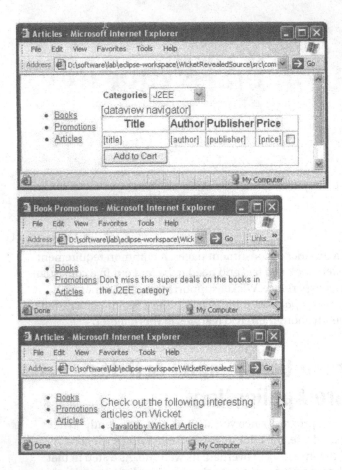

Figure 4-1. *Online bookstore pages with links to other application pages*

Refer to Listings 4-1 and 4-2 for the Book Promotions template and the corresponding Page class, respectively.

Listing 4-1. *Book Promotions Page with Links to Other Pages*

```
<?xml version="1.0" encoding="UTF-8"?>
<html xmlns="http://www.w3.org/1999/xhtml" >
<head>
    <title>Book Promotions</title>
</head>
<body>

<table width="100%">
  <tr>
    <td>
      <ul>
```

```
      <li><a href="#" wicket:id="linkToBooks">Books</a></li>
      <li><a href="#" wicket:id="linkToPromotions">Promotions</a></li>
      <li><a href="#" wicket:id="linkToArticles">Articles</a></li>
    </ul>
   </td>
  <td>
   <!-- Page content starts here -->
   Don't miss the super deals on the books in the J2EE category
   <!-- Page content ends here -->
  </td>
 </tr>
</table>
</body>
</html>
```

Listing 4-2. *The Corresponding Page Class*

```java
import wicket.markup.html.link.BookmarkablePageLink;

public class BookPromotions extends WebPage {

  public BookPromotions(){
    addLinksToOtherPages();
  }

  protected void addLinksToOtherPages(){
    add(new BookmarkablePageLink("linkToBooks", ViewBooks.class));
    add(new BookmarkablePageLink("linkToPromotions", BookPromotions.class));
    add(new BookmarkablePageLink("linkToArticles", Articles.class));
  }
}
```

Wicket ships with several flavors of links, and BookmarkablePageLink happens to be one of them. It is used to represent a stable link to pages within the Wicket application that can be cached in a web browser and used at a later time. As the name suggests, bookmarkable links to pages can be bookmarked or added to a list of favorite links.

The Articles page also needs to carry the links (see Listing 4-3).

Listing 4-3. *A Page for Displaying Links to Interesting Articles Along with Page Links*

```html
<?xml version="1.0" encoding="UTF-8"?>
<html xmlns="http://www.w3.org/1999/xhtml" >
<head>
    <title>Articles</title>
</head>
<body>
```

```
<table width="100%">
  <tr>
    <td>
      <ul>
        <li><a href="#" wicket:id="linkToBooks">Books</a></li>
        <li><a href="#" wicket:id="linkToPromotions">Promotions</a></li>
        <li><a href="#" wicket:id="linkToArticles">Articles</a></li>
      </ul>
    </td>
    <td>
      <!-- Page content starts here -->
      Check out the following interesting articles on Wicket <br/>
      <li wicket:id="articles">
      <a href="" wicket:id="webPageLink"/><span wicket:id="display">
          Javalobby Wicket Article</span>
      </li>
      <!-- Page content ends here -->
    </td>
  </tr>
</table>
</body>
</html>
```

Note that you could have used hard-coded link references (via <a href= /> tags) only if you knew of a fixed set of links up front. Typically, links are stored in a persistence store for later dynamic retrieval. So you need to have a Wicket component that does just that.

In this case, the POJO (POJO stands for plain old Java object) ArticleLink holds onto the link-related information—the display text and the actual link to the article. Wicket models these links to destinations outside of Wicket through the class ExternalLink. If you don't prefer to display the external link in the same window as the Articles page, you can also get Wicket to open the external link in a pop-up window as follows. Wicket has a PopupSettings class that allows you to specify the pop-up settings through flags as shown in Listing 4-4.

Listing 4-4. *The Articles Page Class*

```
import wicket.markup.html.link.BookmarkablePageLink;
import wicket.markup.html.link.ExternalLink;
import wicket.markup.html.list.ListItem;
import wicket.markup.html.list.ListView;
import wicket.markup.html.link.PopupSettings;

public class Articles extends WebPage {

    public Articles(){
      addLinksToOtherPages();
      add(new ListView("articles",fetchArticlesFromStore() ){
        private static final long serialVersionUID = 1L;
```

```
      protected void populateItem(ListItem item){
        // Initialize PopupSettings.
        PopupSettings popupSettings = new PopupSettings(
            PopupSettings.RESIZABLE
            | PopupSettings.SCROLLBARS
            | PopupSettings.LOCATION_BAR
            | PopupSettings.TOOL_BAR
            | PopupSettings.MENU_BAR
            | PopupSettings.STATUS_BAR);
        ArticleLink link = (ArticleLink)item.getModelObject();
        // Configure the ExternalLink with the PopupSettings.
        item.add(new ExternalLink("webPageLink",link.getHref()).
            setPopupSettings(popupSettings));
        item.add(new Label("display", link.getDisplay()));
      }
    });
  }

  protected void addLinksToOtherPages(){
    add(new BookmarkablePageLink("linkToBooks", ViewBooks.class));
    add(new BookmarkablePageLink("linkToPromotions", BookPromotions.class));
    add(new BookmarkablePageLink("linkToArticles", Articles.class));
  }

  // Links are typically fetched from some repository store
  // like Database. For now, return an in-memory list.

  private List fetchArticlesFromStore(){
    return Arrays.asList(
      new ArticleLink[]{
        new ArticleLink("Javalobby Wicket Article",
            "http://www.javalobby.org/java/forums/t60786.html"),
        new ArticleLink("Why Somebody Loves Wicket",
"http://weblogs.java.net/blog/gfx/archive/2005/08/get_to_love_web.html")
      }
    );
  }

  // Holds onto the link's href and display

  class ArticleLink{
    private String display;
    private String href;

    public ArticleLink(String display, String href){
      this.display = display;
      this.href = href;
    }
```

```
      public String getDisplay() {
        return display;
      }

      public String getHref() {
         return href;
      }
      private static final long serialVersionUID = 1L;
   }
}
```

Repeat the preceding steps for the ViewBooks page as well (see Listing 4-5).

Listing 4-5. *ViewBooks Page Modified Similarly to Accommodate Page Links*

```
public class ViewBooks extends..

   //..
   public ViewBooks(){
      addLinksToOtherPages();
      //..
   }

   protected void addLinksToOtherPages(){
      add(new BookmarkablePageLink("linkToBooks", ViewBooks.class));
      add(new BookmarkablePageLink("linkToPromotions", BookPromotions.class));
      add(new BookmarkablePageLink("linkToArticles", Articles.class));
   }

}
```

The preceding changes are good enough to achieve what you set out for. But it's probably not too difficult to infer that there are quite a few places in the code that could do away with the duplication. For example, in the HTML markup of all the pages, only the content demarcated by the following XML comments is actually unique to a page:

```
<!-- Page content starts here -->
<!-- Page content ends here -->
```

The rest of the content is the same for all the pages. The routine that adds the links to the pages is also found in every page.

Providing a Common Layout

It's probably a good idea to store the repeating markup someplace common, as shown in Listing 4-6. Call it BookShopTemplatePage.html.

Listing 4-6. *BookShopTemplatePage.html with the Markup Common to All Pages*

```
<?xml version="1.0" encoding="UTF-8"?>
<html xmlns="http://www.w3.org/1999/xhtml" >
<head>
    <title>No Title</title>
</head>
<body>
<table width="100%">
  <tr>
    <td>
      <ul>
      <li><a href="#" wicket:id="linkToBooks">Books</a></li>
      <li><a href="#" wicket:id="linkToPromotions">Promotions</a></li>
      <li><a href="#" wicket:id="linkToArticles">Articles</a></li>
      </ul>
    </td>
    <td>
      <!-- This part of the markup, indicated by <wicket:child/>
      will be contributed by the page inheriting
      this template. -->
      <wicket:child/>
    </td>
  </tr>
</table>
</body>
</html>
```

The tag `<wicket:child/>` is of prime importance here. The tag indicates that while rendering, it will be replaced by the content of another markup file that is likely to extend from the current one. Like any other Wicket template, this one needs to have a `Page` class of its own, too. Note that you have taken care of the code duplication as a result of having the links in all the pages (see Listing 4-7).

Listing 4-7. *BookShopTemplatePage.java Representing the Common Template*

```
import wicket.markup.html.link.BookmarkablePageLink;

public abstract class BookShopTemplatePage extends WebPage {
  public BookShopTemplatePage(){
    addLinksToOtherPages();
  }

  protected void addLinksToOtherPages() {
    add(new BookmarkablePageLink("linkToBooks", ViewBooks.class));
    add(new BookmarkablePageLink("linkToPromotions", BookPromotions.class));
    add(new BookmarkablePageLink("linkToArticles", Articles.class));
  }
}
```

Even though there isn't anything *abstract* about the class, it is still marked as abstract just to convey the intent that the template/page is not to be used stand-alone. It is meant to be extended by other concrete pages, and it specifies just the common page layout. Now that you have extracted the markup common to all the pages, modify the respective templates as indicated in Listings 4-8 and 4-9.

Listing 4-8. *Book Promotions Page Extracted into a Container of Its Own*

```
<?xml version="1.0" encoding="UTF-8"?>
<wicket:extend>
   <!-- child content -->
   Don't miss super deals on the books in the J2EE category
   <!-- End child content -->
</wicket:extend>
```

Listing 4-9. *Modified Articles.html*

```
<?xml version="1.0" encoding="UTF-8"?>
<wicket:extend>
   <!-- child content -->
   Check out the following interesting articles on Wicket <br/>
   <li wicket:id="articles">
    <a href="" wicket:id="webPageLink"/>
      <span wicket:id="display">
        Javalobby Wicket Article
      </span>
   </li>
   <!-- child content -->
</wicket:extend>
```

Note that in all the templates, you now just retain content unique to those particular pages. Also of importance is the fact that the content unique to those pages is specified within Wicket's <wicket:extend> tag. This is to let Wicket know that when it renders this page, it is supposed to replace the <wicket:child/> element of the *base template* with the markup placed within the <wicket:extend> tag.

Modify the page classes Articles, BookPromotions, and ViewBooks to extend BookShop➥ TemplatePage. You can remove the call to the method addLinksToOtherPages as well.

In case your template editor insists that the pages need to be enclosed within <html><body>, </body></html> tags, you can include them around the <wicket:extend> tag for the sake of completeness. Wicket will ignore anything that doesn't fall within the <wicket:extend> tag. Essentially, having something like what appears in Listing 4-10 should keep Wicket and the template editor happy.

Listing 4-10. *Articles.html As an HTML Document*

```
<?xml version="1.0" encoding="UTF-8"?>
<html>
<body>
<wicket:extend>
   <!-- Child content -->
   Check out the following interesting articles on Wicket <br/>
   <li wicket:id="articles">
       <a href="" wicket:id="webPageLink"/><span wicket:id="display">
       Javalobby Wicket Article</span>
   </li>
   <!-- Child content -->
</wicket:extend>
</body>
</html>
```

Make sure that the changes in Listing 4-10 have actually not altered the user experience.

Click the page links and verify the HTML page title that shows up on the browser. It displays "No Title" for all the pages. Well, the BookShopTemplatePage has no way of determining the page it is currently displaying. It's pretty easy to fix this though, and you will see how next.

Getting the Pages to Display Corresponding Titles

Modify the *static* <title> to a dynamic one by attaching a *wicket:id* attribute, as shown in Listing 4-11.

Listing 4-11. *BookShopTemplate.html Modified for Dynamic Title Rendering*

```
<?xml version="1.0" encoding="UTF-8"?>
<html xmlns="http://www.w3.org/1999/xhtml" >
<head>
    <title wicket:id="pageTitle">No Title</title>
</head>
<body>

<!- REST SNIPPED -->
```

This obviously requires a corresponding Wicket component to be added to the Page class. The PropertyModel linked to the component needs to source the title text from somewhere. BookShopTemplatePage doesn't know where it's going to come from. The onus rests on the class that is likely to extend it. So make the intent clear by marking the "title getter" abstract, as in Listing 4-12.

Listing 4-12. *BookShopTemplatePage.java*

```java
public abstract class BookShopTemplatePage extends WebPage {

    public BookShopTemplatePage (){
      add(new Label("pageTitle",new PropertyModel(this,"pageTitle")));
      addLinksToOtherPages();
    }
    protected void addLinksToOtherPages() {
      //..
    }

    // To be overridden by "child" templates
    public abstract String getPageTitle();

}
```

Provide an implementation of the abstract method in all the concrete pages, as shown in Listings 4-13, 4-14, and 4-15.

Listing 4-13. *BookPromotions.java*

```java
public class BookPromotions extends BookShopTemplatePage {
  //..
  public String getPageTitle() {
    return "Book Promotions";
  }
}
```

Listing 4-14. *Articles.java*

```java
public class Articles extends BookShopTemplatePage {
 //..
 public String getPageTitle() {
   return "Articles";
 }
}
```

Listing 4-15. *ViewBooks.java*

```java
public class ViewBooks extends BookShopTemplatePage{
  //..
  //..
  public String getPageTitle() {
    return "Books";
  }

}
```

The page titles should show up fine now. The same technique can be used for any element that needs to be different between the related pages. Note that the markup inheritance shown in the example is just one level deep: all application pages extend the common BookShopTemplatePage. You could have a deeper hierarchy depending upon the specific needs of the application being developed and still get markup inheritance to work. Also note that BookShopTemplatePage is like any other Wicket page. The base page could be composed of any number and type of Wicket components like Panels and Borders. We will look at Wicket's Border component now and defer the discussion on Panels to Chapter 7, which covers custom Wicket components.

Separating Navigation Links and the Associated Page Content Through Border Components

In a nutshell, Wicket has two types of components—one that can have an associated markup template and another that can't. Wicket's Panel, Border, and Page are components that belong to the former category. This will be discussed in detail in Chapter 7. For now, let's concentrate on Wicket's Border components.

Quoting from the wicket.markup.html.border.Border Javadoc:

> *A border component has associated markup which is drawn and determines placement of any markup and/or components nested within the border component. The portion of the border's associated markup file which is to be used in rendering the border is denoted by a <wicket:border> tag. The children of the border component instance are then inserted into this markup, replacing the first <wicket:body> tag in the border's associated markup.*

If this isn't quite clear to you, it would probably help to look at an example. What Listings 4-16 and 4-17 show is a Page with a Label.

Listing 4-16. *MyPage.html*

```
<html>
<body>
<span wicket:id="label">Label content goes here</span>
</body>
</html>
```

Listing 4-17. *MyPage.java*

```
import wicket.markup.html.basic.Label;
public class MyPage extends WebPage{
  public MyPage(){
    add(new Label("label", new Model(" Wicket Rocks 8-) "));
}
```

The page would render as shown in Figure 4-2.

Figure 4-2. *A simple page with a label*

Now let's say you want to draw a box around the text and render it in a yellow background. Listing 4-18 shows how you could probably do this.

Listing 4-18. *MyPage.html with the Text Inside a Box*

```
<html>
<body>
<table width = "0%" border = "1" cellspacing = "0"
cellpadding = "1" bgcolor = "yellow">
  <tr>
    <td width = "100%" valign = "top">
      <span wicket:id="label">Label content goes here</span>
    </td>
  </tr>
</table>
</body>
</html>
```

Figure 4-3 illustrates how `MyPage.html` should now display in your browser (except the gray will appear yellow on your screen).

Figure 4-3. *The same page with the label highlighted*

Now imagine that you are required to draw such boxes around several labels that occur within the same page or for that matter labels that occur across pages. Wicket allows you to model them as Border components so that you don't have to be copying the same layout around other labels. The actual Border markup needs to be specified within the <wicket:border> tag in its template, as shown in Listing 4-19 (remember, Wicket Border components have their own associated markup template).

Listing 4-19. *MyBorder.html*

```
<wicket:border>
<table width = "0%" border = "1" cellspacing = "0"
       cellpadding = "1" bgcolor = "yellow">
 <tr>
   <td width = "100%" valign = "top">
     <wicket:body/>
   </td>
 </tr>
</table>
</wicket:border>
```

A corresponding Border class doesn't do much at the moment (see Listing 4-20). But Borders could themselves carry Wicket components similar to a Wicket Page.

Listing 4-20. *MyBorder.java*

```
import wicket.markup.html.border.Border;

public class MyBorder extends Border{
  public MyBorder(String id){
    super(id);
  }
}
```

Now remove the markup that adds the box from MyPage.html and add a span element to accommodate the contents of MyBorder.html instead as shown in Listing 4-21.

Listing 4-21. *MyPage.html with a Border Component*

```
<html>
<body>
<span wicket:id="myborder">
   <span wicket:id="label">Label content goes here</span>
</span>
</body>
</html>
```

Listing 4-22 shows the modified Page class.

Listing 4-22. *MyPage.java with a Border Component*

```
import wicket.markup.html.border.Border;

public class MyPage extends WebPage {
  public MyPage(){
    Border border = new MyBorder("myborder")
    add(border);
    border.add(new Label("label",
            new Model(" Wicket Rocks 8-) ")));
  }
}
```

In other words, the body of the "myborder" component (i.e., the span with a *wicket:id* "label") is substituted into the MyBorder's associated markup at the position indicated by the <wicket:body> tag. Now that you understand a little about Wicket Borders, let's explore another Wicket component—BoxBorder. wicket.markup.html.border.BoxBorder is a subclass of the Border component.

Now let's say you want to separate the navigation links and the associated page content through some kind of demarcation. Wicket has a BoxBorder class that does just that. It draws a thin black line around its child components (see Listing 4-23).

Listing 4-23. *BookShopTemplate.html Modified to Accommodate Borders*

```
<?xml version="1.0" encoding="UTF-8"?>
<html xmlns="http://www.w3.org/1999/xhtml" >
<head>
    <title wicket:id="pageTitle">No Title</title>
</head>
<body>

<table width="100%">
 <tr height="100%">
    <td valign="top" height="100px">
     <!-- Place the BoxBorder component around links -->
      <span wicket:id="pageLinksBorder">
        <ul>
        <li><a href="#" wicket:id="linkToBooks">Books</a></li>
        <li><a href="#" wicket:id="linkToPromotions">Promotions</a></li>
        <li><a href="#" wicket:id="linkToArticles">Articles</a></li>
      </ul>
      </span>
    </td>
    <td valign="top" height="100px">
     <!-- Place the BoxBorder component around the page being displayed -->
```

```
    <span wicket:id = "pageBorder">
      <wicket:child/>
    </span>
  </td>
 </tr>
</table>
</body>
</html>
```

Earlier the application page links were being added to the Page directly. Now they have to be added to the enclosing BoxBorder in accordance with the template hierarchy. Accordingly, the Page class needs some modification, as shown in Listing 4-24.

Listing 4-24. *BookShopTemplate.java*

```java
import wicket.markup.html.border.BoxBorder;
//..

public abstract class BookShopTemplate extends WebPage {

    public BookShopTemplate(){
    add(new Label("pageTitle", new PropertyModel(this, "pageTitle")));
    Border pageLinksBorder = null;
    add(pageLinksBorder = new BoxBorder("pageLinksBorder"));
    // Add the links to the 'pageLinksBorder' BoxBorder
    addLinksToOtherPages(pageLinksBorder);
    // Add the Border components
    add(new BoxBorder("pageBorder"));
    }


    protected void addLinksToOtherPages(MarkupContainer container) {
    container.add(new BookmarkablePageLink("linkToBooks", ViewBooks.class));
    container.add(new BookmarkablePageLink("linkToPromotions",
BookPromotions.class));
    container.add(new BookmarkablePageLink("linkToArticles", Articles.class));
    }
}
```

Now try accessing the ViewBooks page. It should result in the error shown in here:

ViewBooks Page Error on Rendering After Adding the BoxBorder Component

```
02:27:21.890 ERROR! [SocketListener0-1]
wicket.RequestCycle.step(RequestCycle.java:993) >19> Unable to find
component with id 'bookForm' in [MarkupContainer [Component id =
_extend, page = com.apress.wicketbook.layout.ViewBooks, path =
0:pageBorder:_child:_extend.MarkupInheritanceResolver$
```

TransparentWebMarkupContainer, isVisible = true, isVersioned
= true]]. This means that you declared wicket:id=bookForm in your
smarkup, but that you either did not add the component to your page
at all, or that the hierarchy does not match.

It should not be too difficult to reason this out if you observe that the <wicket:child> tag is enclosed within the "pageBorder" component. This also means that the templates that extend from BookShopTemplate need to have their components fall under the "pageBorder" Border component in the page hierarchy. You can no longer add the child template components to the parent page; you need to be adding them to the parent template's Border component instead. This introduces a certain amount of ambiguity in the child template Page class, as it mandates that the Page content be always wrapped using a Border. If you decide to remove the parent page's Border component later, you will be forced to change pages that inherit from it. Relax—Wicket, as always, has a simple solution. You still get to retain the child templates as they are if you make the existing "pageBorder" component transparent by calling setTransparentResolver(true), as shown in Listing 4-25. This setting allows you to add the components to the pageBorder component's parent. Wicket will take care of the rest, even though the page hierarchy doesn't exactly match that of the template. Even if you remove the parent's Border component later, the child templates will still continue to work properly. This setting is recursive, in that it also allows you to have transparent borders embedded inside other transparent borders.

Listing 4-25. *The Base Template Page with Transparent Borders*

```
import wicket.markup.html.border.BoxBorder;
//..

public abstract class BookShopTemplate extends WebPage {

    public BookShopTemplate(){
      add(new Label("pageTitle", new PropertyModel(this, "pageTitle")));
      // Let's also make the 'pageLinksBorder' transparent.
      add(new BoxBorder("pageLinksBorder").setTransparentResolver(true));
      // Now you aren't required to add the links to the Border.
      // The links can be added to the Page class as was the case
      // earlier.
      addLinksToOtherPages();
      // Add the Border components.
      add(new BoxBorder("pageBorder").setTransparentResolver(true));
    }
//..
}
```

On the browser, this renders as shown in Figure 4-4.

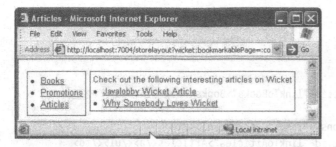

Figure 4-4. *The improved online bookstore application home page with BoxBorder*

If you are interested, you can take a look at the BoxBorder HTML template file that drew those lines around the page content (the Wicket distribution comes with the source code).

Say you don't like the way BoxBorder renders, and you want to make an attempt at rolling out your own by attaching a CSS to the Page. Create a folder called style under your context folder and make a style sheet named style.css with the content shown in Listing 4-26. You can decide the name and the location of the style sheet; Wicket doesn't dictate anything. It should be accessible from the Wicket pages, however.

Listing 4-26. *style.css*

```css
.borderedBlock {
  background: #DEDEDE;
  color: gray;
  font-weight: bold;
  border: solid #E9601A;
  border-width: thin;
  padding: 2px 2px 2px 6px;
  margin: 2px;
}
```

Note that the style can be specified inline as well within the <style>, </style> tags. When applied to an HTML widget, this style draws a border around that widget with the preceding attributes.

Modify the BookShopTemplate layout as you see in Listing 4-27.

Listing 4-27. *BookShopTemplate.html with CSS*

```html
<?xml version="1.0" encoding="UTF-8"?>
<html xmlns="http://www.w3.org/1999/xhtml" >
<head>
    <title wicket:id="pageTitle">No Title</title>
    <link rel="stylesheet" type="text/css" href="style/style.css"/>
</head>
<body>
```

```
<table width="100%">
  <tr>
    <td class="borderedBlock">
      <table>
      <tr>
        <td><ul><a href="#" wicket:id="linkToBooks">Books</a></ul></td>
        <td><ul><a href="#"
          wicket:id="linkToPromotions">Promotions</a></ul></td>
        <td><ul><a href="#" wicket:id="linkToArticles">Articles</a></ul></td>
      </tr>
      </table>
    </td>
  </tr>
  <tr>
    <td valign="top" colspan="3" class="borderedBlock">
      <wicket:child/>
    </td>
  </tr>
</table>
</body>
</html>
```

Since you have your own style sheet, remove the references to BoxBorder from the
BookShopTemplate class. Now the pages will have an improved look and feel (see Figure 4-5).

Figure 4-5. *The online bookstore application home page with CSS-styled border*

Note that you didn't have to change the markup in the application pages. This is the
advantage of having a common layout specified external to the application pages.

Disabling Links to the Page Currently Being Displayed

Currently, irrespective of the page that the user is viewing, the link to that very page shows up in an enabled state. If you want the links to show up disabled in such cases, call setAutoEnable(true) on the link class. The fact that the method returns the reference to the link also helps (you can chain your methods calls, as shown in Listing 4-28).

Listing 4-28. *BookShopTemplate Modified to Autodisable Links*

```
class BookShopTemplate..
    //..
    protected void addLinksToOtherPages() {
        add(new BookmarkablePageLink("linkToBooks",
ViewBooks.class).setAutoEnable(true));
        add(new BookmarkablePageLink("linkToPromotions",
BookPromotions.class).setAutoEnable(true));
        add(new BookmarkablePageLink("linkToArticles",
Articles.class).setAutoEnable(true));
    }
}
```

Figure 4-6 shows how the links would show up with the "Promotions" link clicked. Note that other than the "Promotions" link, all other links show up in an enabled state.

Figure 4-6. *The online bookstore home page with automatically enabled links*

Employing wicket:link to Generate Links

As if the preceding code weren't simple enough, Wicket allows you to generate links through the wicket:link (see Listing 4-29). Why would you use wicket:link for the same purpose? Well, as it turns out, you get all of the link functionality for free.

Listing 4-29. *Links Represented Through wicket:link*

```
<?xml version="1.0" encoding="UTF-8"?>
<html xmlns="http://www.w3.org/1999/xhtml" >
<head>
    <title wicket:id="pageTitle">No Title</title>
    <style>
     .borderedBlock {
       background: #DEDEDE;
       color: gray;
       font-weight: bold;
       border: solid #E9601A;
       border-width: thin;
       padding: 2px 2px 2px 6px;
       margin: 2px;
     }
    </style>
</head>
<body>

<table width="100%">
   <tr>
    <td class="borderedBlock">
    <table>
     <tr>
     <wicket:link>
      <td>
         <li><a href="ViewBooks.html">Books</a></li>
      </td>
      <td>
         <li><a href="BookPromotions.html">
             Promotions</a>
         </li>
      </td>
      <td>
         <li><a href="Articles.html">
             Articles</a>
         </li>
      </td>
     </wicket:link/>
     </tr>
    </table>
    </td>
   </tr>
   <tr>
    <td valign="top" colspan="3" class="borderedBlock">
       <wicket:child/>
    </td>
```

```
    </tr>
  </table>
</body>
</html>
```

As a result, `BookShopTemplate` would be reduced to the code in Listing 4-30.

Listing 4-30. *The Base Template Page with Link Components Removed*

```java
public abstract class BookShopTemplate extends WebPage {

    // Note that you don't need addLinksToOtherPages anymore.

    public BookShopTemplatePage (){
      add(new Label("pageTitle",new PropertyModel(this,"pageTitle")));
    }

    public abstract String getPageTitle();
}
```

There is a caveat to using `<wicket:link>`: although it's great for linking to pages that are in the same package as or in a subpackage of the page whose markup contains `wicket:link`, if you want to link to pages outside the package, then `<wicket:link>` will not work. In that respect, `wicket:link` is not a silver bullet.

Borders Are Not Just About Boxes

If the previous examples seem to suggest that Borders are only good at drawing boxes around components, let's quickly put that misconception to rest by looking at another example. You will see how to develop a collapsible border component that decorates the markup, to be expanded or collapsed based on user interaction. You will use a JavaScript function that will toggle the display style of the component it is decorating. You will also add a little style to the border component to aid better display (see Listing 4-31). Also note the usage of the `<wicket:head>` tag to specify this `CollapsibleBorder` component's contribution to the final HTML `<head>` element when the Page is rendered.

Listing 4-31. *A Template That Models a Collapsible Border*

```html
<wicket:head>
  <style>
    .header {color:#729ac2; cursor:pointer; font-weight:bold; border-top:1px solid
      #300;}
    .collapsibleBorder {display:none;}
  </style>
  <script>
    // The JavaScript function that toggles the visibility of the div element
    // encloses the markup that it is decorating.
    function toggle(collapsibleBorderId) {
```

```
      var styleObj = document.getElementById(collapsibleBorderId).style;
      styleObj.display = (styleObj.display == 'block')? 'none': 'block';
    }
  </script>
</wicket:head>

<wicket:border>
<div>
  <!-- This holds on to the header text -->
  <div class="header" wicket:id="header">+
<span wicket:id="headerText"></span></div>
  <!-- The collapsible border -->
  <div wicket:id="collapsibleBorder" class="collapsibleBorder">
    <wicket:body/>
  </div>
</div>
</wicket:border>
```

Let's look at the corresponding Border component. Note that the Border component can be used multiple times in the same page. So it wouldn't be prudent to associate an ID with the div identified by the Wicket ID header up front. Wicket can assign a unique ID to the element at runtime, and you should make use of that ability in this case. This also means that you have to defer the call to the JavaScript toggle function until runtime. How do you bind the JavaScript method call to the element at runtime? Wicket invokes certain callback functions that allow you to modify the markup during render phase. We will look at them in greater detail in Chapter 7. For now, it should suffice to know that Wicket calls the Component. onComponentTag(ComponentTag) method, passing in the Java representation of the tag— wicket.markup.ComponentTag—while rendering the template. You will bind the JavaScript function in the callback method (see Listing 4-32).

Listing 4-32. *The Java Representation of the Collapsible Border*

```
package com.apress.wicketbook.layout;

import wicket.markup.ComponentTag;
import wicket.markup.html.WebMarkupContainer;
import wicket.markup.html.basic.Label;
import wicket.markup.html.border.Border;
import wicket.model.PropertyModel;

public abstract class CollapsibleBorder extends Border {

  public CollapsibleBorder(String id) {
    super(id);
    WebMarkupContainer collapsibleBorder = new
        WebMarkupContainer("collapsibleBorder");
```

```
    // It's essential that the div outputs its
    // "id" for the JavaScript to toggle its
    // display property at runtime.

    collapsibleBorder.setOutputMarkupId(true);

    WebMarkupContainer header = new Header("header", collapsibleBorder);
    add(header);
    add(collapsibleBorder);
    // The text to identify
    header.add(new Label("headerText", new PropertyModel(this,"header")));
  }

  public abstract String getHeader();

  private class Header extends WebMarkupContainer {

    // The CollapsibleBorder element reference is required in order
    // to determine its "id" at runtime.

    WebMarkupContainer collapsibleBorder;

    public Header(String id, WebMarkupContainer collapsibleBorder) {
      super(id);
      this.collapsibleBorder = collapsibleBorder;
    }

    protected void onComponentTag(ComponentTag tag) {
      String collapsibleBorderId = collapsibleBorder.getMarkupId();

      // This will add an attribute "onclick" that might show up as follows:
      //< <div class="header" wicket:id="header"
      //onclick="toggle('border_collapsibleBorder')">

      tag.put("onclick", "toggle('" + collapsibleBorderId + "')");
    }
  }
}
```

Now let's look at a sample page that uses the preceding Border component (see Listing 4-33). The page essentially has a search panel that allows you to enter the search criteria and another that displays the search results. For now, the search results are hard-coded. This example was incorporated just to give you a feel of one of the ways of designing and using a Border component.

Listing 4-33. *A Search Page That Uses the Collapsible Border Component*

```html
<html>
<head><title>Employee Search</title></head>
<body>
    <!-- A span to accommodate the Border -->
    <span wicket:id="search">
      <input type="text"/><input type="submit" value="Search"/>
    </span>
    <!-- A span to accommodate the Border -->
    <span wicket:id="searchResults">
      <table border="1">
        <tr>
           <th>Employee</th>
           <th>Department</th>
        </tr>
        <tr><td>Tom</td><td>Finance</td></tr>
        <tr><td>Chris</td><td>IT</td></tr>
        <tr><td>John</td><td>Marketing</td></tr>
      </table>
    </span>
</body>
</html>
```

Figure 4-7 shows how the template described in the Listing 4-33 renders on the browser.

Figure 4-7. *The Employee Search screen with a collapsed border*

On clicking the + symbol, the Employee Search and the Employee Search Results panels are expanded, as you see in Figure 4-8.

Figure 4-8. *The Employee Search screen with the border expanded*

Refer to Listing 4-34 for the corresponding Page class.

Listing 4-34. *A Page That Uses the Collapsible Border Component*

```
package com.apress.wicketbook.layout;

import wicket.markup.html.WebPage;

public class CollapsibleLinksPage extends WebPage {
  public CollapsibleLinksPage() {
    add(new CollapsibleBorder("search") {
      // Specify the header for the search panel.
      public String getHeader() {
        return "Employee Search";
      }
    });
    add(new CollapsibleBorder("searchResults") {
      // Specify the header for the search results panel.
      public String getHeader() {
        return "Employee Search Results";
      }
    });
  }
}
```

Summary

In this chapter, you learned how Wicket extends the concept of inheritance supported by object-oriented languages to template markup as well. Wicket encourages the use of markup inheritance to provide a common layout and consistent look and feel to the application pages. You also learned that components can also be decorated using Wicket's Border class. Note that you could use Wicket's Border component as well in place of markup inheritance. But the latter is easier to work with when it comes to providing a common layout. You also were introduced to some flavors of Link components supported by Wicket. Toward the end, just so you would have an idea of what Wicket Border components are capable of, you were shown a way of creating a *collapsible* Border component.

■ ■ ■

CHAPTER 5

Integration with Other Frameworks

Up to this point, I have shown you how Wicket handles various aspects of web development. It's quite self-sufficient that way, and it ships with all the bells and whistles to tackle enterprise Java web development requirements. That said, it's just a web framework, and there will always be a need to integrate with other frameworks that excel in a particular area that Wicket doesn't really address and is probably not even designed for. Wicket nevertheless ships with quite a few integration modules that give you access to features available in other frameworks. Accordingly, we will look at Wicket's integration with templating technologies like FreeMarker and Velocity. You will see how trivial it is to embed a Velocity or a FreeMarker template in a Wicket Page. The past couple of years have witnessed the meteoric rise of one particular J2EE application framework—Spring. In this chapter, you will see how the difference in the design ideology of Wicket and Spring makes the integration difficult. Having some insight into the integration problems, you will then be exposed to the Wicket way of getting past these hurdles. The discussion that follows assumes that you have some form of familiarity with the frameworks just listed.

Wicket and Velocity

Velocity is a Java-based templating engine that can be used as an alternative to other templating technologies, like JSPs. A Velocity template typically consists of static markup interspersed with some dynamic code that is evaluated at runtime. The template needs to be supplied with a context object known as `VelocityContext` (as is typically the case).

While Wicket works with plain-vanilla HTML templates, it integrates with Velocity at a certain level through the Wicket-Velocity subproject. You can directly embed the Velocity template in a Wicket page through the `wicket.contrib.markup.html.velocity.VelocityPanel` component. It is just a `MarkupContainer` that accepts the location of the Velocity template expressed through one of several implementations of `wicket.util.resource.IString➥ResourceStream`. You will learn how to use one such implementation, `wicket.util.resource.UrlResourceStream`, which allows you to specify the Velocity template location through the `java.net.URL` class.

`VelocityPanel` also needs to be configured with the context (a map) required by the Velocity template. Let's look at an example to clarify things a little more.

OBTAINING THE SOURCE

Wicket and all its associated projects employ Maven in order to build a distributable artifact. The Velocity and FreeMarker integration modules, for example, can be found here—`http://svn.sourceforge.net/viewcvs.cgi/wicket-stuff/trunk/`. The Wicket-Spring integration module that we will be looking at later is available for download here—`http://sourceforge.net/project/showfiles.php?group_id=119783&package_id=182494`.

In order to get you started quickly, the book source code ships with the required jar files bundled along with it.

The Velocity Framework is available for download at `http://jakarta.apache.org/velocity/`, while the FreeMarker library can be downloaded from `http://freemarker.org/`. But you really don't have to be downloading their respective jars if you were building using Maven.

The Velocity template to display the books in a tabular format is shown in Listing 5-1. It just expects to be supplied with a list of Book objects. A Velocity template generally sources its data from the Velocity context in the form of a Map. Essentially, you need to supply a map model that maps the list of Book objects to the key bookList.

Listing 5-1. *Velocity Template for Displaying Book Details*

```
<table border="1">
<tr>
  <th>Title</th>
  <th>Author</th>
  <th>Publisher</th>
  <th>Price</th>
</th>
#foreach ($book in $bookList)
<tr>
  <td>$book.title</td>
  <td>$book.author</td>
  <td>$book.publisher</td>
  <td>$book.price</td>
</tr>
#end
</table>
```

Let's have a Wicket Page that displays the books for a selected book category using the same example as the one in Chapter 3 (see Listing 5-2). This example also demonstrates how you can mix and match Wicket and Velocity components in the same Wicket template.

Listing 5-2. *Books.html*

```
<html>
<head><title>Browse Books</title></head>
<body>
<form name="viewBookForm" wicket:id="viewBookForm">
 <table>
  <tr>
    <td><b>Categories</b></td>
    <td>
      <select wicket:id="categories">
        <option>J2EE</option>
        <option>ASP.NET</option>
        <option>Scripting</option>
      </select>
    </td>
  </tr>
 </table>
 <span wicket:id="bookDetails">
    Velocity Panel goes here
 </span>
</form>
</body>
</html>
```

The VelocityPanel needs a model to fetch the data for populating the VelocityContext. Since the data is dependent on the selected book category, you need a model that determines the model object lazily. You also know that a model allows you to do just that through its IModel.getObject(Component component) method. So let's create one. Also, note the usage of Wicket's MicroMap class in Listing 5-3. It is an implementation of the java.util.Map interface, which can only hold a single object. This is particularly useful to control memory usage in Wicket and particularly makes sense in this case.

Listing 5-3. *VelocityPanel Model*

```
import wicket.util.collections.MicroMap;
class BookDetailsModel extends Model {



/* Since the category that is selected isn't known until runtime, you
 * need to make use of the indirection introduced by the model. The
 * component will call this method on the model every time it needs
 * access to the underlying "model object."
 */
```

```
  public Object getObject(Component comp) {
    Map data = new  MicroMap();

   // Fetch the books belonging to the selected book category.

    data.put("bookList", getBookDao().findBooksForCategory(
         getCategory()));
    return data;
  }

  public BookDao getBookDao() {
    BookStoreApplication application =
        (BookStoreApplication) getApplication();
    return application.getBookDao();
  }

}
```

Now that you have the VelocityPanel model in place, let's put it to work in the Page class corresponding to the template, as shown in Listing 5-4.

Listing 5-4. *The Page Class Corresponding to the Books Template*

```
import wicket.util.resource.UrlResourceStream;
import wicket.contrib.markup.html.velocity.VelocityPanel;
import com.apress.wicketbook.shop.model.BookDao;
import wicket.util.resource.IStringResourceStream;

public class Books extends WebPage{

  // By default books belonging to ALL categories will be displayed.
  private String category = BookDao.CATEGORY_ALL;
    class BookDetailsModel extends Model{
       //..
    }

    public Books() {
      Form form = new Form("viewBookForm");
      BookDetailsModel bookDetailsModel = new BookDetailsModel();

      // The DropDownChoice model is mapped to the Page property
      // ("category") and is directly accessed by
      // the VelocityPanel model. Therefore, nothing special
      // needs to be done in DropDownChoice.onSelectionChanged().
```

```
        DropDownChoice categories = new CategoryDropDownChoice("categories",
            new PropertyModel(bookDetailsModel, "category"),
                getBookCategories());

        form.add(categories);

        // Read the velocity template in the form of a stream first.
        IStringResourceStream velocityTemplateStream =
          new UrlResourceStream(getClass().getResource("BookDetails.vm"));

        // Initialize VelocityPanel with the stream and the model.
        VelocityPanel bookDetailsPanel = new VelocityPanel("bookDetails",
                velocityTemplateStream, bookDetailsModel);

        form.add(bookDetailsPanel);

        bookDetailsPanel.setThrowVelocityExceptions(true);
        add(form);
    }

    public String getCategory() {
      return category;
    }

    public void setCategory(String category) {
      this.category = category;
    }

    public List getBookCategories() {
      BookStoreApplication application = (BookStoreApplication)
            getApplication();
      return application.getBookDao().getSupportedCategories();
    }

    class CategoryDropDownChoice extends DropDownChoice {
      public CategoryDropDownChoice(String id, IModel model,
            List choices) {
        super(id, model, choices);
      }
     // You would require a server-side notification when
     // the book category is changed.
      public boolean wantOnSelectionChangedNotifications() {
        return true;
      }
    }
  }
}
```

The page should render as shown in Figure 5-1 on the browser.

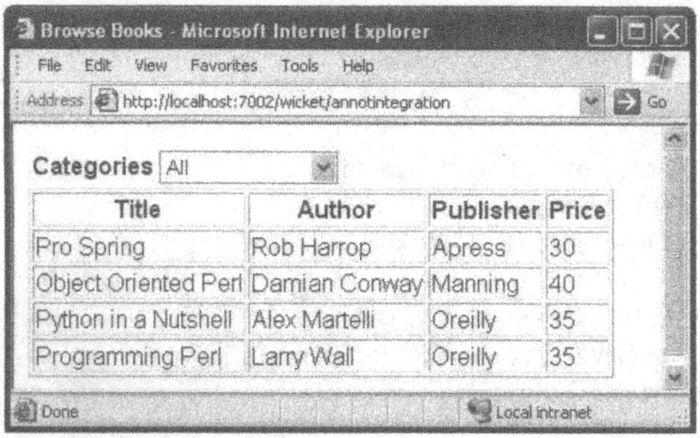

Figure 5-1. *A page that uses a Velocity template to list all the available books*

The VelocityPanel essentially gets the Velocity framework library to process the Velocity template based on the data passed to it through the BookDetailsModel. Then it just replaces the <span> tag body content identified by the *wicket:id* bookDetails with the one generated by Velocity. That pretty much sums up Wicket's integration with Velocity. Note that next we will look at how Wicket integrates with Velocity's close cousin—FreeMarker.

Wicket and FreeMarker

FreeMarker is another templating engine along the lines of Velocity, albeit more powerful. On the surface it also requires a template similar to Velocity that abides by FTL (FreeMarker Templating Language) and a context for the template to render dynamic data. We looked at the Velocity template BookDetails.vm earlier. Listing 5-5 shows the FreeMarker equivalent.

Listing 5-5. *FreeMarker Template for Displaying Book Details—BookDetails.ftl*

```
<table border="1">
<tr>
  <th>Title</th>
  <th>Author</th>
  <th>Publisher</th>
  <th>Price</th>
</th>
<#list bookList as book>
<tr>
  <td>${book.title}</td>
  <td>${book.author}</td>
  <td>${book.publisher}</td>
  <td>${book.price}</td>
</tr>
</#list>
</table>
```

Since `wicket.contrib.markup.html.freemarker.FreeMarkerPanel` mimics the `VelocityPanel` API specifications to quite an extent, you are not required to make any sweeping changes to the existing Books page to make it work with the FreeMarker template. The `BookDetailsModel`, for example, still makes lot of sense. Listing 5-6 presents the code.

Listing 5-6. *Books.java Modified to Work with a FreeMarker Template*

```
import wicket.contrib.markup.html.freemarker.FreeMarkerPanel;

public class Books extends WebPage{
 //..
  public Books(){
   IStringResourceStream freemarkerPanelStream =
     new UrlResourceStream(getClass().getResource("BookDetails.ftl"));

   FreeMarkerPanel bookDetailsPanel = new FreeMarkerPanel("bookDetails",
       freemarkerPanelStream, bookDetailsModel);
   bookDetailsPanel.setThrowFreeMarkerExceptions(true);
   form.add(bookDetailsPanel);
  }
 //..
}
```

This concludes the section on Wicket-FreeMarker integration. Note that neither Velocity nor FreeMarker support Wicket URLs or `Form` components. They are just there for the sake of presentation. This integration module makes sense, for example, if you already have a prede-fined Velocity or FreeMarker template stored in a database.

Let's move on to discuss Wicket's integration with the Spring Framework.

The Spring Framework

The *Spring Framework* is founded on the principles of *inversion of control* (IoC). It builds a powerful programming model around POJO (Plain Old Java Object) beans through its aspect-oriented features. It is also known as a *dependency injection* (DI) container. Spring is basically an object factory at its heart—an advanced one at that. An excellent Spring reference is avail-able if you are looking for in-depth treatment of Spring: *Pro Spring* by Rob Harrop (Apress, 2005). Spring documentation is a very good source of information on this topic and can be found here: `http://static.springframework.org/spring/docs/1.2.x/reference/index.html`. You can also refer to Martin Fowler's article on IoC and DI in general here: `http://martinfowler.com/articles/injection.html`. Here, I will restrict this discussion to Spring's integration with Wicket.

If you want Wicket Pages to take advantage of Spring's nifty DI capabilities, they need to integrate with Spring well. But there are some difficulties in this, and we will explore them next.

Difficulties in Spring Integration

The two main reasons that make Wicket-Spring integration difficult are as follows:

- Wicket is an *unmanaged* framework.

- Wicket components and models are often serialized.

Let's take a closer look at these obstacles to Wicket-Spring integrations.

Wicket Is an Unmanaged Framework

As just mentioned, one difficulty in making Wicket and Spring work together stems from the fact that Wicket is an *unmanaged* framework. There are lots of *managed* frameworks out there. Spring is one such framework, and it offers tremendous capabilities through dependency injection. Maven is another, and it doesn't expect a detailed build script, unlike Ant, in order to build your project. But all good things come at a cost—Maven expects you to organize your folder structure in a particular way, and as for Spring, it takes away your ability to instantiate or "do a new" on objects.

It would be appropriate to look at Struts-Spring integration at this point, as this would help you appreciate the Wicket-Spring integration issue better. In the case of Struts, Action classes are where all the "action" takes place. The framework expects you to extend the built-in Action class by overriding the execute method. What it doesn't allow you to do is instantiate your Action classes. This ability still rests with the framework. In other words, Struts RequestProcessor manages the Action classes for you. There is a central point in the framework where it "does a new" in your stead. The Spring equivalent would be the ApplicationContext class. The user never instantiates the bean. The context hands it over to the user on request. The context takes care of all the other details as well.

Spring seems to be a natural fit with such managed frameworks. Struts allows you to configure a different RequestProcessor if required, and Spring takes advantage of it by providing one. It overrides the processActionCreate() hook method to return an Action class instance configured in a Spring context, thereby conferring DI capabilities on them. Simply because you can swap one implementation for the other at the point an initialization needs to be done and the fact that there is only one place where you need to do it makes the implementation trivial. Contrary to this, Wicket allows you to *instantiate* a Page class at any point in the application, making it almost impossible to use a Spring-ified Page class transparently to the user. Earlier, you saw two main reasons that make Wicket-Spring integration difficult. You now have some idea of the first one. Let's look at the other.

MANAGED AND UNMANAGED FRAMEWORKS

Managed frameworks are those that manage the life cycle of your objects—they instantiate them, destroy them, and thereby handle the object life cycle on your behalf. In order to manage your objects, the Framework somehow has to wrap them. Therefore, the preferred model is to work with interfaces and not objects because interfaces can be easily wrapped with proxies. Such a model makes sense for larger objects like services—but very little sense for small objects like components. Also, since the instantiation is taken care of for you, you have very little control over the constructor, so the objects are usually beans. Constructors have very important properties such as atomicity, and all this is lost in a managed framework when you need to pass in different parameters to the constructor at different times. In an unmanaged framework, you are in charge of the object's life cycle and therefore in control of instantiation.

DI Issue Due to Wicket Model and Component Serialization

Wicket keeps its tree of components in an ISessionStore implementation. It turns out to be an HTTP session by default. But there is nothing that stops you from storing the session information in a database or a file, for example. You are just required to provide a custom ISessionStore implementation. In a clustered environment, session data needs to be replicated across the cluster. This is done by serializing objects in a cluster node's session and deserializing them on another cluster node's session. Dependencies are normally held as instance variables in a Page. This presents a problem for dependency injection because it is not desirable to serialize the dependency; dependencies often have references to other dependencies in the container, and so if one is serialized, it will probably serialize a few others and can possibly cascade to serializing the entire container. Even if the cascading is not a problem and the dependency is serialized, when it deserializes, it will no longer be part of the container—it will be a stand-alone clone. This is also undesirable. Also, a singleton ceases to remain one after deserialization unless handled with care.

This amply demonstrates the integration issue in regards to component serialization. As with most cases, Wicket introduces another level of indirection to solve this problem: injecting an instance of a dynamic proxy into the Page that in turn directs all the calls invoked on it on to the original Spring object. The injected proxy requires a minimal memory footprint and contains just enough information to locate the dependency from the context. This is especially required to keep the serialization impact to a minimum. Wicket employs the dynamic byte code enhancement capabilities of CGLIB library when proxying a class.

Wicket proposes two distinct approaches to integration with Spring:

- Integration through the framework's global SpringWebApplication class

- Integration using the @SpringBean Java 5 annotation and the AnnotSpringWebApplication class

Accessing the Spring ApplicationContext Through the WebApplication Class

You know that Wicket applications have a global application object that is a subclass of Wicket's WebApplication class. This global application object is created only once per application and is never serialized (since it contains no user-specific data and thus remains the same across all nodes in the cluster). These qualities make it a good candidate to act as a service locator for the rest of the application. A Spring ApplicationContext is one such global object factory. If Wicket's WebApplication class were to be made aware of the Spring ApplicationContext, this would enable Page classes to access services configured within Spring. Also, Spring makes its ApplicationContext available to all those beans that implement the ApplicationContextAware interface, only if they are *configured within Spring itself*. If this indeed were the case, how to let WicketServlet know that it needs to pull the WebApplication from within Spring? As is often the case, most problems in computer science are indeed solved by having another level of indirection.

Recall from the discussion in Chapter 1 that WicketServlet looks for an IWebApplication➡ Factory implementation first under the context param-name applicationFactoryClassName. The Wicket-Spring module provides such a factory, wicket.spring.SpringWebApplication➡ Factory, that, instead of creating an instance of WebApplication, pulls it out of the Spring application context. Wicket keeps the instance of the application object in a ThreadLocal variable and provides various helper methods in components to get to it, so that it is easy to retrieve dependencies in Wicket components. When adopting this approach, the dependencies are *not* held as instance variables in the Page that requires access to them. The Page instead does a lookup on the WebApplication class to resolve the dependencies.

The web.xml needs to register Spring's ContextLoaderListener listener class, which also needs to know the location of the Spring application context configuration file (see Listing 5-7). ContextLoaderListener then initializes the Spring ApplicationContext, passing in the configuration file content. This is the default Spring set up for initializing the ApplicationContext.

Listing 5-7. *web.xml*

```
<?xml version="1.0" encoding="ISO-8859-1"?>
<!DOCTYPE web-app
    PUBLIC "-//Sun Microsystems, Inc.//DTD Web Application 2.3//EN"
    "http://java.sun.com/dtd/web-app_2_3.dtd">

<web-app>

    <display-name>wicket-spring-examples</display-name>
```

```
<!-- Spring's ContextLoader will look for Spring xml files specified here -->
<!--
  Spring by default looks for a file named applicationContext.xml under the
  WEB-INF folder.
  This default configuration is therefore commented.
<context-param>
  <param-name>contextConfigLocation</param-name>
  <param-value>/WEB-INF/applicationContext.xml</param-value>
</context-param>
-->
<!--
  Spring ships with this listener that loads the above
  applicationContext.xml and binds it
  to the servlet context that is later used by SpringWebApplicationFactory
  to look up SpringWebApplication.
-->

<listener>
  <listener-class>
    org.springframework.web.context.ContextLoaderListener
  </listener-class>
</listener>
<servlet>
  <servlet-name>BookStoreApplication</servlet-name>
  <servlet-class>wicket.protocol.http.WicketServlet</servlet-class>
  <init-param>
      <param-name>applicationFactoryClassName</param-name>
      <param-value>wicket.spring.SpringWebApplicationFactory</param-value>
  </init-param>
  <load-on-startup>1</load-on-startup>
</servlet>

<servlet-mapping>
  <servlet-name>BookStoreApplication</servlet-name>
  <url-pattern>/integration/*</url-pattern>
</servlet-mapping>
</web-app>
```

Figure 5-2 depicts the sequence of events just discussed.

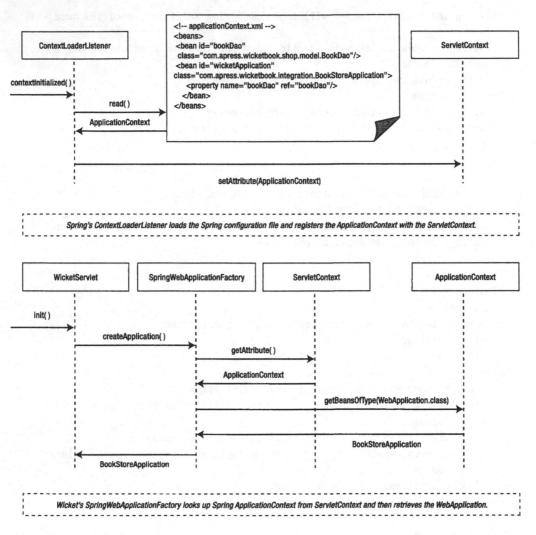

Figure 5-2. *How Wicket configures itself with a WebApplication configured within a Spring context*

"Programming to an interface" is always a good thing. It allows you to swap the underlying interface implementation transparently to the clients of the interface. The fact that it facilitates *test-driven development* is all the more reason that you religiously follow it (wherever applicable). This is one of the underlying principles of working with Spring. Currently you have a BookDao that maintains an in-memory list of books. So let's decouple the implementation from the interface specification so that later you can swap it for an implementation that works with a database, for example (see Listing 5-8). Even though you started off with the implementation first, a quick look at the refactoring catalog (http://refactoring.com/catalog/index.html) tells you that applying the extract interface refactoring should get you the interface specification you are looking for. Most of the IDEs support this refactoring method. This is what you are likely to end up with if you accept the default behavior—i.e., all methods in the implementation class will show up in the "extracted" interface.

Listing 5-8. *IBookDao*

```
package com.apress.wicketbook.shop.model;

import java.util.List;

public interface IBookDao {
    // Move the constants to the interface so that
    // it will be visible to all the DAOs.

    /* Some Publishers */
    public static String APRESS = "Apress";
    public static String MANNING = "Manning";
    public static String OREILLY = "Oreilly";

    /* Some categories */
    public static String CATEGORY_J2EE = "J2EE";
    public static String CATEGORY_SCRIPTING = "Scripting";
    public static String CATEGORY_ALL = "All";

    public static String[] categories = new String[] {
     CATEGORY_J2EE, CATEGORY_SCRIPTING, CATEGORY_ALL };

    public void addBook(Book book);
    public Book getBook(int id);
    public List getBooksForCategory(String category, int start, int count);
    public int getBookCount(String category);
    public List findBooksForCategory(String category);
    public List findAllBooks();
    public List getAllCategories();
    public List getSupportedCategories();

}
```

Accordingly, you will get the Page class to program to IBookDao instead of BookDao, as shown in Listing 5-9.

Listing 5-9. *Books.java*

```
public class Books extends WebPage {

  class BookDetailsModel extends Model {

    public Object getObject(Component comp) {
      Map data = new HashMap();
      data.put("bookList", getBookDao().findBooksForCategory(
            getCategory()));
      return data;
    }
```

```
    public IBookDao getBookDao() {
      BookStoreApplication application = (BookStoreApplication)
          getApplication();
      return application.getBookDao();
    }
  }        //..
}
```

The custom application class needs to extend wicket.spring.SpringWebApplication provided by Wicket (see Listing 5-10).

Listing 5-10. *Spring-ified BookStoreApplication Class*

```
package com.apress.wicketbook.integration;

import wicket.spring.SpringWebApplication;
import com.apress.wicketbook.shop.model.IBookDao;

public class BookStoreApplication extends SpringWebApplication {
   // This dependency will be resolved by Spring during instantiation.
   private IBookDao bookDao;

  // Use Spring's setter injection technique to have the dependency resolved.
  public void setBookDao(IBookDao bookDao){
    this.bookDao = bookDao;
  }

  public IBookDao getBookDao(){
    return bookDao;
  }
//
}
```

Since you want the BookStoreApplication class to be "Spring-aware," you need to configure it within the Spring configuration file. Note that the you can specify any value for the id attribute identifying the WebApplication. Wicket's SpringWebApplicationFactory class looks for a bean of type WebApplication in Spring's ApplicationContext, shown in Listing 5-11, and uses that as the application-specific WebApplication class. If more than one WebApplication class is found in the ApplicationContext, it will result in a runtime error.

Listing 5-11. *applicationContext.xml*

```
<?xml version="1.0" encoding="UTF-8"?>
<!DOCTYPE beans PUBLIC "-//SPRING//DTD BEAN//EN"
"http://www.springframework.org/dtd/spring-beans.dtd">
```

```
<beans>
    <bean id="bookDao" class="com.apress.wicketbook.shop.model.BookDao"/>
    <!-- setup wicket application -->
    <bean id="wicketApplication"
class="com.apress.wicketbook.integration.BookStoreApplication">
        <property name="bookDao" ref="bookDao"/>
    </bean>
</beans>
```

Spring looks for the XML configuration file by the name applicationContext.xml by default under the context/WEB-INF folder.

The location and name of the application context file is immaterial as long as you let the ContextLoaderListener know where to find it. In fact, you could specify more than one application context file as well. But discussing that is beyond the scope of this book. For now, save your applicationContext.xml in the context/WEB-INF folder.

CUSTOM APPLICATION CLUTTER

One disadvantage of treating the Application class as a global registry is that the CustomApplication class is likely to get cluttered with getters and setters as the number of service objects that the Page depends upon increases.

Note that access to Spring's ApplicationContext is just one method call away: SpringWeb➡ Application.internalGetApplicationContext(). You have access to the ApplicationContext as SpringWebApplication implements Spring's ApplicationContextAware interface. If you intend to use this context class, you wouldn't be required to specify the IBookDao dependency in your Page class. You can directly pull it out of the ApplicationContext as shown in Listing 5-12.

Listing 5-12. *BookStoreApplication Accessing BookDao Through Spring's ApplicationContext*

```
import org.springframework.context.ApplicationContext;

public class BookStoreApplication extends SpringWebApplication {
    public IBookDao getBookDao(){
        ApplicationContext springApplicationContext =
            getSpringApplicationContext();
        return (IBookDao)springApplicationContext.getBean("bookDao");
    }

    public ApplicationContext getSpringApplicationContext(){
        return internalGetApplicationContext();
    }
}
```

One advantage of this is that depending upon the way the BookDao class is configured in the Spring context file (singleton or prototype), you can return a different instance of the BookDao class for every method call. Note that if you were to specify the BookStoreApplication's IBookDao dependency in the Spring context file, you will, by virtue of the fact that there is only one instance of the WebApplication class per web application, end up with a singleton instance of the BookDao class.

Even though the preceding solution works well, the Page class still needs to "pull" data from the WebApplication class. Hence this falls under the category of dependency lookup rather than dependency injection—i.e., the control still remains *uninverted*. Luckily, this is not so much of a problem, as Wicket ships an IoC solution for Spring integration, and we shall discuss that next.

Configuring Injection Through an IComponentInstantiationListener Implementation

For enabling IoC on the Page, you need a way by which you can resolve the dependencies without doing an explicit lookup. You also need to make sure that the fields that need their dependencies resolved are pointing to valid Spring bean references before the Page constructor executes. That way their services can be employed by other components when constructing the Page. Wicket's IComponentInstantiationListener has been specifically designed to support such custom processing during component instantiation. An IComponentInstantiationListener implementation when registered with Wicket's Application class gets called whenever a component is instantiated. (In Chapter 3, you saw how Wicket addresses the component authorization/authentication centrally though the same interface.) Wicket supplies an implementation, wicket.injection.ComponentInjector, that resolves dependencies during component construction. This of course needs to be registered with the Wicket's Application class.

In practice, you don't need to be doing all this. It's automatically taken care of as long as your Application class extends the appropriate WebApplication subclass that ships with Wicket—wicket.spring.injection.annot.AnnotSpringWebApplication.

LIGHTWEIGHT MODEL AND PAGE

Irrespective of whether you use Spring with Wicket or not, it's still a good Wicket programming practice to keep Page and Wicket model classes as lightweight as possible.

WICKET-SPRING INTEGRATION THROUGH AOP

Employing *aspect-oriented programming* (AOP) implementations like AspectJ to intercept the new operator is also a possible solution for the Spring-Wicket integration problem. But it appears that the Wicket developers have steered clearly away from introducing another framework to address this problem. Also, Spring 2.0 is likely to ship with the ability to dependency inject domain objects created using the new operator. It remains to be seen how Wicket can benefit from this feature. *AspectJ In Action* by Ramnivas Laddad (Manning, 2003) is an excellent source to learn about AOP in general and AspectJ in particular.

The ComponentInjector makes use of the wicket.injection.Injector subclass to do the actual DI. It first introspects all the fields of a component (which is a Page in this case) and then looks up the Spring ApplicationContext, asking for the object that maps to the field name or the type, and if found, sets it as the value for the field. It does this through Java reflection.

Specifying Target Field for Dependency Injection

If you notice, there is still an issue with the preceding Injector implementation. It has no way of knowing the fields that actually require dependency injection. What is required is an ability to specify which fields are interested in having their dependencies resolved through the Injector. Essentially, what you need is a way to specify *meta* information about the field itself. Injector can then infer from the meta information whether the field requires DI and move from there. Java 5 made a giant leap in that regard by providing *annotations*—a way to specify metadata on top of your code. What you need here is an annotation that needs to be retained in the Java class file for runtime introspection and something that can be supported on a Java instance variable. Wicket's wicket.spring.injection.annot.SpringBean annotation satisfies all of the preceding requirements (see Listing 5-13).

Listing 5-13. *SpringBean.java*

```
package wicket.spring.injection.annot;

import java.lang.annotation.Documented;
import java.lang.annotation.ElementType;
import java.lang.annotation.Retention;
import java.lang.annotation.RetentionPolicy;
import java.lang.annotation.Target;
```

```
@Retention(RetentionPolicy.RUNTIME)
@Target( {/* ElementType.METHOD, */ElementType.FIELD})
@Documented
public @interface SpringBean {
    /**
    * Optional attribute for specifying the name of the bean.
    * If not specified,the bean will be looked up by the type
    * of the field with the annotation.
    *
    * @return name attr
    */
    String name() default "";
}
```

Injector now knows that only those fields that carry @SpringBean need to be dependency injected.

You could configure Injector with any kind of object factory. The Wicket-Spring module provides nice abstractions to achieve a good level of loose coupling. Today you have implementation to support Spring integration. You can contribute one for HiveMind, for example. (HiveMind is another IoC container like Spring and is available for download here: http://jakarta.apache.org/hivemind/.)

DI AND FIELD INITIALIZATION

Never set the field that requires dependency injection explicitly to null. Note that the dependency injection happens from within the base class (wicket.Component) constructor (IComponentInstantiation➡ Listeners are called within the wicket.Component class constructor.) In Java, a derived class is initialized after the super class initialization is complete. If the derived class's instance variables are explicitly initialized to null, all the work done by ComponentInjector will boil down to nothing since the former's initialization process will kick in after ComponentInjector is done with its work. This will result in the references being set back to null.

Specifying Spring Dependency Through Java 5 Annotation

If you like the DI method that we discussed earlier, you need to be doing the following:

- Extend your application class from Wicket-Spring's AnnotSpringWebApplication class. This class takes care of configuring Wicket's AnnotSpringInjector, which injects class based on annotation. It also makes sure that wicket.injection.ComponentInjector is registered as an IComponentInstantiationListener.

- Annotate the fields that require DI with the wicket.spring.injection.annot. SpringBean annotation.

- Configure SpringWebApplicationFactory as the Application factory class in web.xml.

- Configure your AnnotSpringWebApplication subclass in applicationContext.xml.

@SpringBean annotation accepts an optional attribute for specifying the name of the bean as identified in Spring's XML configuration or ApplicationContext. If not specified, the bean will be looked up based on the Java type of the field with the annotation (see Listing 5-14).

Listing 5-14. *AnnotBookStoreApplication Setup for Spring Annotations*

```
package com.apress.wicketbook.integration;

import wicket.spring.injection.annot.AnnotSpringWebApplication;

public class AnnotBookStoreApplication extends AnnotSpringWebApplication{

    public ISessionFactory getSessionFactory() {
    return new ISessionFactory() {
      public Session newSession() {
       return new BookStoreSession(AnnotBookStoreApplication.this);
      }
    };
    }

    public Class getHomePage() {
    // You will be developing this class next.
    return BooksWithDI.class;
    }
}
```

Now that you have the WebApplication class ready, you just need to specify the @SpringBean annotation on the fields that require DI. Rest assured that by the time the Page is instantiated, all dependencies will have been wired up. Since dependency injection happens before the Page constructor actually executes, you can access the Spring-annotated instance variable safely within the Page.

Listing 5-15 presents the modified Books page with Spring-annotated variables. Note that you need not look up the BookStoreApplication class any longer to access the DAO object. It automatically gets injected for you. Note that the class presented in Listing 5-15 and the template (see Listing 5-16) is same as the ViewBooks class that you developed in Chapter 3. The significant difference lies in the way BookDataProvider accesses the DAO. Earlier, it was doing a static look up from the ThreadLocal variable:

```
public class BookDataProvider implements IDataProvider{
    //..,
    private BookDao getBookDao(){
        return ((BookStoreApplication)Application.get()).getBookDao();
    }
    //..
}
```

Listing 5-15. *BookWithDI.java—A Page That Carries @SpringBean Annotations*

```java
import wicket.spring.injection.annot.SpringBean;

public class BooksWithDI extends WebPage {
    private String category = BookDao.CATEGORY_ALL;

    // Get IBookDao injected from Spring Application context.
     @SpringBean private IBookDao bookDao;
    // @SpringBean private IBookDao bookDao = null; -> Avoid this by all means!

    //..
    public BooksWithDI() {
      Form form = new Form("viewBookForm");

      // Pass the reference of the injected Spring Object.
      IDataProvider dataProvider = new BookDataProvider(bookDao);
      form.add(new BookDataView("books",dataProvider));

      // Directly look up categories using bookDao.
      DropDownChoice categories = new CategoryDropDownChoice("categories",
        new PropertyModel(this, "category"), bookDao.getAllCategories());
      form.add(categories);
      //..
    }

    class BookDataView extends DataView{

      public BookDataView(String id,
               IDataProvider dataProvider) {
        super(id, dataProvider);
      }

      protected void populateItem(final Item item) {
        Book book = (Book) item.getModelObject();
        item.setModel(new CompoundPropertyModel(book));
        item.add(new Label("title"));
        item.add(new Label("author"));
        item.add(new Label("publisher"));
        item.add(new Label("price"));
      }
    }
    // Note that the helper method getBookCategories() is not needed any longer.
}
```

Listing 5-16. *BookWithDI.html*

```html
<html>
<head>
<title>Browse Books</title>
</head>
<body>
<form name="viewBookForm" wicket:id="viewBookForm">
  <table>
    <tr>
    <td><b>Categories</b></td>
    <td>
      <select wicket:id="categories">
        <option>J2EE</option>
        <option>ASP.NET</option>
        <option>Scripting</option>
      </select>
    </td>
    </tr>
  </table>
  <table border-"1">
    <!-- The column headers have been ignored -->
    <tr wicket:id="books">
      <td><span wicket:id="title">[Book Title]</span></td>
      <td><span wicket:id="author">[Book Author]</span></td>
      <td><span wicket:id="publisher">[Book Publisher]</span></td>
      <td><span wicket:id="price">[Book Price]</span></td>
    </tr>
  </table>
</form>
</body>
</html>
```

You can do something along the lines of Listing 5-17 instead. It is *important* that the DAO passed to the data provider be a *proxy* from Wicket-Spring integration module when used in production environment. This is necessary to avoid the issue that could arise out of Wicket model and component serialization that we discussed earlier. The proxy obtained from Wicket's Injector only serializes information it needs to locate the DAO when it is deserialized instead of serializing the DAO itself.

Listing 5-17. *BookDataProvider Directly Storing a Reference to the DAO*

```java
public class BookDataProvider implements IDataProvider{

  private String category;
    // Make sure that this points to a Proxy as returned from
    // Wicket's Injector.
  private IBookDao bookDao;
```

```
    public BookDataProvider(IBookDao bookDao,String category){
      this.category = category;
      this.bookDao = bookDao;
    }

    public BookDataProvider(IBookDao bookDao){
      this(bookDao,BookDao.CATEGORY_ALL);
    }
    //..
}
```

Spring Integration Through Commons Attributes

You saw how succinct Wicket-Spring integration through Java 5 annotation is. But not every project under the sun gets to use Java 5 as the base platform. It might still be using a Java version that shipped prior to Java 5. In order to please everyone, Wicket now has support for Spring integration through Commons Attributes as long as one doesn't mind the "attribute compilation" step required by the Jakarta utility. Instead of specifying @wicket.spring. injection.annot.SpringBean Java 5 annotation as suggested in the previous section, you need to annotate the field with the @@wicket.spring.injection.cattr.SpringBean Commons Attribute as a Javadoc-like tag (see Listing 5-18).

Listing 5-18. *BooksWithDI.java When Used in Conjunction with Commons Attributes*

```
public class BooksWithDI extends WebPage {

  /**
  * @@wicket.spring.injection.cattr.SpringBean("bookDao")
  */
  private IBookDao bookDao;
  //..

}
```

This time around, your Application class needs to extend the wicket.spring.injection. cattr.CommonsAttributeSpringWebApplication class though. One of the primary reasons you program to the IBookDao interface is that it allows you to switch the DAO implementation in a transparent fashion.

The BookDao class that you looked at just holds onto the book references in memory. Let's consider a persistent solution instead.

How Wicket Integrates with EJB 3

In this section, you will look at one of the ways of integrating an enterprise-level persistence solution like EJB 3 with Wicket. Hibernate is used as the EJB 3 implementation in the examples.

A Quick EJB 3 Entity Bean Refresher

EJB3 entity beans are just plain POJOs that represent persistent domain entities. "User," "Sales Order," and "Catalog Item" are typical examples of concepts that make up a domain model and are prime candidates to be persisted to a back-end store. Typically, the bean attributes map to the columns of the table, and this mapping is expressed through Java 5 annotations. These annotations in turn are defined by the EJB 3 Java Persistence Architecture (JPA) specifications. An XML descriptor file could also be used to specify the "bean attribute to database column" mapping information. You can use the XML descriptor entries to override the annotations specified in the bean class as well. The backing EJB implementation then generates the appropriate database SQL queries based on the information you specify using annotations. The container runs these queries transparently to the client in response to the calls executed on the bean. You just deal with the POJOs and class associations while the container takes care of the interactions with the back-end store. For a thorough discussion on JPA, you could refer to *Pro EJB 3: Java Persistence API* by Mike Keith and Merrick Schincariol (Apress, 2006).

Choosing an EJB3 Implementation

JPA is after all a specification, and to actually see it working, you require an implementation. At the time of writing this book, Hibernate 3 was one of the more popular implementations of JPA, and thus it is used in this chapter. The EJB 3 support is available as three separate downloads:

1. Hibernate Core

2. Hibernate Annotations

3. Hibernate EntityManager

These libraries are available for download at `http://hibernate.org`. At the time of writing this chapter, the Hibernate–EJB 3 release was not final. The following versions were known to support EJB JPA—`Hibernate-3.2.0.cr2`, `Hibernate-annotations-3.2.0.CR1`, and `Hibernate-entitymanager-3.2.0.CR1`. You would require all the jar files that come with each of these libraries.

If Eclipse is your IDE of choice, then it would be a good idea to define a `User_Library` variable to add all the required Hibernate jar files to the web application classpath.

Now that you understand what an EJB 3 entity bean is and have downloaded an implementation as well, the next logical step would be to actually code the bean class.

Listing 5-19 represents the `Book` entity that you have been using throughout. It uses the following JPA annotations:

Annotation	Description
`@Entity`	A class-level annotation to mark a class as an EJB 3 entity bean
`@Table`	Annotation to provide the backing database table information
`@Basic`	Simplest type of mapping to database column
`@Column`	Annotation for providing the table column name and column constraints
`@Id`	Primary key that uniquely identifies the entity
`@GeneratedValue`	Annotation for specifying the generation strategies for values of primary keys

There is a very high probability that you will use a database as the persistence store for the majority of the applications that you develop. The EJB 3 container will then generate the required Entity bean-to-database mapping, the SQL queries to manage the actual persistence to the back end, etc., based on the Java 5 annotations that you specify on the POJO. Note that not all annotations in the Listing 5-19 have to be necessarily supplied. The underlying JPA implementation is very likely to provide for "intelligent defaults" in the absence of certain annotations.

Listing 5-19. *Book Bean Converted to EJB 3 Entity Bean Using annotationspackagecom. apress.wicketbook.shop.model;*

```java
import java.io.Serializable;

/** EJB3 imports **/

import javax.persistence.Basic;
import javax.persistence.Column;
import javax.persistence.Entity;
import javax.persistence.GeneratedValue;
import javax.persistence.GenerationType;
import javax.persistence.Id;
import javax.persistence.Table;

@Entity
@Table(name="Book")

public class Book implements Serializable {

  @Id
  @GeneratedValue(strategy=GenerationType.AUTO)
  protected int id;

  @Basic
  @Column(name="TITLE", nullable=false,updatable=false)
  protected String title;

  @Basic
  @Column(name="AUTHOR", nullable=false,updatable=false)
  protected String author;

  @Basic
  @Column(name="PRICE", nullable=false,updatable=true)
  protected float price;

  @Basic
  @Column(name="PUBLISHER", nullable=false,updatable=false)
  protected String publisher;
```

```
@Basic
@Column(name="CATEGORY", nullable=false,updatable=false)
protected String category;

public Book(){ }
/** The rest is the same as the Book class you developed in Chapter 3 **/
//..
}
```

This is not all; you still have to provide a little more information before you can have a fully functioning EJB 3 entity bean. JPA defines an EntityManager interface that manages entities within a persistence context. The set of entities that can be managed by a given EntityManager instance is defined by a persistence unit. A persistence unit defines the set of all classes that are related or grouped by the application, and that must be colocated in their mapping to a single database.

A persistence.xml file defines a persistence unit. It may be used to specify managed persistence classes included in the persistence unit, object/relational mapping information for those classes, and other configuration information for the persistence unit and for the entity manager(s) and entity manager factory for the persistence unit. The persistence.xml file is usually located in the META-INF directory of the root of the persistence unit.

Defining the persistence.xml

The persistence.xml in Listing 5-20 does the following:

1. Identifies the persistence unit as "wicketPersistenceManager".

2. Specifies the transaction setting as Local Transaction. You might want to switch to a JTA implementation when running in a J2EE container.

3. Identifies the entity bean by specifying the fully qualified class name.

4. Configures Hibernate to work with HSQLDB.

Listing 5-20. *persistence.xml As Required by EJB 3 Specification*

```
<persistence>
  <persistence-unit name="wicketPersistenceManager" transaction-
type="RESOURCE_LOCAL">
    <!--the bean that needs to be persisted -->
    <class>com.apress.wicketbook.shop.model.Book</class>
    <!--
    Vendor specific properties goes here. You will use Hibernate3 EJB3
    implementation with HSQL Db configured
    -->
    <properties>
      <property name="hibernate.dialect" value="org.hibernate.dialect.HSQLDialect"/>
      <property name=
         "hibernate.connection.driver_class"value="org.hsqldb.jdbcDriver"/>
```

```
    <property name="hibernate.connection.username" value="sa"/>
    <property name="hibernate.connection.password" value=""/>
    <property name="hibernate.connection.url" value="jdbc:hsqldb:."/>
    <property name="hibernate.max_fetch_depth" value="3"/>
    <property name="hibernate.hbm2ddl.auto" value="create-drop"/>
    <property name="hibernate.show_sql">true</property>
    <property name="hibernate.jdbc.batch_size" value="0"/>
  </properties>
  </persistence-unit>
</persistence>
```

Make sure that you place persistence.xml in the src/META-INF folder. The information specified in Listing 5-20 is enough to get a minimalistic Hibernate EJB 3 configuration up and running. You could term the EntityManager class as the gateway to the interaction with the entity. In addition to several other features, it has methods to persist, find, and delete entities from the persistence store. The example in Listing 5-21 also makes use of EJB Query Language (EJBQL), which is quite similar to standard SQL. EJBQL works on entities, associations, and properties instead of database tables and columns.

Listing 5-21. *IBookDao Implementation Using Hibernate 3*

```java
package com.apress.wicketbook.integration;

import java.util.Arrays;
import java.util.List;

// EJB 3 imports
import javax.persistence.EntityManager;
import javax.persistence.EntityManagerFactory;
import javax.persistence.EntityTransaction;
import javax.persistence.Query;

import com.apress.wicketbook.shop.model.Book;
import com.apress.wicketbook.shop.model.IBookDao;

public class HibernateBookDao implements IBookDao {

  private EntityManagerFactory entityManagerFactory;

  public HibernateBookDao(EntityManagerFactory entityManagerFactory) {
    this.entityManagerFactory = entityManagerFactory;

    addBook(new Book("Rob Harrop", CATEGORY_J2EE, "Pro Spring", 30.00f,
        APRESS));
    addBook(new Book("Damian Conway", CATEGORY_SCRIPTING,
        "Object Oriented Perl", 40.00f, MANNING));
```

```
    addBook(new Book("Alex Martelli", CATEGORY_SCRIPTING,
        "Python in a Nutshell", 35.00f, OREILLY));
    addBook(new Book("Alex Martelli", CATEGORY_SCRIPTING,
        "Python Cookbook", 35.00f, OREILLY));
}

private EntityManager getEntityManager() {
    return getEntityManagerFactory().createEntityManager();
}

public void addBook(final Book book) {
    EntityManager manager = getEntityManager();
    EntityTransaction trans = manager.getTransaction();
    try{
        trans.begin();
        manager.persist(book);
        trans.commit();
    }catch(Exception e){
        trans.rollback();
    }finally{
        manager.clear();
        manager.close();
    }
}

public Book getBook(final int id) {
    EntityManager manager = getEntityManager();
    try {
        return manager.find(Book.class, new Integer(id));
    } finally {
        manager.close();
    }
}

public List getBooksForCategory(String category, int start, int count) {
    EntityManager manager = getEntityManager();
    try {
        Query query = manager.createQuery(
            " select book from Book book where book.category=?1")
            .setParameter(1, category).setFirstResult(start).setMaxResults(count);
        return query.getResultList();
    } finally {
        manager.close();
    }
}
```

```java
public int getBookCount(String category) {
  EntityManager manager = getEntityManager();
  try {
    Query query = manager
        .createQuery("select count(*) from Book where category = ?1");
    query.setParameter(1, category);
    return ((Integer) query.getSingleResult()).intValue();
  } finally {
    manager.close();
  }
}

public List findBooksForCategory(String category) {
  EntityManager manager = getEntityManager();
  if (CATEGORY_ALL.equals(category)){
    return findAllBooks();
  }
  try {
    Query query = manager
        .createQuery("select book from Book as book where book.category = ?1");
    query.setParameter(1, category);
    return query.getResultList();
  } finally {
    manager.close();
  }
}

public List findAllBooks() {
  EntityManager manager = getEntityManager();
  try {
    return manager.createQuery("select book from Book as book")
        .getResultList();
  } finally {
    manager.close();
  }

}

public List getAllCategories() {
  return null;
}

public List getSupportedCategories() {
  return Arrays.asList(categories);
}
```

```
  public List getSearchResult(String bookNameStartsWith) {
    EntityManager manager = getEntityManager();
    try {
      String strQuery = " select book from Book as book where book.title like ?1% ";
      Query query = getEntityManager().createQuery(strQuery);
      query.setParameter(1, bookNameStartsWith);
      return query.getResultList();
    } finally {
      manager.close();
    }
  }

  public EntityManagerFactory getEntityManagerFactory() {
    return entityManagerFactory;
  }
}
```

Note that the EntityManagerFactory interface is used by the application to obtain an application-managed entity manager and needs to be injected as well. Listing 5-22 shows how this can be done. Only one instance of EntityManagerFactory should exist per application. Spring's ObjectFactory class allows us to do just that. When Spring notices that a bean depends on an ObjectFactory and not a bean reference directly, it calls the ObjectFactory. getObject() method to fetch the actual bean reference. Refer to Listing 5-23 for one such implementation.

Listing 5-22. *EntityManageFactoryObjectFactory That Returns the EntityManagerFactory Implementation*

```
package com.apress.wicketbook.integration;

import javax.persistence.EntityManagerFactory;
import javax.persistence.Persistence;

import org.springframework.beans.BeansException;
import org.springframework.beans.factory.BeanCreationException;
import org.springframework.beans.factory.ObjectFactory;

public class EntityManageFactoryObjectFactory implements ObjectFactory {
  private EntityManagerFactory entityManagerFactory;

  public Object getObject() throws BeansException {
    /*
     * Only one instance of EntityManagerFactory should exist per
     * application
     */
    if (entityManagerFactory != null)
      return entityManagerFactory;
```

```
    try {
      entityManagerFactory = Persistence
          .createEntityManagerFactory("wicketPersistenceManager");
      return entityManagerFactory;
    } catch (Throwable ex) {
      throw new BeanCreationException(
          "Error creating EntityManagerFactory ", ex);
    }
  }
}
```

Listing 5-23. *applicationContext.xml for IBookDao Implementation Using Spring 1.2 and EJB 3 Based on Hibernate*

```
<beans>
    <bean id="Ej3BookDao"
    class="com.apress.wicketbook.integration.HibernateBookDao">
    <!--HibernateBookDao specifies its dependency on an ObjectFactory
    implementation -->
    <constructor-arg><ref bean="entityManagerFactoryObjectFactory"/> ➡
</constructor-arg>
    </bean>

<!-- setup wicket application -->
<bean id="wicketApplication"
class="com.apress.wicketbook.integration.AnnotBookStoreApplication"/>

    <bean id="entityManageFactoryObjectFactory"
       class="com.apress.wicketbook.integration.EntityManageFactoryObjectFactory"/>
</beans>
```

How Spring 2.0 Further Simplifies EJB 3 Programming

Even though programming to the EJB 3 persistence API (also known as *Java Persistence Architecture*, or JPA) is way simpler compared to its 2.1 counterpart, it is still tedious to be repeating the redundant code that deals with EntityManager lookup, query creation, and subsequent cleanup. Listing 5-21 demonstrates this problem. At the time of writing this chapter, Spring 2.0 M5 had built-in support for JPA. As is the case with Spring, the EJB 3 support doesn't mean that Spring 2.0 ships with a JPA implementation. It instead provides support through its library classes like JpaTemplate, JpaCallback, and JpaDaoSupport.

For more information on Spring 2.0's JPA support, refer to the info at this URL: http://static.springframework.org/spring/docs/2.0.x/reference/orm.html#orm-jpa.

Spring also has a JpaDaoSupport class that your DAO can subclass. This class has lots of helper methods that give you access to the persistent store. It allows access to the JpaTemplate class through the getJpaTemplate() method. This way you can still perform operations that require access to the EntityManager, for example (see Listing 5-24).

Listing 5-24. *IBookDao Implementation Using Spring 2.0 and EJB 3 Based on Hibernate*

```java
package com.apress.wicketbook.integration;

// Other imports

// Spring 2.0 imports
import org.springframework.orm.jpa.JpaCallback;
import org.springframework.orm.jpa.support.JpaDaoSupport;

public class Spring2EJB3BookDao extends JpaDaoSupport implements IBookDao{

  public void addBook(final Book book) {
    getJpaTemplate().persist(book);
  }

  public Book getBook(final int id) {
    return getJpaTemplate().find(Book.class, new Integer(id));
  }

  public List getBooksForCategory(final String category, final int start,
      final int count) {

    return (List) getJpaTemplate().execute(
      new JpaCallback() {
        public Object doInJpa(EntityManager manager)
            throws PersistenceException {
          Query query = manager.createQuery(
            " select book from Book book where book.category=?1")
            .setParameter(1, category).setFirstResult(start)
            .setMaxResults(count);
          return query.getResultList();
        }
      }
    );
  }

  public int getBookCount(final String category) {
```

```
    Integer count = (Integer)getJpaTemplate().execute(new JpaCallback() {
      public Object doInJpa(EntityManager manager)
          throws PersistenceException {
        Query query = manager
          .createQuery("select count(*) from Book where category = ?1");
        query.setParameter(1, category);
        return query.getSingleResult();
      }
    });
    return count.intValue();
  }

  public List findBooksForCategory(String category) {
    return getJpaTemplate().find(
        "select book from Book as book where book.category = ?1",
        category);
  }

  public List findAllBooks() {
    return getJpaTemplate().find("select book from Book as book");
  }

  // Other method implementations are not shown here but are available in the book's
  // source code.

  /*
   * Concrete subclasses can override this for custom initialization behavior.
   * Gets called after population of this instance's bean properties by Spring's
   * JpaDaoSupport class. In this case, the Dao initialization routine goes here.
   *
   */

  protected void initDao(){
    addBook(new Book("Rob Harrop", CATEGORY_J2EE, "Pro Spring", 30.00f,
        APRESS));
    addBook(new Book("Damian Conway", CATEGORY_SCRIPTING,
        "Object Oriented Perl", 40.00f, MANNING));
    addBook(new Book("Ted Husted", CATEGORY_J2EE, "Struts In Action",
        40.00f, MANNING));
    addBook(new Book("Alex Martelli", CATEGORY_SCRIPTING,
        "Python in a Nutshell", 35.00f, OREILLY));
    addBook(new Book("Larry Wall", CATEGORY_SCRIPTING, "Programming Perl",
        35.00f, OREILLY));
    addBook(new Book("Alex Martelli", CATEGORY_SCRIPTING,
        "Python Cookbook", 35.00f, OREILLY));
  }
}
```

But you need to configure the JpaDaoSupport class with an EntityManagerFactory instance, however. This is a classic case for using Spring dependency injection. Accordingly, you need to declare the EntityManageFactory and then wire it into JpaDaoSupport through the Spring configuration file (see Listing 5-25).

Listing 5-25. *Spring applicationContext.xml Configured with Spring2Hibernate3BookDao*

```xml
<?xml version="1.0" encoding="UTF-8"?>
<!DOCTYPE beans PUBLIC "-//SPRING//DTD BEAN//EN"
"http://www.springframework.org/dtd/spring-beans.dtd">

<beans>

  <!-- Declare the EJB3-compliant Dao -->
  <bean id="Ej3Spring2BookDao"
      class="com.apress.wicketbook.integration.Spring2Hibernate3BookDao">
    <!-- Spring's JpaDaoSupport needs a reference to the
      EntityManagerFactory -->
      <property name="entityManagerFactory" ref="entityManagerFactory"/>
  </bean>

  <!-- LocalEntityManagerFactoryBean will look for the presence of
  META-INF/persistence.xml in classpath by default -->

  <bean id="entityManagerFactory"
      class="org.springframework.orm.jpa.LocalEntityManagerFactoryBean">

    <!-- The persistence unit to look for in the persistence.xml. Remember you named
    it 'wicketPersistenceManager' -->

    <property name="persistenceUnitName" value="wicketPersistenceManager"/>
  </bean>

  <!-- Set up Wicket application -->
  <bean id="annotWicketApplication"
      class="com.apress.wicketbook.integration.AnnotBookStoreApplication"/>

</beans>
```

You will notice that the Page injection errors out on container restart! But this shouldn't get you worried. Wicket's Spring injector, by default, looks for a bean based on the Java type of the field that carries the @SpringBean annotation. If more than one implementation is found in the Spring's ApplicationContext for a given type, Wicket-Spring throws an error to the same effect. So it's very reassuring that Wicket's Spring injector actually detects the conflict and reports the error. Now there are couple of solutions to address this trivial problem: you can either remove the reference to the BookDao bean from the Spring configuration file or supply the bean ID Ej3Spring2BookDao to the @SpringBean annotation explicitly. Listing 5-26 shows how this can be done.

Listing 5-26. *persistence.xml As Required by the EJB 3 Specification*

```
package com.apress.wicketbook.integration;
public class BooksWithDI extends WebPage {

  @SpringBean(name="Ej3Spring2BookDao") private IBookDao bookDao;
```

Summary

In this chapter, we looked at how Wicket integrates with other frameworks, namely Velocity, FreeMarker, and Spring. We looked at Velocity and FreeMarker integration through VelocityPanel and FreemarkerPanel, respectively. Then we discussed the all-important integration with the popular J2EE application framework Spring. You learned the difficulties in making them work together.

You saw that Wicket's integration with Spring through the SpringWebApplication class amounts to dependency pull, and that it also provides for a nonintrusive, consistent IoC solution through the use of the AnnotSpringWebApplication class and SpringBean annotation. Then you looked at Spring–EJB 3 integration using Hibernate 3. You also had a sneak peek at EJB 3 support built into Spring 2.0 through the JpaDaoSupport and JpaTemplate classes.

Note that Wicket integrates well with frameworks other than the ones listed in this chapter. The ones discussed here should serve as a good starting point for understanding others.

CHAPTER 6

■■■

Localization Support

Internationalization is a vast topic on its own, and this chapter doesn't attempt to explain all aspects of internationalizing a web application. It instead focuses on Wicket's support for internationalization. Wicket allows you to externalize locale-specific messages and also provides for flexible formatting of messages through the powerful StringResourceModel class. You could specify messages at different levels in the component hierarchy, thereby enabling you to override messages intelligently. We shall discuss these and more in the following sections.

Localization Through the <wicket:message> Tag

By working through the following examples, you will first make an attempt at localizing the labels on the UserProfilePage: name, address, etc. Wicket allows you to achieve this by adding a level of indirection through the <wicket:message> tag. You can specify the <wicket:message> tag instead of hard-coding the label. More importantly, you are required to specify a key whose value will be looked up from the locale-specific properties file. Listing 6-1 shows the first attempt at localizing the UserProfilePage.

Listing 6-1. *Internationalized UserProfilePage with All Labels Replaced by the* <wicket:message> *Tag*

```
<head>
  <!-- Internationalized page title -->
  <title><wicket:message key="page.title"></wicket:message></title>
</head>
<body>
 <span wicket:id="feedback"></span>
 <!-- Internationalized page labels -->
 <form wicket:id="userProfile">
  <wicket:message key="name"></wicket:message>
    <input type="text" wicket:id="name"/><br/>
  <wicket:message key="address"></wicket:message>
    <input type="text" wicket:id="address"/><br/>
  <wicket:message key="city"></wicket:message>
    <input type="text" wicket:id="city"/><br/>
  <wicket:message key="country"></wicket:message>
```

```
  <select wicket:id="country">
    <option>Country-1</option>
    <option>Country-2</option>
    <option>Country-3</option>
  </select><br/>
<wicket:message key="pin"></wicket:message>
  <input type="text" wicket:id="pin"/><br/>
<wicket:message key="phoneNumber"></wicket:message>
  <input type="text" wicket:id="phoneNumber"/>
  <br/>
```

Note that you can use the shortcut

```
<wicket:message key="name"/>
```

for

```
<wicket:message key="name"></wicket:message>
```

In order to provide locale-specific messages, you need a way for the application to find the messages specific to a given locale. In Java, such messages are typically specified through the java.util.PropertyResourceBundle class. PropertyResourceBundle is a concrete subclass of java.util.ResourceBundle that manages resources for a locale using a set of static strings from a property file. These properties files should contain a set of key=value pairs, mapping the keys you want to use to look up the text to the correct text for that locale. Java's ResourceBundle support typically takes into consideration the locale information when looking for resource bundles, while Wicket supports a concept of style and variation in addition to locale. We shall discuss this in detail in the section "Support for Skinning and Variation in Addition to Locale-Specific Resources."

The next thing you need to do is to make sure that the locale-specific properties file has all the wicket:message keys that you specified in the Page along with the corresponding locale-specific messages. The label or the display text will be picked up from the default UserProfilePage.properties file if the locale is en_US, as shown in Listing 6-2. The messages could also be specified in a properties file corresponding to a component containing the tag in the hierarchy, that is, UserProfileForm. You would be required to call this file UserProfilePage$UserProfileForm.properties though, as the Form component is an inner class. We will discuss the message search order in the upcoming section. For now, specify the messages in the page properties file.

Listing 6-2. *UserProfilePage.properties*

```
page.title= User Profile
name= Name
address= Address
pin = Pin
city = City
country = Country
phoneNumber = Phone Number
```

And it will get picked up from `UserProfilePage_es.properties` if the locale is switched to Spanish (identified by es), as shown in Listing 6-3.

Listing 6-3. *UserProfilePage_es.properties*

```
page.title=perfil de usuario
name= Nombre Del Usuario
address= Dirección
pin = Número de identificación
city = Ciudad
country = País
phoneNumber = Teléfono
```

Likewise, Wicket will look for `UserProfilePage_fr.properties` for French and `UserProfilePage_de.properties` for German, and so on. Remember that Wicket will default to the body of the `<wicket:message>` tag if the key is not found.

Having a good understanding of the way Wicket searches for the localized message is key to developing internationalized web applications with Wicket. As mentioned previously, we will discuss the search order next.

Sources for Localized Messages and Their Search Order

In Wicket, the process of searching for locale-specific messages is delegated to the `Localizer` class. The `Localizer` searches for the resource files (or properties files) based on the component that is passed in. You can specify message texts at different levels, with more specific texts taking precedence over more general ones.

Wicket tags in a template are typically resolved using several `wicket.markup.resolver.IComponentResolver` implementations. This resolving process usually involves mapping the element's *wicket:id* to the corresponding Wicket component, in addition to other things. `<wicket:message>` tags, for example, are resolved using the `WicketMessageResolver` class. When the `Localizer` looks for a message text, it searches for a resource bundle based on a class or object given to it. In this case, `WicketMessageResolver` typically passes in the Wicket component class within which the `<wicket:message>` tag is contained. For example, when searching for the message key name, the class `UserProfileForm` is passed to the `Localizer`.

When supplied with a component or a class, the `Localizer` first builds the search order. It's always the enclosing `Page` first, and from there on Wicket traverses the `Page` component tree until it reaches the component you passed in. All child components that it encounters along the way are added to the search path. Then it starts looking for the message based on the mechanism described next. Remember that once the message is found, Wicket halts the search process.

Let's consider a Page hierarchy that looks like this:

```
Page (wicket:id = page_id,class=UserProfilePage) extends BasePage
|
|__Form (wicket:id = form_id,class = UserProfileForm)
  |
  |__Panel (wicket:id = panel_id,class=UserProfilePanel)
    |
    |__Label (wicket:id = label_id, class = Label)
    |
    |__TextField (wicket:id = text_id, class = TextField)
```

This process looks for a properties resource file with the same name and package as the class passed in. It also searches based on the superclass of the class passed in. So you have the ability to specify messages not only at the parent component level, but also at the component superclass level. Note that Wicket will pass the appropriate class to the Localizer when required (You can also pass the class to the Localizer when explicitly looking for a locale-specific message). For example, you saw in Chapter 2 that validation messages typically need the component label for display. When Wicket looks up label text corresponding to the Label component (label_id), it would search for the messages in the following order, passing in the class to the Localizer as indicated and moving to the next level if a message is not found:

1. Page (UserProfilePage)

2. BasePage

3. Form (UserProfileForm)

4. Panel (UserProfilePanel)

5. WebApplication (LocalizationApplication.properties) and then Application. properties

Here's a more detailed look at the preceding sequence:

1. Page (UserProfilePage):

   a. Look for the message mapped to the key component ID (label_id) in the UserProfilePage.properties file.

   b. If not found, construct the search path from Page to the label relative to the Page (as you would traverse a tree), with each component ID in the search path separated by a dot (.). This evaluates to form_id.panel_id.label_id. Look for a message mapped to this key.

2. BasePage: If the preceding search doesn't yield a result, check with the parent class of the UserProfilePage (note that the parent component is different from the parent class), BasePage.properties if present. This allows you to define the default messages at the BasePage level that all your application pages are likely to extend. Then you can override those messages in specific Pages as needed. If the message is still not found, move on to the next component in the search path—UserProfileForm.

3. Form (UserProfileForm):

    a. Look for the message mapped to the key component ID (label_id) in the UserProfileForm.properties file. This is a common search step that is executed by default on all resource files. (Note that if UserProfileForm is modeled as an inner class within UserProfilePage, as is usually the case, Wicket will look for a resource file named UserProfilePage$UserProfileForm.properties. This is consistent with the way Java represents inner class files.)

    b. If not found, construct the search path from Form to the label relative to Form (as you would traverse a tree) with each component ID in the search path separated by a dot (.). This evaluates to panel_id.label_id. Look for a message mapped to this key. If the message still isn't found, move on to the next component in the search path—UserProfilePanel.

4. Panel (UserProfilePanel):

    a. Look for the message mapped to the key component ID (label_id) in the UserProfilePanel.properties file.

    b. If not found, construct the search path from Form to the label relative to Form (as you would traverse a tree), with each component ID in the search path separated by a dot (.). This evaluates to label_id. Now this has already been taken care of in the earlier step, and hence would not be executed. If the message text still isn't found, Wicket searches the Application class hierarchy.

5. Look for label_id in the properties file named after your WebApplication subclass (LocalizationApplication.properties) and if even this search turns out to be futile, look for the same key under the default Application.properties that ships with Wicket. It is highly unlikely that the search for a page label in Application.properties will succeed.

If all of the preceding steps fail, Wicket will use the label_id as the Label by default.

Although the search order just listed is very intuitive, it deserves a second look. Let's take the example of the UserProfilePage hierarchy explained earlier. Wicket is all about components, and there is every possibility that the UserProfilePanel was identified as a reusable component even before UserProfilePage was developed. The component developer would have no idea of the other components that are likely to use it later. This could also mean that the localized messages required by the Panel were decided before it could actually be used by the Page. If the Page were to specify different labels for the components contained within the Panel, the only way they could take effect is through the reverse lookup order as employed by Wicket. This allows you to override the Panel labels without actually modifying the Panel properties itself.

This is the case as far as searching for labels is concerned. Wicket does something very similar when searching for validator keys as well. The key that is used to get the validator messages can be located by either consulting the Javadoc of the validator class (an IValidator implementation) or the default Application.properties file that contains localized messages for all validators.

Let's consider the same Page hierarchy as shown earlier. If the TextField component fails the required validation check, Wicket will start looking for the error message that it needs to display as a part of feedback.

The search order for a validator (RequiredValidator in this case) attached to a component (text_id) remains the same:

1. Page (UserProfilePage)

2. BasePage

3. Form (UserProfileForm)

4. Panel (UserProfilePanel)

5. WebApplication (LocalizationApplication)

It's the key that differs from the earlier case.

Following is a detailed look at the validator search order just given:

1. Page (UserProfilePage):

    a. In UserProfilePage.properties, look for the key text_id.RequiredValidator.

    b. If not found, look for form_id.panel_id.text_id.RequiredValidator.

    c. If not found, look for the key RequiredValidator.

2. BasePage: If the preceding search doesn't yield a result, check with the parent class of the UserProfilePage, BasePage.properties if present. If still not found, search in UserProfilePage$UserProfileForm.properties.

3. Form (UserProfileForm):

    a. In UserProfilePage$UserProfileForm.properties, look for the key text_id.RequiredValidator.

    b. If not found, look for panel_id.label_id.RequiredValidator.

    c. If not found, look for the key RequiredValidator.

    d. If not found, UserProfilePanel.properties is the resource file where the search steps will be executed.

4. Panel (UserProfilePanel):

    a. In UserProfilePanel.properties, look for the key text_id.RequiredValidator.

    b. If not found, look for the key RequiredValidator.

    c. If not found, the next place to look through is the Application hierarchy.

5. Look for the message corresponding to the key text_id.RequiredValidator in the properties file named after your WebApplication subclass (LocalizationApplication. properties). The other place to look for the message would be RequiredValidator if the preceding fails.

If all of the preceding turns out to be futile, Wicket looks for same set of keys under the default `Application.properties` file.

How to Switch the Locale Programmatically

Now that you have some insight into Wicket's way of locating localized messages, let's revisit the example that you saw at the beginning of the chapter: internationalizing `UserProfilePage`.

You already have required `<wicket:message>` tags and the labels in Spanish; what you need is a way to programmatically switch the locale to verify that the `<wicket:message>` tag indeed works as advertised. Well, you could change the browser settings to specify the preferred language. But for now, you will see how locale can be programmatically changed in Wicket. You will include HTML radio buttons to help you switch the locale easily, as shown in Listing 6-4.

Listing 6-4. *UserProfilePage.html Modeled Using Radio Buttons*

```
<!-- Continuing from the earlier code snippet -->
    <hr/>
   <span wicket:id="locale">
   <input type="radio">English</input>
   <input type="radio">Spanish</input>
  </span>
  <input type="submit" value="Save"/>
 </form>
</body>
</html>
```

Note that since you want the locale changed on the selection of a radio button, you need to set up the corresponding Wicket component `RadioChoice` for a server-side form submit by returning `true` from the `RadioChoice.wantOnSelectionChangedNotifications()` method. In that respect, the `wicket.markup.html.form.RadioChoice` component works similarly to the `DropDownChoice` and `CheckBox` components that we looked at in Chapter 3. `RadioChoice` is configured with the `PropertyModel` that updates the session with the selected locale (see Listing 6-5).

Listing 6-5. *UserProfilePage.java*

```
import java.util.Locale;

public class UserProfilePage extends WebPage {

  /** Relevant locales wrapped in a list. */
  private static final List LOCALES = Arrays.asList(new Locale[] {
    Locale.ENGLISH, new Locale("es") });
```

```java
/* Set the locale on the session based on user selection. */
public void setLocale(Locale locale) {
  if (locale != null) {
    getSession().setLocale(locale);
  }
}

// RadioChoice when rendering the radio buttons adds a line break after
// each button.
// Since you don't need one, you will set it to blank
public UserProfilePage() {
  //..in addition to already existing code.
  form.add(new LocaleRadioChoice("locale", new PropertyModel(this,
    "locale"), LOCALES).setSuffix(""));
  //..
}

class LocaleRadioChoice extends RadioChoice {

    public LocaleRadioChoice(String id, IModel model, List choices) {
        super(id, model, choices, new LocaleChoiceRenderer());
    }

    protected boolean wantOnSelectionChangedNotifications() {
        return true;
    }
}

private final class LocaleChoiceRenderer extends ChoiceRenderer {
    public LocaleChoiceRenderer() { }

    /**
     * @see wicket.markup.html.form.IChoiceRenderer#getDisplayValue(Object)
     */
    public Object getDisplayValue(Object object) {
        Locale locale = (Locale) object;
        String display = locale.getDisplayName(getLocale());
        return display;
    }
}
```

When you bring up the page in a browser and click the radio button labeled Spanish, you should see something like what appears in Figure 6-1.

Figure 6-1. *UserProfilePage with locale set to Spanish*

Even though the Spanish version of the page renders fine, there is still a problem with the page title. Wicket does not remove the `<wicket>` tags associated with a template by default while rendering. So the localized title text shows up along with the associated `<wicket:message>` tag. You need to tweak the markup settings to tell Wicket that it needs to strip the Wicket tags when rendering. You typically specify this in the `WebApplication` class as shown in Listing 6-6.

Listing 6-6. *LocalizationApplication Set Up to Strip Wicket Tags When Rendering the Page*

```
public class LocalizationApplication extends WebApplication {
//..
public void init() {
    super.init();
    //..
    // Strip Wicket tags when rendering. This will ensure that the page title
    // renders correctly.
    getMarkupSettings().setStripWicketTags(true);
}
//..
}
```

Incorporate the preceding changes and restart the servlet container, and the HTML page title should show up fine. Actually, all is not well with the page. Enter -1 for the PIN and the value **abc** for the phone number and click Save, as shown in Figure 6-2.

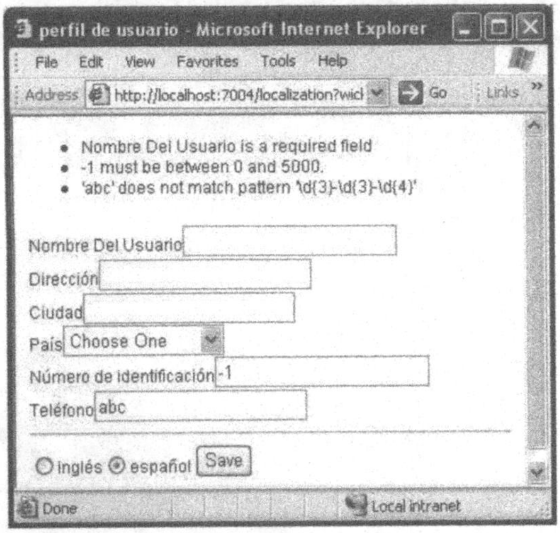

Figure 6-2. *The Validator message display is inconsistent with the current user locale.*

Now where did the validation message come from? Wicket picked it up from the default Application.properties. Actually, Wicket looks for a locale-specific properties file (Application_es.properties), and since you don't have one yet for the Spanish locale, it ended up picking the default file. In fact, before looking for Application_es.properties, Wicket looks for a UserProfilePage_es.properties file as well.

If you remember, in Chapter 2, you got the converter to display a different error message on entering an ill-formed phone number. Since you needed a message unique to the TypeValidator that you used on your page, you specified the error message in a page-specific properties file. You need to do the same in this example by adding the following line to the UserProfilePage.properties:

```
TypeValidator.PhoneNumber=${label} must be all numeric in the form xxx-xxx-xxxx
(e.g., 123-456-7890).${input} does not conform to the format
```

This also reminds you that validation messages need to be localized as well. We will address that issue in the next section.

How to Localize Validation and Error Messages

When using the <wicket:message> tag, you are required to maintain the key=value pairs in the locale-specific properties. This is probably OK for a simple page, like the UserProfilePage, that doesn't have too many labels that need to be localized. But with larger pages with lot of content to internationalize, the level of indirection offered by the message tag in the form of a key=value mapping in a properties file is probably not worth it. You are better off having locale-specific pages that have the localized text directly embedded in it. Wicket by default looks for a locale-specific template when rendering. For example, if the locale happens to be German, it will look for UserProfilePage_de.html, and switching the locale to Spanish in the

UserProfilePage should result in Wicket displaying UserProfilePage_es.html if present. It will default to UserProfilePage.html if the Spanish version of the page is not found. But there is a big drawback associated with this approach too: all locale-specific templates need to be constantly updated throughout the development process, else the template and the corresponding Page class might go out of sync.

The Spanish version of UserProfilePage is shown in Listing 6-7. You already know how the English equivalent looks.

Listing 6-7. *Spanish Version of UserProfilePage, UserProfilePage_es.html*

```
<html>
  <head>
    <title>perfil de usuario</title>
  </head>

  <body>
    <span wicket:id="feedback"></span>
    <form wicket:id="userProfile">
      Nombre Del Usuario <input type="text" wicket:id="name"/><br/>
      Dirección <input type="text" wicket:id="address"/><br/>
      Ciudad <input type="text" wicket:id="city"/><br/>
      País <select wicket:id="country">
        <option>India</option>
        <option>USA</option>
        <option>UK</option>
      </select><br/>
      Número de identificación <input type="text" wicket:id="pin"/><br/>
      Teléfono <input type="text" wicket:id="phoneNumber"/><br/>
      <hr/>
      <input type="submit" value="Save"/>
      <span valign="top" wicket:id="locale">
        <input type="radio">inglés</input>
        <input type="radio">español</input>
      </span>
      <hr/>
    </form>
  </body>
</html>
```

You may be thinking that you can safely get rid of the data in the form of key=value pairs from UserProfilePage.properties, but this isn't really the case: you still need to retain the labels for the components that have validators attached to them. The validation messages will display the *wicket:id* of the component by default when displaying the validation messages in the absence of the labels. With the labels out of your way, let's look at validation error messages (see Listing 6-8).

Listing 6-8. *UserProfilePage_es.properties*

```
userProfile.name= Nombre Del Usuario
userProfile.pin = Número de identificación
userProfile.phoneNumber = Teléfono
RequiredValidator=${label} es un campo requerido
NumberValidator.range=Entre por favor ${label} en la gama ${minimum} - ${maximum}
TypeValidator.PhoneNumber=${label} debe conformarse con el formato xxx-xxx-xxxx
(e.g., 123-456-7890).${input} no se conforma con el formato
```

Figure 6-3 shows the resulting page.

Figure 6-3. *Validation error messages in Spanish*

The error messages corresponding to RequiredValidator and NumberValidator are quite generic (the one corresponding to TypeValidator is not) and accordingly should be stored someplace common so that all pages corresponding to the locale in question can access them centrally. As discussed earlier, you could specify them in a locale-specific (Spanish in this case) Application_es.properties file. In fact, you can contribute your locale-specific Application_*. properties file to the Wicket core if it doesn't already ship with one. In Chapter 2, you took a look at all the messages configured in the default Application.properties. If you want to override any of these default messages and make them available to the entire application, you can specify them in a properties file named after your WebApplication class. For example, you could have LocalizationApplication.properties located in the same package as the LocalizationApplication class. Of course, you can have similar locale-specific properties files as well.

Localization is not just about having a locale-specific properties file. It in fact requires quite a bit of planning in advance. Even a simple page like UserProfilePage, for example, has a problem that was overlooked: it has to do with the way the user country is being represented. Currently, you are storing the locale-specific name of a country in the UserProfile bean, and the moment you switch the locale, you would observe that the country field display reflects an altogether different locale (United States, for example, might show up as Estados Unidos). So it's in your best interest that you store the ISO code of the country instead and then change the display per the user locale (see Listings 6-9 and 6-10).

Listing 6-9. *Storing the ISO Code of the Country to Localize the Display*

```
package com.apress.wicketbook.localization;

public class UserProfile implements Serializable,Cloneable {
    // Store the ISO code of the country so that you can switch country display
    // per locale.
    private Locale country;

    // Define corresponding getters and setters.
}
```

Listing 6-10. *Displaying Country Names per Locale*

```
private final class CountryRenderer extends ChoiceRenderer {
    /**
     * Constructor
     */
    public CountryRenderer() {
    }

    /**
     * @see wicket.markup.html.form.IChoiceRenderer#getDisplayValue(Object)
     */
    public Object getDisplayValue(Object object) {
      Locale locale = (Locale) object;
      String display = locale.getDisplayCountry(getLocale());
      return display;
    }

    /**
     * @see wicket.markup.html.form.IChoiceRenderer#getIdValue(Object,int)
     *       * Store Locale ISO code of the country
     */
    public String getIdValue(Object object, int index) {
      return object.toString();
    }
}
```

If you want to see what implementing CountryRenderer.getIdValue() actually brings you, enter valid values on the UserProfilePage for a given locale (make sure you select a country though) and click Save. On refresh, right-click, select View Source, and you should see something similar to Listing 6-11.

Listing 6-11. *On Selecting View Source*

```
<!-- Rest snipped for clarity -->

  Country<select name="country">
    <option value="en_US">United States</option>
    <!-- I had chosen Spain as my place of residence. "es_ES" is what gets stored in
UserProfile -->
    <option selected="selected" value="es_ES">Spain</option>
    <option value="en_GB">United Kingdom</option>
    <option value="hi_IN">India</option>
  </select><br/>

<!-- Rest snipped for clarity -->
```

You would see the same for the HTML select value attribute irrespective of the locale you are in.

Click the Save button after filling in all the required details. Assuming that the page passes all the validation checks, it refreshes with a message in plain English that informs you of everything you typed in. This is OK if the locale is en_US, for example. But displaying this message even with locale set to Spanish is probably not acceptable. The obvious way to localize this message would be to place it against a key in a locale-specific properties file, as shown in Listing 6-12.

Listing 6-12. *Default Display Message in UserProfilePage.properties*

```
user.message= Mr ${name} lives in the city of ${city} and
can be reached at ${phoneNumber} in ${country}
```

Note that the user.message has placeholders for information that needs to filled in dynamically. You will use the wicket.Localizer class to fill in values at runtime. Wicket's Localizer has helper methods to determine locale-specific messages and also accepts a model (see Listing 6-13) that can help in determining the values for the placeholders in the messages as indicated previously. Wicket just looks for Java bean–like getters when filling up the values. For example, on encountering ${city} in the message, Wicket will call the model object's getCity() method: it translates to UserProfile.getCity() in this case.

Listing 6-13. *Localizer Class Accepting a Model to Perform Variable Substitution*

```
package com.apress.wicketbook.localization;
import wicket.Localizer;

class UserProfilePage extends WebPage{

  class UserProfileForm extends Form {
```

```
    public UserProfileForm(String id, IModel model) {
        super(id, model);
    }

    public void onSubmit() {
        UserProfile usrProf = (UserProfile)getModelObject();
        // All Wicket components can access the Localizer class
        // through the getLocalizer() method.
        Localizer localizer = getLocalizer();
        String infoMessage = localizer.getString("user.message",this,
                            new Model(usrProf));
        info(infoMessage);
    }
  }
}
```

Just to ensure consistency, let's have a Spanish translation for the message as well, as shown in Listing 6-14.

Listing 6-14. *Spanish Version of the Message in UserProfilePage_es.properties*

```
user.message=Senor ${name} reside en la ciudad ${city} y puede ser alcanzado en
${phoneNumber} en el país ${country}
```

Putting Wicket's StringResourceModel to Work

On entering the values for the fields and clicking Save, you should see a message like the one in Figure 6-4.

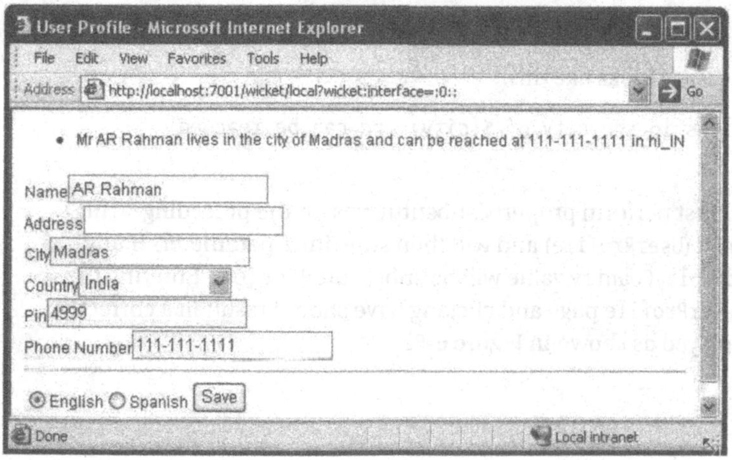

Figure 6-4. *The country needs to be displayed in a readable format.*

The Localizer did substitute the values correctly from the supplied model object consisting of the UserProfile instance. But then the country translation just isn't easy on the eyes. Not many people can figure out that "hi_IN" actually represents India. What you need here is the ability to do a little bit of processing in addition to plain value substitution.

One way of fixing this issue is by using another of Wicket's powerful model classes—wicket.model.StringResourceModel. It combines the flexible Wicket resource loading mechanism with property expressions, property models, and standard Java MessageFormat substitutions (see Listing 6-15).

Listing 6-15. *Localization Through Wicket's StringResourceModel*

```
class UserProfileForm extends Form {
    //..
    public void onSubmit() {
        Locale currLocale = getLocale();
        UserProfile up = (UserProfile) getModelObject();

        // Get the country representation in accordance with
        // the current locale.

        String displayCountry =
up.getCountry()==null?"":up.getCountry().getDisplayCountry(
            currLocale);

        String infoMessage = new StringResourceModel("user.message", this,
            new Model(up), new Object[] {displayCountry}).getString();
        info(infoMessage);
    }
    //..
}
```

Before formatting, the message looks like this:

```
user.message= Mr ${name} lives in the city of ${city} and can be reached
at ${phoneNumber} in {0}
```

StringResourceModel will first perform property substitutions on the preceding string using the supplied model object (UserProfile) and will then substitute parameters if any (specifically in this case, the displayCountry value will be substituted for {0}). Entering the same values as earlier in the UserProfile page and clicking Save should result in a correctly formatted message being displayed as shown in Figure 6-5.

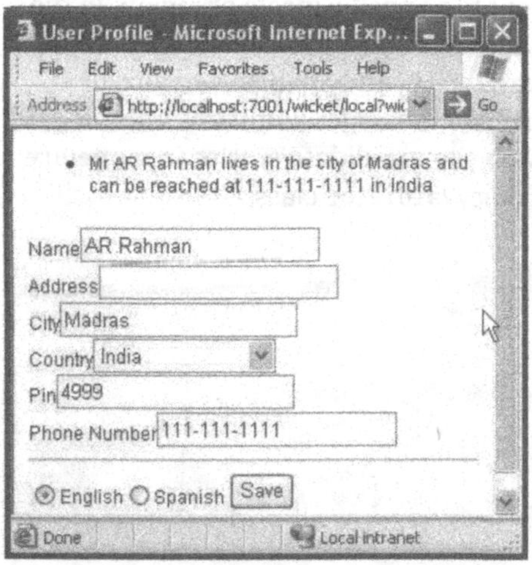

Figure 6-5. *Wicket's StringResouceModel class at work*

Wicket has a model class that represents a localized resource string—wicket.model. ResourceModel. This is a lightweight version of the StringResourceModel. It lacks the ability to perform parameter substitutions, but is easier to use. The reason you need this model is because you haven't localized the Save button display yet. You need to add a *wicket:id* attribute to the button in the template:

```
<input type="submit" wicket:id="save" value="Save"/>
```

and in the Page class specify the ResourceModel along with the Button component:

```
form.add(new Button("save",new ResourceModel("userProfile.save")));
```

You need to specify the localized message in the properties file (UserProfilePage. properties, for example):

```
userProfile.save = Save
```

The equivalent Spanish translation in UserProfilePage_es.properties is

```
userProfile.save = Grabar
```

Locale-Specific Validation

In addition to localizing web pages and validation error messages, there might be a need for tailoring the actual validation to a specific locale as well. Currency validation, for example, falls under this category. Let's consider the US dollar. US currency requires commas to separate dollar values and a period to demarcate cents (i.e., 123,456.78), whereas in the European Union, periods are used to separate Euro currency amounts along with a comma to demarcate cents (i.e., 123.456,78).

Internationalization is the process of tailoring content to a specific locale or region. In the validator's case, it means tailoring validation error messages to a specific locale and/or tailoring actual validation routines to a specific locale. This way, the US and Spanish versions of a web site can have their own language-specific validation error messages. Similarly, internationalization enables the US and Spanish versions of a web site to validate entries in monetary fields differently. Refer to Listing 6-16 for a localized CurrencyValdiator class.

Listing 6-16. *Localized CurrencyValidator*

```java
package com.apress.wicketbook.localization;

import java.io.Serializable;
import java.util.HashMap;
import java.util.Locale;
import java.util.Map;
import java.util.regex.Pattern;

import wicket.markup.html.form.validation.IValidator;
import wicket.markup.html.form.validation.PatternValidator;

public class CurrencyValidator implements Serializable {

  /* Maintain a mapping of locale to currency pattern. */
  private static final Map localeCurrencyPatternMap = new HashMap();

  static {
    localeCurrencyPatternMap.put(Locale.US, Pattern
        .compile("^\\d{1,3}(,?\\d{3})*\\.?(\\d{1,2})?"));
    localeCurrencyPatternMap.put(new Locale("es"), Pattern
        .compile("^\\d{1,3}(\\.?\\d{3})*,?(\\d{1,2})?"));
  }

  /* When requested for a CurrencyValidator, return
   * a PatternValidator for the locale-specific pattern.
   */

  public static IValidator forLocale(Locale locale) {
    Pattern pattern = (Pattern) localeCurrencyPatternMap.get(locale);
    return new PatternValidator(pattern);
  }
}
```

In order to verify that the CurrencyValidator works, add an attribute to the UserProfile bean that represents salary (see Listing 6-17).

Listing 6-17. *UserProfile Bean Modified to Reflect User's Salary*

```
package com.apress.wicketbook.localization;

public class UserProfile implements Serializable{
 //..in addition to other things, handle salary as well.
  private double salary;
  //..
  public double getSalary() {
    return salary;
  }

  public void setSalary(double salary) {
    this.salary = salary;
  }
  //..
}
```

Add an input field to the page template and modify the Page class as shown in Listing 6-18.

Listing 6-18. *UserProfile Bean with the Component to Represent Salary with the CurrencyValidator Attached*

```
public class UserProfilePage extends WebPage{
    public UserProfilePage(){
      //..
      TextField txtAmount = new TextField("salary");
      // Associate the CurrencyValidator with the locale.
      txtAmount.add(CurrencyValidator.forLocale(getLocale()));
      form.add(txtAmount);
      //..
    }
}
```

Wicket associates a new session with a user on first access. It also sets the locale information on the session depending upon the request parameters, which in turn depend on the user browser setting. This happens at the time of Session object creation. All browsers provide a way for changing the browser language settings. In case of Internet Explorer (IE), you can do the following to change the preferred language setting to Spanish: select Tools ➤ Internet Options, and on the General tab, click the Languages button. Click the Add button and select Spanish (International). Then click the Move Up button so that Spanish becomes your preferred language setting. When a request for a page from the browser originates with this setting, Wicket will initialize the session locale setting to Spanish and look for a Spanish version of the page henceforth.

In Internet Explorer, opening a new browser is equivalent to starting a new session. So the language setting will immediately kick in when opening a new browser. This is not the case with Firefox browser, for example. So let's provide a way to invalidate the session programmatically (see Listing 6-19).

Listing 6-19. *Adding the "Invalidate Session" Link to UserProfilePage.html*

```
<!-- Rest snipped for clarity -->
   <input type="submit" value="Save"/>
   </form>
   <a href="" wicket:id="link">Invalidate Session</a>
 <!-- Rest snipped for clarity -->
```

On clicking the "Invalidate Session" link, invalidate the session as demonstrated in Listing 6-20.

Listing 6-20. *Programmatic Session Invalidation*

```
public class UserProfilePage extends WebPage{
   //..
   public UserProfilePage(){
 add(new Link("link"){
   @Override
   public void onClick() {
     getSession().invalidate();
   }
});
   }
   //..
}
```

Now you don't require the radio buttons that you used earlier to programmatically switch locales for testing. You could just click the link that invalidates the session and then modify the browser language setting to switch the locale.

Support for Skinning and Variation in Addition to Locale-Specific Resources

Wicket ResourceBundles are different from the usual Java resource bundles, as the latter have no support for *style* and *variation* in addition to locale. Wicket pages can be skinned by setting the style attribute in the user's session. Styles are intended to give a particular look to a component or resource that is independent of its locale. For example, a style might be a set of resources, including images and markup files, that gives the design the look of, say, an ocean to the user. Wicket expects the resources names be suffixed with ocean in this case.

There is also a variation attribute that is additive to the style attribute. Whereas styles are session (user) specific, variations are component specific. For example, if the style is ocean and the variation is NorthSea, the resources are given the names suffixed with

NorthSea_ocean. If no style attribute has been set, the variation takes the place of the style in the resource name. If the style is set, the variation and "" are prepended to the style name, which is then returned by getStyle().

As mentioned previously, Java resource bundles do not take into consideration style and variation as supported by Wicket. So Wicket's localization support is not based on Java resource bundles in that respect. But Wicket does default to Java resource bundle–like behavior in the absence of a style or a variation attribute.

We discussed the resource lookup order in the last section. Remember that in the presence of style and variation attributes on the session and component respectively, the resource matches will be attempted in the following order (this assumes the user session has been configured with a style named ocean):

1. <path>_style_locale.properties (e.g., UserProfilePage_ocean_es.properties)

2. <path>_locale.properties (e.g., UserProfilePage_es.properties)

3. <path>_style.properties (e.g., UserProfilePage_ocean.properties)

4. <path>.properties (e.g., UserProfilePage.properties)

Loading Messages from a Database

Wicket manages the resource lookup through a wicket.settings.IResourceSettings implementation. wicket.settings.Settings is the default implementation. It maintains a chain of IStringResourceLoader instances that are searched in order to obtain string resources used during localization. By default, the chain is set up to first search for resources against a particular component (e.g., Page) and then against the application. Wicket provides this functionality by using wicket.resource.loader.ComponentStringResourceLoader and wicket.resource.loader.wicket.resource.loader.ClassStringResourceLoader, respectively in that order. The latter is configured to look up messages against the Application class. These components search for a properties file by default (see Listing 6-21).

Listing 6-21. *IStringResourceLoader for Loading of Resource Strings for an Application*

```
public interface IStringResourceLoader{
 String loadStringResource(Class clazz, String key, Locale locale, String style);
}
```

So if you need to pull localized strings from a database, you have to embed the database lookup logic in the loadStringResource method, as shown in Listing 6-22.

Listing 6-22. *DatabaseResourceLoader for Loading Message Strings from a Database*

```
public class DatabaseResourceLoader implements IStringResourceLoader{
   String loadStringResource(Class clazz, String key, Locale locale, String style){
   // Lookup database
   }
}
```

Then you need to let the Settings class know that you would like to use Database→
ResourceLoader for searching localized messages, as you see in Listing 6-23.

Listing 6-23. *WebApplication Modified to Register the DatabaseResourceLoader with the*
Settings Object

```
public class LocalizationApplication extends WebApplication {
 //..
 public void init() {
    super.init();
    getResourceSettings().addStringResourceLoader(new DatabaseResourceLoader());
 }
//..
}
```

Remember that this setting overrides the default Wicket settings. So you can add other
available IStringResourceLoader implementations as well. The order in which you add them
to the Resource settings is also the order in which Wicket looks up resources.

Summary

Internationalization is a vast topic. In this chapter, we specifically looked at the localization
support built into Wicket. You saw how to use <wicket:message> tags to externalize localized
messages first. Then we discussed the case where it makes sense to maintain locale-specific
pages.

We then looked at the Wicket way of searching localized messages, the search order being
key to developing internationalized web applications. Having covered that, I also showed
you that Wicket's StringResourceModel allows for powerful message formatting capabilities.
Messages are not the only items that need to be localized. Even validators might need to take
locale information into consideration.

The chapter concluded by looking at the abstraction built by Wicket over resources and
also discussed how you could have your own IStringResourceLoader implementations,
and how you could get Wicket to use those implementations by registering them in your
WebApplication subclass.

CHAPTER 7

∎∎∎

Custom Wicket Components and Wicket Extensions

All the pages that you have developed until now have been composed of Wicket core components, or Wicket-Extensions subproject components, or a combination of both. In fact, when you started off, the first thing you did was to write a component: the Login page is a Wicket Page that in turn is a Wicket component. Components like DataView and PagingNavigator have a lot of functionality built into them, and you could put them to use with very little effort (i.e., lines of code) on your part. The less code you have to maintain, the fewer the bugs and the higher the productivity. In this chapter, you will see how you can extend components that ship with the core of Wicket and its extensions. Later, you will see how you can build and distribute your own. Wicket specifies the types of components you can define through a component class hierarchy. Before we proceed further, let's take a look at this hierarchy.

Wicket Component Hierarchy

wicket.Component sits right at the top of the Wicket component hierarchy. Its immediate subclass—wicket.MarkupContainer—allows you to have components nested within itself. But it does not have a markup template of its own. Its markup is contained (inline) within the page or component that actually uses it. Wicket's Panel components, on the other hand, have an associated markup template file. Wicket clearly distinguishes between components that have their own markup and those that don't by modeling them as two distinct classes within its component hierarchy. Essentially, wicket.MarkupContainer and its subclass wicket.markup.html.WebMarkupContainer represent components whose markup is inline. On the other hand, wicket.markup.html.WebMarkupContainerWithAssociatedMarkup and more specifically its subclass, wicket.markup.html.panel.Panel, model reusable components that hold markup and other components and have a markup template of their own. You are likely to use Panels extensively when you start developing your custom components. Wicket's Border component is also a special type of WebMarkupContainerWithAssociatedMarkup and ships with its own markup. Figure 7-1 summarizes Wicket's component hierarchy.

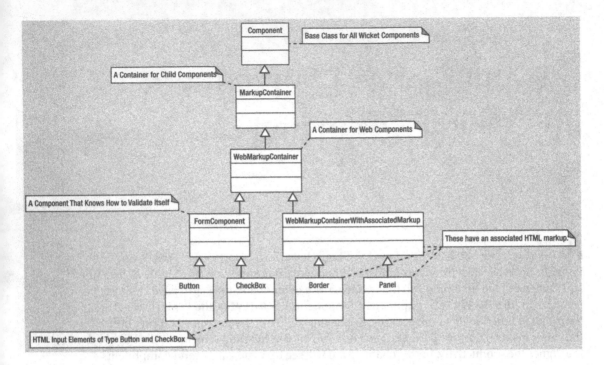

Figure 7-1. *The Wicket Component hierarchy. Note that this class diagram does not represent the entire built-in component hierarchy. Only the significant components have been included.*

This concludes a quick-fire introduction to Wicket component hierarchy, which will become more clear as you extend or develop custom components. As a starting point, let's customize a component that you used earlier—PagingNavigator.

Improving the PagingNavigator Component's Look and Feel

In Chapter 3, you used Wicket's PagingNavigator component when displaying books in the example online bookstore application. Here you'll develop a customized navigator that provides information about the total number of items that is likely to be retrieved by the IDataProvider implementation and the relative position of the items (being displayed at a given point in time) in the list.

First, you need to get hold of the existing PagingNavigator template. Download the Wicket source distribution and extract the PagingNavigator template, which is reproduced here for your convenience:

```
<html xmlns:wicket>
<body>
  <wicket:panel>
    <a wicket:id="first">&lt;&lt;</a> <a wicket:id="prev">&lt;</a>
    <span wicket:id="navigation">
```

```
  <a wicket:id="pageLink" href="#"><span wicket:id="pageNumber">5</span>
  </a>
  </span>
  <a wicket:id="next">&gt;</a> <a wicket:id="last">&gt;&gt;</a>
  </wicket:panel>
</body>
</html>
```

Now change this template as shown in Listing 7-1.

Listing 7-1. *CustomPagingNavigator.html*

```
<html xmlns:wicket>
<body>
  <wicket:panel>

    <!-- Added a label to display the user friendly message -->
    <span wicket:id="headline">a headline above the navigator</span><br/>

    <!-- Modified link text -->
    [<a wicket:id="first">First</a>/<a wicket:id="prev">Prev</a>]
    <span wicket:id="navigation">
    <a wicket:id="pageLink" href="#"><span wicket:id="pageNumber">5
    </span></a>
    </span>

    <!-- Modified link text -->
    [<a wicket:id="next">Next</a>/<a wicket:id="last">Last</a>]
  </wicket:panel>
</body>
</html>
```

You will create a custom navigator class whose name is the same as the template, as required by Wicket (see Listing 7-2). The custom navigator just needs to add the ability to configure headline text to the existing PagingNavigator component. The "headline" component is a typical example of a component of type WebComponent. It really doesn't have a template of its own. The PagingNavigator within which the "headline" component is contained has an associated markup and is in fact a Panel component.

Listing 7-2. *CustomPagingNavigator.java*

```
package com.apress.wicketbook.components;

import wicket.extensions.markup.html.repeater.data.DataView;
import wicket.markup.ComponentTag;
import wicket.markup.MarkupStream;
import wicket.markup.html.WebComponent;
import wicket.markup.html.navigation.paging.PagingNavigator;
```

```java
public class CustomPagingNavigator extends PagingNavigator {

    public CustomPagingNavigator(String id, DataView dataView) {
        super(id, dataView);
        add(new HeadLine("headline", dataView));
    }

    class HeadLine extends WebComponent {
        private DataView dataView;

        public HeadLine(String id, DataView dataView) {
            super(id);
            this.dataView = dataView;
        }

        // Wicket callback method - explained after the code snippet.

        protected void onComponentTagBody(final MarkupStream markupStream,
                final ComponentTag openTag) {
            String text = getHeadlineText();
            replaceComponentTagBody(markupStream, openTag, text);
        }

        // Custom text providing more information about the items being displayed,
        // etc.

        public String getHeadlineText() {
            int firstListItem = dataView.getCurrentPage()
                    * dataView.getItemsPerPage();
            StringBuffer buf = new StringBuffer();
            // Construct the display string.
            buf.append(String.valueOf(dataView.getRowCount())).append(
                    " items found, displaying ").append(
                    String.valueOf(firstListItem + 1)).append(" to ").append(
                    String.valueOf(firstListItem
                            + Math.min(dataView.getItemsPerPage(), dataView
                                    .getRowCount()))).append(".");
            return buf.toString();
        }

    }
}
```

The CustomPagingNavigator has quite a few interesting things going on in it. During the render phase, Wicket calls Component.onComponentTag() on the contained components, passing in the Java representation of the tag—ComponentTag. Typically, additional attributes can be added or the existing ones can be modified in the callback method. Note that even though you are allowed to add or modify a tag attribute, Wicket doesn't permit you to remove an existing tag attribute. This is an important stipulation because graphic designers may be setting attributes on component tags that affect visual presentation. It's not just components that are allowed to add or modify the tag attributes. Wicket's IBehavior implementations also get an opportunity to add or modify component tag attributes through a similar onComponentTag callback method. Wicket's SimpleAttributeModifier, which you used in Chapter 3 to add tag attributes to HTML table rows, does exactly that through the onComponentTag(Component component,ComponentTag tag) callback method. If a tag allows for its body (text or component) to be specified, it calls onComponentTagBody() as well later where you can control what needs to go into the tag body.

For example, the following will result in onComponentTag and onComponentTagBody being called:

```
<span wicket:id="allowsForBodyComponent">Body goes here </span>
```

whereas this next example will result in only onComponentTag being called, as the latter does not allow for the tag body to be specified:

```
<span wicket:id="someComponent"/>
```

Wicket's Label component, for example, replaces the tag body with the string representation of the associated model object, and it does so through Component.replaceComponentTagBody().

In your custom navigator, the body ("a headline above the navigator") of the label

```
<span wicket:id="headline">*a headline above the navigator*</span><br/>
```

is replaced with the text returned at runtime by MyPagingNavigator.getHeadlineText().

As you can see in Figure 7-2, the custom navigator now has a look and feel that is more informative.

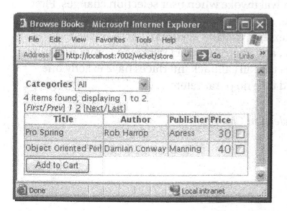

Figure 7-2. *The Browse Books display page configured with a custom PagingNavigator component*

Note that you could have used the Label component with the PropertyModel instead of the HeadLine component:

```
import wicket.markup.html.basic.Label;

public class CustomPagingNavigator extends PagingNavigator {
    DataView dataView;
    public CustomPagingNavigator(String id, DataView dataView) {
        super(id, dataView);
        this.dataView = dataView;
        add(new Label("headline",new PropertyModel(this,"headlineText")));
    }
    //..
}
```

A WebComponent was used in Listing 7-2 to demonstrate the significant onComponentTagBody render-time callback method.

Now this has been neat, but it's probably time to move on to another component that you can customize to suit your needs—Wicket's DropDownChoice. In fact, you've already seen how to make changes to this particular component in Chapter 3. To recap: the default behavior of the DropDownChoice component is *not* to update the form component models when the user selection changes. To get this component to update the form, you called Form.process() in the DropDownChoice.onSelectionChanged method. If there are other Pages in a project that expect this kind of customized behavior from DropDownChoice, instead of resorting to copy-and-paste programming it's probably a good idea to create a customized component out of it and encourage reuse.

Customizing the DropDownChoice Component

The main objective of your customized DropDownChoice component is to make sure that a form component's models are updated when the user selection changes. You can do this in a "selection change listener" method that Wicket will invoke when user selection changes. First, you'll specify that method through an interface.

Note that all such listener interfaces *must* extend Wicket's IRequestListener (see Listing 7-3). This interface is a marker interface, and you can expect Wicket to complain at runtime if you don't extend it. Wicket mandates that all callback interfaces have exactly one method, and that method must return void and take no parameters.

Listing 7-3. *A Custom Listener for Drop-Down Selection Changes*

```
package com.apress.wicketbook.components;

import wicket.IRequestListener;
import wicket.RequestListenerInterface;

public interface MyOnChangeListener extends IRequestListener {
```

```
    public static final RequestListenerInterface INTERFACE =
        new RequestListenerInterface(MyOnChangeListener.class);
    // Expect Wicket to call this method when user selection changes.
    void userSelectionChanged();
}
```

Before you build your component, access the ViewBooks page on the browser, right click, and select View Source. The code on your screen should look like Listing 7-4.

Listing 7-4. *DropDown onchange Script Generated by Wicket*

```html
<html>

<!- Rest of the source snipped for clarity -->

<form action="/wicket/store?wicket:interface=:1:tabs:panel
:bookForm::IFormSubmitListener" wicket:id="bookForm"
  name="viewBookForm" method="post" id="tabs:panel:bookForm">
  <input type="hidden" name="tabs:panel:bookForm:hf:0"
id="tabs:panel:bookForm:hf:0"/>
  <table>
   <tr>
   <td><b>Categories</b></td>
   <td>
   <select wicket:id="categories" onchange="
    document.getElementById(
    'tabs:panel:bookForm:hf:0').value=
    '/wicket/store?wicket:interface=:1:tabs:panel:bookForm
    :categories::IOnChangeListener';
    document.getElementById('tabs:panel:bookForm').submit();"
      name="categories">
        <option value="0">J2EE</option>
        <option value="1">Scripting</option>
        <option value="2">ASP.NET</option>
        <option value="3">Design Patterns</option>
        <option selected="selected" value="4">All</option>
   </select>
   </td>
   </tr>
  </table>

<!- Rest of the source snipped for clarity -->
```

The HTML select element with the ID categories is of interest. Note the JavaScript event, onchange, that encodes the information needed by Wicket's RequestCycle to invoke IOnChangeListener on DropDownChoice. As you see here, it basically describes the path to navigate to the component and the interface method to invoke:

```
'/wicket/store?wicket:interface=:1:tabs:panel:bookForm:categories::
IOnChangeListener'
```

Also note that returning true from DropDown.wantOnSelectionChangedNotifications()
results in document.getElementById('tabs:panel:bookForm').submit(); being generated by
Wicket on the onchange event (which results in the form submit).

The DropDownChoice component generated this code, and your custom component will
have to do this too. Even though all components are nested within a Page, it's probably unfair
to expect the component developer to traverse all the way up to the Page to figure out the URL
path to navigate to itself. Luckily, Wicket instead places that responsibility on the Page class
and provides a helper method, Component.urlFor(), to determine the URL. The Form component also ships with a helper method that generates the accompanying JavaScript code. Now
it's all about setting an attribute (onchange) and the corresponding JavaScript that needs to
trigger on encountering that event on the HTML select widget. Wicket provides you with that
opportunity through the onComponentTag callback method when it runs into the <select
wicket:id="categories"> markup in the markup stream, passing in the ComponentTag—the
Java representation of the HTML tag. Listing 7-5 shows the partial implementation of the
custom DropDownChoice component that you will develop.

Listing 7-5. *Custom DropDownChoice Component's onComponentTag Implementation*

```
public class FormSubmittingDropDownChoice extends DropDownChoice{
    //..
    protected void onComponentTag(final ComponentTag tag){
        // Invoke the default behavior.
        super.onComponentTag(tag);
        // URL that points to this component's MyOnChangeListener method.
        // This call falls on the base component class, which in turn calls
        // the Component class method discussed earlier, passing itself
        // as the reference.

        final String url = urlFor(MyOnChangeListener.INTERFACE).toString();
        Form form = getForm();
        tag.put("onchange", form.getJsForInterfaceUrl(url));

        // Print it out just in case you are curious.
        System.out.println("URL for our listener " + url);
        System.out.println("Javascript code for our URL " +
            form.getJsForInterfaceUrl(url));
    }
```

Now Wicket will call MyOnChangeListener.useSelectionChanged when the user changes the
drop-down selection. You need to process the Form component so that it ends up updating
the model.

```
public void userSelectionChanged() {
  // Access the parent form and process it.
  // It will validate and update the model.
  getForm().process();
  // Call onSelectionChanged.
  onSelectionChanged(getModelObject());
}
```

Essentially, your custom component, FormSubmittingDropDownChoice, extends
DropDownChoice and adds the custom behavior required by your project. Listing 7-6 is
just a complete version of this custom component.

Listing 7-6. *FormSubmittingDropDownChoice.java*

```
package com.apress.wicketbook.components;

import java.util.List;
import wicket.markup.ComponentTag;
import wicket.markup.html.form.DropDownChoice;
import wicket.markup.html.form.Form;
import wicket.model.IModel;

public class FormSubmittingDropDownChoice extends DropDownChoice
    implements MyOnChangeListener{

  public FormSubmittingDropDownChoice(String id, IModel model, List choices) {
    super(id, model, choices);
  }

  public void userSelectionChanged() {
    getForm().process();
    onSelectionChanged(getModelObject());
  }

  protected void onComponentTag(final ComponentTag tag){
    super.onComponentTag(tag);
    // URL that points to this component's IOnChangeListener method
    final String url = urlFor(listenerInterface).toString();
    Form form = getForm();
    tag.put("onChange", form.getJsForInterfaceUrl(url) );
    System.out.println("URL for our listener " + url);
    System.out.println("Javascript code for our URL " +
      form.getJsForInterfaceUrl(url));
    }

}
```

Now you can modify the code for the ViewBooks page, as shown in Listing 7-7, to use the preceding component in place of DropDownChoice. Note that this also enables you to directly work with Wicket's Form instead of MyForm.

Listing 7-7. *ViewBooks.java*

```
import com.apress.wicketbook.components.FormSubmittingDropDownChoice;

public class ViewBooks..

    public ViewBooks(){

        // Note that you don't need MyForm now.
        Form form = new Form("bookForm");
        // Rest is the same.
        // Instead of DropDownChoice you need the following.

        FormSubmittingDropDownChoice categories = new
            FormSubmittingDropDownChoice("categories",
              new PropertyModel(dataProvider, "category"),
              getBookCategories()) {

            public void onSelectionChanged(Object newSelection){
                books.setCurrentPage(0);
            }
        };
        form.add(categories);
        //..
    }
}
```

Actually, there was no need to define a custom listener, but you did so here only to give you some idea of the inner workings of Wicket. There should never be a need to define your own custom listener interfaces when working with Wicket.

Everything that you did in the method userSelectionChanged() could have instead been done in the DropDownChoice.onSelectionChanged() method and by returning true from the DropDownChoice.wantOnSelectionChangedNotifications() method.

Other Variations of the urlFor() Method

Earlier, you used the Component.urlFor(RequestListenerInterface) to generate the URL to access the custom listener that you developed. While we are on this topic, let's look at other variations of this method, as some might come in handy when developing custom components.

```
Component.urlFor(PageMap pageMap, java.lang.Class pageClass,
        PageParameters parameters)
```

This method can be used to return a bookmarkable URL that references a given Page class using a given set of page parameters. Since the URL that is returned contains all the information necessary to instantiate and render the page, it can be stored in a user's browser as a stable bookmark. It is also used internally by Wicket's BookmarkableLink component to generate the required URL to access the page.

Component.urlFor(ResourceReference resourceReference)

This method returns a URL that references a shared resource through the provided resource reference. You will see later in this chapter that many Wicket components have their own CSS style sheet and/or JavaScript files. They are normally packaged along with the component in the form of jar files. The component template refers to them in their HTML <head> section. The preceding method provides you with the URL to refer to those packaged resources from within the template.

In the upcoming text, we will look at some components that ship with the Wicket-Extensions subproject. Of these, there are a couple of alternatives to components that you used in the ViewBooks page. For example, you could replace DataView with the wicket. extensions.markup.html.repeater.data.table.DataTable component. We will discuss Wicket-Extension's DataTable component in the next section.

Getting the Online Bookstore to Use the Wicket-Extensions DataTable Component

The DataTable component, as the name suggests, is used to display tabular data. It also introduces the concept of toolbars, which can be used to display sortable column headers, paging information, filter controls, and other information. DataTable also provides its own markup for the associated HTML table. Since the component generates the HTML table by itself, it allows you to specify the table header information in the form of a list. This could be useful in scenarios where the headers are retrieved dynamically from a database, for example.

wicket.extensions.markup.html.repeater.data.table.IColumn and its implementation wicket.extensions.markup.html.repeater.data.table.PropertyColumn represent a column in the table. You need to supply the column header information along with the Wicket property expression (same as that used by PropertyModel) that is evaluated against the current row's model object to determine the table cell's value.

It is also important to note that DataTable works with wicket.extensions.markup.html. repeater.util.SortableDataProvider instead of the IDataProvider that you are so familiar with by now. SortableDataProvider, while implementing the IDataProvider interface, keeps the sort information inside the data provider implementation because it makes that information easy to access within the data provider. So you really aren't required to change your IDataProvider implementation except that the BookDataProvider now needs to inherit from SortableDataProvider and use the sort information if applicable (see Listing 7-8). Sorting on a column can be specified when creating a PropertyColumn as you will see shortly.

Listing 7-8. *BookDataProvider.java Modified to Extend Wicket's SortableDataProvider*

```
import wicket.extensions.markup.html.repeater.util.SortParam;
import wicket.extensions.markup.html.repeater.util.SortableDataProvider;

public class BookDataProvider extends  SortableDataProvider{

  // Rest of the code remains unchanged.

  public Iterator iterator(final int first, final int count){

    // SortableDataProvider tells you which column was actually clicked and
    // whether the data needs to be displayed in an ascending manner or otherwise.

    SortParam sortParam =  getSort();

    // Use this information. Incorporating sorting in the application is
    // left as an exercise to the user.

    // Whether you need to retrieve in ascending or descending fashion
    boolean isAscending = sortParam.isAscending();
    // Information regarding the column header that was clicked for sorting
    String column = sortParam.getProperty();

    // You might want to modify this to incorporate sorting as an exercise.
    return bookDao.getBooksForCategory(category,first,count).iterator();
  }

}
```

Enabling Sortable Columns on the DataTable

Remember that DataTable specifies the HTML table structure in its template. As long as the
data you want displayed in the table cells is plain text, PropertyColumn works like a charm.
But in this case, one of the columns happens to include a check box to remember the user
selection. The DataView component that you used earlier knew about it because you explicitly
specified the check box in the template. However, there is no way for DataTable to know about
this information. This is a tricky problem that you are faced with, but Wicket has an acceptable
solution: a Wicket Panel component can wrap any other component and will render it as is.
So the solution is to wrap the component you want rendered in a Panel and supply the Panel
in turn to the DataTable's HTML cells through an AbstractColumn implementation (see
Listing 7-9). In this case, the CheckBox component is wrapped by the Panel represented
by the inner class BookSelectionPanel. Since this would result in an inner class file,
ViewBooks$BookSelectionPanel, the panel template also needs to be named similarly:
ViewBooks$BookSelectionPanel.html.

Listing 7-9. *Supplying the DataTable Columns Through IColumn Implementations*

```
import wicket.extensions.markup.html.repeater.data.table.AbstractColumn;
import wicket.extensions.markup.html.repeater.data.table.IColumn;
import wicket.extensions.markup.html.repeater.data.table.PropertyColumn;
import wicket.extensions.markup.html.repeater.refreshing.Item;

public class ViewBooks extends WebPage{

  //..
  // A helper method that constructs the columns required by the
  // DataTable component.
  protected IColumn[] getColumnsForTable() {

    List columns = new ArrayList();

    // Create a column with header "Title", make it sortable, and
    // pass the property "title" to the SortableDataProvider and
    // use "title" as the property expression against the current row's model
    // object.The model object is the actual row from the BookDao (i.e., a Book
    // instance).

    columns.add(new PropertyColumn(new Model("Title"), "title","title"));

    // Create a column with header "Author" and
    // use "author" as the property expression against the current row's model
    // object.

    columns.add(new PropertyColumn(new Model("Author"), "author"));
    columns.add(new PropertyColumn(new Model("Publisher"),
          "publisher","publisher"));
    columns.add(new PropertyColumn(new Model("Price"), "price","price"));

    // Special handling of the check box through the AbstractColumn class
    columns.add(new AbstractColumn(new Model("")) {

      // DataTable will call this method when rendering the table cell,
      // passing in the ID used in the template, the IModel, and Item.

      public void populateItem(Item cellItem, String componentId,
          IModel rowModel) {

        // rowModel represents the data from the database for each row
        // so the model object (not the model!) is the Book object from the
        // database. Set it as the model.
```

```
        setModel(rowModel);

        // Access the model object again to retrieve the Book instance.
        Book book = (Book)getModelObject();
        // Add the component to Item as in DataView.
        cellItem.add(new BookSelectionPanel(componentId, book));
      }

    });
    return (IColumn[]) columns.toArray(new IColumn[0]);
  }
  //..
  //..
}
```

The custom panel template that wraps a check box element is shown in Listing 7-10.

Listing 7-10. *ViewBooks$BookSelectionPanel.html Encloses the Check Box*

```
<!-- A pair of <wicket:panel> tags are used to demarcate the
panel markup -->
<wicket:panel>
  <input type="checkbox" wicket:id="selected"/>
</wicket:panel>
```

As you would expect, you are just required to add Wicket's CheckBox component to the Panel (see Listing 7-11).

Listing 7-11. *ViewBooks.BookSelectionPanel Wraps the CheckBox Component*

```
public class BookSelectionPanel extends Panel {

    public BookSelectionPanel(String id, Book book) {
      super(id);
      add(new CheckBox("selected", new CheckBoxModel(book.getId()))) {
        protected boolean wantOnSelectionChangedNotifications() {
          return true;
        }
      });
    }

}
```

Configure the DataTable as shown in Listing 7-12.

Listing 7-12. *ViewBooks Modified to Use DataTable*

```
import wicket.extensions.markup.html.repeater.data.table.HeadersToolbar;
import wicket.extensions.markup.html.repeater.data.table.NavigationToolbar

public class ViewBooks..
  //..
  public ViewBooks(){
    final DataTable books = new DataTable("books",
     getColumnsForTable(),dataProvider,4);
    // Adds the default navigation toolbar
    books.addTopToolbar(new NavigationToolbar(books));
    // Adds the column headers with sorting enabled through links
    books.addTopToolbar(new HeadersToolbar(books,dataProvider));
  }
}
```

Remember, you added an `AttributeModifier` to `DataView` component rows in Chapter 3. The `AttributeModifier` was configured to add the `class` attribute to the `<tr>` element and initialize it to the values odd or even. The `DataTable` does not add the `class` attribute to the HTML table rows, but it does provide factory methods to create the `Item` component that represents the HTML row (`<tr>`) on the server side. You may choose to return the `Item` with a `AttributeModifier` attached to it as shown in Listing 7-13.

Listing 7-13. *Customized DataTable*

```
class CustomDataTable extends DataTable{

  public CustomDataTable(String id, IColumn[] columns,
      IDataProvider dataProvider, int rowsPerPage) {
    super(id, columns, dataProvider, rowsPerPage);
  }

  // Item represents a table row (<tr>). Add the class attribute using the
  // factory method provided specifically for such custom processing.

  protected Item newRowItem(final String id, int index, final IModel model){
    Item item = new Item(id, index, model);
    item.add(new AttributeModifier("class",true,
              new Model(index%2==0?"odd":"even")));
    return item;
  }
}
```

If that seems like a lot of code, you can use DefaultDataTable instead. All of the code in Listing 7-13 translates to the following when using DefaultDataTable:

```
public class ViewBooks..
  //..
  public ViewBooks(){
    final DataTable books = new DefaultDataTable("books",getColumnsForTable(),
      dataProvider, 4);
  }
}
```

The Page should render just fine now, but depending upon your preference, you might not want to define a Panel just to act as a placeholder for an HTML check box (ViewBooks$Book➡ SelectionPanel.html).

Let's see if there is a way by which you can do away with this Panel. Note that a Panel with a check box can serve as a reusable component by itself.

Wicket Fragments

You just saw that when working with a DataTable, for example, it is a bit awkward to maintain tiny pieces of markup in plenty of Panel markup files. A Wicket Fragment component provides a means to maintain the Panel's tiny piece of markup in the parent component's markup file.

Add a Fragment markup as shown in Listing 7-14 toward the end of the ViewBooks.html template. It looks exactly like the ViewBooks$BookSelectionPanel.html except that instead of being enclosed within a pair of <wicket:panel>,</wicket:panel> tags, it now needs to be enclosed within a <wicket:fragment> tag and needs to be assigned a *wicket:id* attribute as you would when using a Panel in a Page.

Listing 7-14. *The Fragment to Include Toward the End of ViewBooks.html*

```
<wicket:fragment wicket:id="checkBoxFrag">
  <input type="checkbox" wicket:id="selected"/>
</wicket:fragment>
```

Corresponding to this markup, you need an equivalent to Wicket's wicket.markup. html.panel.Fragment component. Note that it looks exactly like the BookSelectionPanel inner class that you wrote earlier. The Fragment needs to know its ID, like any other Wicket component, and the markupId it will be replacing in the parent Page. It also needs to be told the MarkupContainer that actually contains its markup—ViewBooks in this case (see Listing 7-15).

Listing 7-15. *Defining a Fragment Equivalent for a BookSelectionPanel*

```
import wicket.markup.html.panel.Fragment;

class ViewBooks extends WebPage{
//..
public class BookSelectionFragment extends Fragment {
```

```
    // The markupProvider is crucial. It identifies the component
    // whose markup contains the Fragment's markup.

    public BookSelectionFragment(String id, String markupId,
        MarkupContainer markupProvider, Book book) {
      super(id, markupId, markupProvider);
      add(new CheckBox("selected", new CheckBoxModel(book.getId()))) {
        protected boolean wantOnSelectionChangedNotifications() {
          return true;
        }
      });
    }
}
//..
```

Refer to Listing 7-16 to understand how the BookSelectionFragment replaces the BookSelectionPanel in the DataTable component.

Listing 7-16. *Replacing BookSelectionPanel with BookSelectionFragment*

```
class ViewBooks extends WebPage{
 //..
 protected IColumn[] getColumnsForTable() {
  //..
  columns.add(new AbstractColumn(new Model("")) {
    public void populateItem(Item cellItem, String componentId,IModel rowModel) {
        final Book book = (Book) rowModel.getObject(null);

        // The following Fragment will replace the markup with wicket:id
        // componentId, while its own markup ID is
        // "checkBoxFrag". Also, the Fragment markup
        // can be found within the ViewBooks page itself.

        Fragment frag = new BookSelectionFragment(componentId,
          "checkBoxFrag", ViewBooks.this, book);
        cellItem.add(frag);
    }
  });
 }
 //..
}
```

Note that the same Fragment can be used in several places throughout the Page if required. It provides a nice way to encapsulate a commonly occurring markup in a Page or other component. Note that in the current scenario, the markup wasn't generic enough and was hence modeled as a Fragment. It would have ended up as a Panel otherwise. (You would have modeled it as a Panel if it were to be included in several other pages.)

Next, we will look at another useful Wicket extension component—TabbedPanel.

Incorporating a Tabbed Panel in the Online Bookstore Application

The TabbedPanel component represents a panel with tabs. These tabs in turn point to different content panels, and the tabs are used to switch between these panels. The template in itself is quite simple, as you can see in Listing 7-17.

Listing 7-17. *TabbedPanel.html*

```
<wicket:panel>
<div class="tab-row">
<ul>
  <li wicket:id="tabs">
    <!-- The Tab link and display text -->
    <a href="#" wicket:id="link"><span wicket:id="title">[[tab title]]</span></a>
  </li>
</ul>
</div>


<!-- Currently active panel falls here -->

<span wicket:id="panel" class="tab-panel">[panel]</span>
</wicket:panel>
```

The TabbedPanel component uses Wicket's Loop component to render the tab display text and Link that activates a given tab. In turn, it expects you to configure the component with a list of wicket.extensions.markup.html.tabs.AbstractTab implementations. The AbstractTab implementations are the server-side representations of the tabs that you see on the browser. Also note that all tab panels have the same ID, panel! How does Wicket accommodate different panels with the same ID? At any given point in time, only one Panel can be active or visible. Wicket allows for this effect by replacing an existing Panel with another Panel with the same ID. It does it through MarkupContainer.replace(Component child). This feature demonstrates Wicket's excellent support for dynamic templates. Let's modify the online bookstore application home page to link to its pages/panels through a TabbedPanel component. The page that holds the tabs just has a div element to hold onto the tabbed panel as shown in Listing 7-18.

Listing 7-18. *BookShopTabbedPanelPage.html*

```
<?xml version="1.0" encoding="UTF-8"?>
<html xmlns="http://www.w3.org/1999/xhtml" >
<head>
    <title>Bookstore</title>
</head>
<body>
<div wicket:id="tabs" class="tabpanel1">[e-Bookstore tabbed panel will be
here]</div>
</body>
</html>
```

Listing 7-19 presents the corresponding Page class.

Listing 7-19. *BookShopTabbedPanelPage*

```
import wicket.extensions.markup.html.tabs.AbstractTab;
import wicket.extensions.markup.html.tabs.TabbedPanel;

public class BookShopTabbedPanelPage extends WebPage {
  public BookShopTabbedPanelPage() {
    configureTabs();
  }

  // A helper method that configures the tabs

  protected void configureTabs() {
    // Create a list of ITab objects used to feed the tabbed panel.
    final List tabs = new ArrayList();

    // The model here represents the tab text.
    // Add Books tab and get it to return the appropriate
    // Panel as well. You will be developing the Panels
    // referenced here next.

    tabs.add(new AbstractTab(new Model("Books")) {
      public Panel getPanel(String panelId) {
        return new ViewBooksPanel(panelId);
      }
    });

    // Add Promotions tab as well.
    tabs.add(new AbstractTab(new Model("Promotions")) {
      public Panel getPanel(String panelId) {
        return new BookPromotionsPanel(panelId);
      }
    });

    // Add Articles tab as well.
    tabs.add(new AbstractTab(new Model("Articles")) {
      public Panel getPanel(String panelId) {
        return new ArticlesPanel(panelId);
      }
    });

    // Configure the TabbedPanel component with the tabs.
    final TabbedPanel panel = new TabbedPanel("tabs", tabs);
    add(panel);
  }
}
```

The Wicket-Extensions TabbedPanel component requires Panels, and you have Pages at your disposal. There is currently no easy way of adapting a Wicket Page to a Panel yet. This is not so much of a problem though. You just have to modify the pages to extend wicket.markup.html.panel.Panel instead of Wicket's WebPage and have a constructor that accepts the component ID (see Listing 7-20).

Listing 7-20. *BookPromotionsPanel.java Is Now a Panel*

```
import wicket.markup.html.panel.Panel;

public class BookPromotionsPanel extends Panel {
  private static final long serialVersionUID = 1L;

  public BookPromotionsPanel(String id) {
    super(id);
  }
}
```

The template now needs to identify itself as a Wicket Panel by enclosing the content within <wicket:panel> start and end tags, as shown in Listing 7-21. The other Page templates and classes need to be modified similarly.

Listing 7-21. *BookPromotionsPanel.html*

```
<wicket:panel>
    <!-- Child content -->
        Don't miss the super deals on the books in the J2EE category
    <!-- End child content -->
</wicket:panel>
```

The source code for the examples used in the book is available for download from the Apress web site (http://www.apress.com). The code for other panels aren't reproduced here to conserve space. However, Figure 7-3 shows how it renders on the browser.

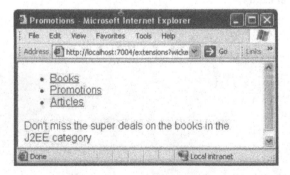

Figure 7-3. *TabbedPanel when used without a style sheet*

Well, the generated HTML is nowhere close to being a tabbed panel (it is just links with text), but you did expect this after having looked at the TabbedPanel template in its current form, didn't you?

Applying a Style Sheet to the Tabbed Panel

As you just saw, the TabbedPanel in its primitive form simply renders a link with text on the browser. On the server side, it swaps the appropriate panel depending upon the link you click. If you really want to have a nice-looking tab, you need to apply your own style sheet on top of the template. For now, use one of the styles specified in this article—http://www.alistapart. com/articles/slidingdoors/. It requires a few images (refer to the source code for these images). You will apply the style sheet shown in Listing 7-22.

Listing 7-22. *panel.css Style Sheet for Displaying the Panel*

```css
table.palette { border:0; }
table.palette td.header { font-weight: bold; font-size: 12pt;
  background-color: #eef7ff; padding: 2px;
  border-top: 1px solid #729ac2;
  border-bottom: 1px solid #729ac2;
}
table.palette td.pane { width: 100px; text-align: center; }
table.palette td.pane select { width: 200px;  }
table.palette td.buttons { text-align: center; padding-left: 10px; padding-right:
10px; }
table.palette td.buttons button { width: 40px; height: 40px; }

div.tabpanel div.tab-row{
  float:left;
  width:100%;
  background:#DAE0D2 url("bg.gif") repeat-x bottom;
  line-height:normal;
}

div.tabpanel div.tab-row ul {
  margin:0;
  padding:10px 10px 0;
  list-style:none;
}

div.tabpanel div.tab-row li {
  float:left;
  background:url("left.gif") no-repeat left top;
  margin:0;
  padding:0 0 0 9px;
}
```

```
div.tabpanel div.tab-row a {
  display:block;
  background:url("right.gif") no-repeat right top;
  padding:5px 15px 4px 6px;
  text-decoration:none;
  font-weight:bold;
  color:#765;
  white-space:nowrap;
}

div.tabpanel div.tab-row a:hover {
  color:#333;
}

div.tabpanel div.tab-row li.selected {
  background-image:url("lefton.gif");
}

div.tabpanel div.tab-row li.selected a {
  background-image:url("righton.gif");
  color:#333;
  padding-bottom:5px;
}
```

Since the Wicket-Extensions TabbedPanel does not have a reference to a style sheet, you need to ensure that you attach it. The images and the style sheet could be copied over to the context root or some folder relative to it, and you could have BookShopTabbedPanelPage reference it. For now, copy over the images and the style sheet to the context root of the web application. Then modify the BookShopTabbedPanelPage to refer to the style sheet, as in Listing 7-23.

Listing 7-23. *BookShopTabbedPanelPage.html with a Reference to panel.css*

```
<?xml version="1.0" encoding="UTF-8"?>
<html xmlns="http://www.w3.org/1999/xhtml" >
<head>
    <title>Bookstore</title>

    <!-- Since the style sheet is located at the context root, this will work.
    If the CSS is stored in the folder <context-root>/styles, href
    points to 'styles/panel.css' -->

    <link rel="stylesheet" type="text/css" href="panel.css"/>
</head>
<body>
<div wicket:id="tabs" class="tabpanel">[e-Bookstore tabbed panel will be here]</div>
</body>
</html>
```

Figure 7-4 shows the improved TabbedPanel appearance after applying the style sheet (refer back to Listing 7-22).

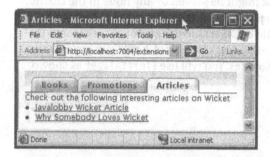

Figure 7-4. *TabbedPanel when used in conjunction with a Cascading Style Sheet*

If this style in conjunction with the TabbedPanel were to be used in another application, you would again be required to copy over the style sheet and images to the context root of the new web application. This doesn't sound too convenient. So let's address this problem in the next section.

Packaging Wicket Components into Libraries

As discussed in the previous section, the style sheet belongs to the TabbedPanel and not the BookShopTabbedPanelPage that uses the component. So you need a way to get the TabbedPanel to refer to the images and the style sheet. But then you don't have access to the TabbedPanel component source code, as it comes packaged with Wicket-Extensions. Well, you sure can get to the source, Wicket being a pure open-source project. But then modifying component source code to accommodate a custom feature probably doesn't seem too object oriented. One option could be to extend the existing TabbedPanel and package the images and the style sheet along with it (see Listing 7-24).

Listing 7-24. *CustomTabbedPanel Component Package Structure*

```
+com
  +apress
    +wicketbook
      +components
          - CustomTabbedPanel.class
          - panel.css
          - bg.gif
          - left.gif
          - lefton.gif
          - right.gif
          - righton.gif
```

The images, the style sheet, and JavaScript files if present are typically referred to as *packaged resources*.

Wicket applications by design are session heavy. So in order to get the framework to scale, it is very likely such applications will be deployed in a cluster. Every server on a cluster is termed a *node*. In clustered applications, a request might be served by any node in the cluster.

Let's say you access a page that has a link to a packaged resource on node A. Now the URL for the resource gets forwarded to node B, but node B doesn't have the resource registered yet because maybe the Page class hasn't been loaded and so its static block hasn't run yet. So the initializer is a place for you to register all those resources. You will use IInitializer as shown in Listing 7-25.

Listing 7-25. *CustomTabbedPanel*

```
package com.apress.wicketbook.components;

import java.util.List;
import java.util.regex.Pattern;

import wicket.Application;
import wicket.AttributeModifier;
import wicket.IInitializer;
import wicket.behavior.HeaderContributor;
import wicket.extensions.markup.html.tabs.TabbedPanel;
import wicket.markup.html.PackageResource;
import wicket.model.Model;

public class CustomTabbedPanel extends TabbedPanel {

  public final static class ComponentInitializer implements IInitializer {
      /**
       * @see wicket.IInitializer#init(wicket.Application)
       */
      public void init(Application application) {
        // Register all .js, .css, and .gif files as shared resources. This allows
        // you to specify a Java regex pattern to capture all images, .css files,
        // etc.
        PackageResource.bind(application, CustomTabbedPanel.class, Pattern
            .compile(".*\\.css|.*\\.gif"));
      }
  }

  public CustomTabbedPanel(String id, List tabs) {
      super(id, tabs);
      // Add a reference to the panel CSS.
      add(HeaderContributor.forCss(CustomTabbedPanel.class, "panel.css"));
      // You shall identify the div that holds the panel through the class
```

CHAPTER 7 ■ CUSTOM WICKET COMPONENTS AND WICKET EXTENSIONS **223**

```
          // "tabpanel".
          // This is necessary because your style sheet uses it.
          add(new AttributeModifier("class", true, new Model("tabpanel")));
    }

}
```

Now every component might have such IInitializer implementations. What you need is a way to get all of them to execute when the application starts up. Wicket's way of achieving the same is by having another IInitializer implementation that calls each of these in turn (see Listing 7-26).

Listing 7-26. *Initializer*

```
package com.apress.wicketbook.components;

import wicket.Application;
import wicket.IInitializer;

/**
 * Initializer for your custom components
 */

public class Initializer implements IInitializer {
  /**
   * @see wicket.IInitializer#init(wicket.Application)
   */
  public void init(Application application) {
   // Call the component initializers.
    new CustomTabbedPanel.ComponentInitializer().init(application);
  }
}
```

But then Wicket needs to know about the Initializer in Listing 7-26 in the first place so that it can call it during application initialization. The way you do this is by having a wicket.properties file with the entry in Listing 7-27. Wicket looks for all properties files named wicket.properties available in the class path and invokes the init method on startup.

Listing 7-27. *wicket.properties*

```
initializer=com.apress.wicketbook.components.Initializer
```

Now you just need to package all of the preceding in a jar file. Accessing the CustomTabbedPanel component is just about dropping the resulting jar file into the <Context>/WEB-INF/lib folder of the target application.

Displaying Appropriate Tab Titles

Clicking a tab should result in the appropriate HTML title being displayed on the page. Since the title needs to dynamically evaluated, add a *wicket:id* attribute to it as shown in Listing 7-28.

Listing 7-28. *Replacing the Static BookShopTemplatePanelPage.html Title with a Dynamic One*

```
<-- Replace <title>Bookstore</title> with -->
<title wicket:id="title">Title goes here</title>
```

The newly added `<span>` element can be modeled as a Label on the Wicket side. The TabbedPanel knows the tab that is being displayed at a given point in time, and the tab in turn knows its title. The Label can then be configured with a model that returns the tab title (see Listing 7-29).

Listing 7-29. *TabTitleModel*

```java
package com.apress.wicketbook.extensions;

public class BookShopTabbedPanelPage extends WebPage {
  //..

  protected void configureTabs() {
    final List tabs = new ArrayList();
    //..
    final TabbedPanel panel = new TabbedPanel();

    // A model that retrieves the currently clicked tab
    // and determines its title.

    class TabTitleModel extends Model{
      public Object getObject(Component comp){
        return
          ((ITab)tabs.get(panel.getSelectedTab()))
            .getTitle()
              .getObject(null);
      }
    }

    add(new Label("title", new TabTitleModel()));
  }
}
```

Restricting the Categories of Books Being Displayed Through Wicket's Palette Component

You might have noticed that you haven't designed any screen related to the administration of the bookstore. You don't have screens that allow you to add new books to the database, for example. You might want to sell books belonging to certain categories only. Currently there is no way for you to specify that filter. So now you'll try developing a screen that allows you to do just that. The BookDao class requires some modifications to accommodate this new requirement though (see Listing 7-30).

Listing 7-30. *BookDao Modified to Accommodate Display Filter*

```
public class BookDao implements Serializable{
//..
List displayFilter;

// Maintain copies of "all" and "select" categories.

private void init(String[] cats) {
   categories = new ArrayList();
   for (int i = 0; i < cats.length; i++) {
     categories.add(cats[i]);
   }
   displayFilter = (List)((ArrayList)categories).clone();
}


public BookDao() {
   init(new String[] { CATEGORY_J2EE, CATEGORY_SCRIPTING,
     CATEGORY_ASP_NET, CATEGORY_DP, CATEGORY_ALL });
   //..
}

// For now, you will not allow empty filters.

public void setDisplayFilter(List displayFilter) {
   if (displayFilter != null && !displayFilter.isEmpty()) {
     if (displayFilter.contains(CATEGORY_ALL)) {
       displayFilter = categories;
     } else {
       this.displayFilter = displayFilter;
     }
   }
}
}
```

```
// Add a method to fetch all categories.
public List getAllCategories() {
   return categories;
}
// Modify this previously existing method to return the filtered values.
public List getSupportedCategories() {
   return displayFilter;
}


}
```

If the web site administrator were to specify this filter, he or she would need to be able to view all the available categories and at the same time select the categories that he or she wants displayed on the ViewBooks page. Designing such a component requires some effort. Luckily, Wicket-Extensions gives it away free under the Apache 2.0 license.

Quoting from the Javadoc of wicket.extensions.markup.html.form.palette.Palette component:

> Palette is a component that allows the user to easily select and order multiple items by moving them from one select box into another.

Well, looks like this is what you need at the moment. Build the Panel that will host this component for you, as shown in Listing 7-31.

Listing 7-31. *AdminPanel.html*

```
<wicket:panel>
<form wicket:id="form">

  <!-- A placeholder for the palette -->
  <span wicket:id="palette"></span>
  <input type="submit"/>
</form>
</wicket:panel>
```

Before you actually use the Palette, take a quick look at Listing 7-32, which shows what it takes to construct one.

Listing 7-32. *Palette Constructor Contract*

```
public class Palette extends Panel{
  public Palette(java.lang.String id,
              wicket.model.IModel model,
              wicket.model.IModel choicesModel,
              wicket.markup.html.form.IChoiceRenderer choiceRenderer,
              int rows,
              boolean allowOrder)
  }
}
```

Here's a brief explanation of the parameters in Listing 7-32:

Argument	Description
id	Component ID
model	Model representing collection of user's selections
choicesModel	Model representing collection of all available choices
choiceRenderer	Renderer used to render choices
rows	Number of choices to be visible on the screen with out scrolling
allowOrder	Argument that allows user to move selections up and down

Except for IChoiceRenderer (identified by the choiceRenderer parameter), the constructor parameters are fairly self-explanatory. So let's take a closer look at what IChoiceRenderer is all about.

Some of the HTML elements such as drop-down lists, multiple choice lists, etc., display or work on a list of values. For an item in such a list, the *display value* on the browser might not be used as the *identifier*, or ID, on the server side. wicket.markup.html.form.IChoiceRender separates the ID values used for internal representation from display values, which are the values shown to the user of components that use this renderer. Now that you are equipped with the information to configure a Wicket Palette, let's put together a functional AdminPanel (see Listing 7-33).

Listing 7-33. *AdminPanel.java*

```java
package com.apress.wicketbook.extensions;

import wicket.extensions.markup.html.form.palette.Palette;
import wicket.markup.html.form.Form;
import wicket.markup.html.form.IChoiceRenderer;
import wicket.markup.html.panel.Panel;

import com.apress.wicketbook.shop.app.BookStoreApplication;
import com.apress.wicketbook.shop.model.BookDao;

public class AdminPanel extends Panel {

        // A helper to retrieve BookDao
    protected BookDao getBookDao() {
      return ((BookStoreApplication) getApplication()).getBookDao();
    }

    public AdminPanel(String id) {
      super(id);
      configurePalette();
    }
```

```
protected void configurePalette() {
  // This will be displayed in the Available choices section
  // of the palette.
  List categories = getBookDao().getAllCategories();

  // The user selection will be displayed here.
  List displayFilter = getBookDao().getSupportedCategories();

  IChoiceRenderer renderer = new CustomChoiceRenderer();

  final Palette palette = new Palette("palette", new Model(
        (Serializable) displayFilter), new Model(
        (Serializable) categories), renderer, 10, true);
  Form form = new PaletteForm("form", palette);
  form.add(palette);
  add(form);
}

// The server-side representation of categories is a list of String objects, and
// they are unique in the online bookstore application. So use those as the
// display and ID.

class CustomChoiceRenderer implements IChoiceRenderer {
  // For a given item in the list, use the String representation for display.
  public Object getDisplayValue(Object object) {
    return object.toString();
  }

  // For a given item in the list, use the String representation for the ID
  // as well.
  public String getIdValue(Object object, int index) {
    return object.toString();
  }
}


class PaletteForm extends Form {
  private Palette palette;

  public PaletteForm(String id, Palette palette) {
    super(id);
    this.palette = palette;
  }

  // On submit, set the selected values as the
  // display filter for categories.
```

```
public void onSubmit() {
    List displayFilter = new ArrayList();
    for (Iterator iter = palette.getSelectedChoices();
            iter.hasNext();) {
        displayFilter.add(iter.next());
    }
    getBookDao().setDisplayFilter(displayFilter);
}

}
}
```

Figure 7-5 shows how the Palette renders on the browser.

Figure 7-5. *AdminPanel configured with a Palette for selecting book categories being displayed*

After selecting the categories you want displayed, click the submit button. On form submission, you ask for the selected choices from the palette, which are the categories that need to be displayed when a user clicks the "Books" link.

Before this chapter concludes, let's take a look at another Wicket-Extensions component—TextTemplateHeaderContributor.

Adding Page Header Contributions Using the TextTemplateHeaderContributor Component

Consider the JavaScript function shown in Listing 7-34. It basically displays a pop-up that returns a boolean value of true or false depending upon whether you click OK or Cancel when prompted. This is the behavior of the built-in JavaScript function confirm.

Listing 7-34. *A JavaScript Function That Allows You to Pop Up a Confirmation Message When Invoked*

```
function confirmDelete(){
  return confirm("Delete yes/no?");
}
```

Consider a page that has two buttons as shown in Listing 7-35 that attaches the confirmDelete() functionality to the onclick event. Note that the message displayed in the pop-up box (as specified by the argument to the confirm function) turns out to be the same for the two buttons. It is highly unlikely that you would want the same message displayed on clicking two different buttons, as they are likely to result in different actions being performed on the server side.

Listing 7-35. *TestDeleteButton.html, Which Uses Buttons with Hard-Coded References to the JavaScript Function confirm*

```
<html>
<body>
<form wicket:id="form">
  <input type="submit" value="Delete1" wicket:id="delete1"
    onclick="return confirmDelete()"/>
  <input type="submit" value="Delete2" wicket:id="delete2"
    onclick="return confirmDelete()"/>
</form>
</body>
</html>
```

Typically, such JavaScript functions are maintained external to the page that uses them in a .js file (call it confirmdelete.js in this example). Say you have a requirement whereby you don't want to be hard-coding the onclick button event in the template. What you want here is the ability to add the onclick attribute to the corresponding server-side Button component dynamically. You know that you can add attributes to a Component through the onComponentTag callback method. But it will probably be more elegant and "Wicket-like" if you can get a custom IBehavior to do the same and then attach the behavior to the component. Let's give this custom behavior a name—ConfirmDeleteBehavior (you will be developing it subsequently).

Even though you can bind the JavaScript confirmDelete function to the onclick event using ConfirmDeleteBehavior, you still are left with a few unaddressed issues:

- You still haven't found a way to include the confirmdelete.js file in your template. Well, you can hard-code the reference to the file in the <head> section of the template. But a more elegant solution would be to get ConfirmDeleteBehavior to include the contents of the .js file in the template at runtime—wicket.extensions.util.resource. TextTemplateHeaderContributor enables a Component or a IBehavior to contribute the contents of the given template (the JavaScript template in this case).

- The JavaScript function still does not provide a way to configure the confirmation message dynamically—Wicket allows you to specify a wicket.extensions.util.resource. TextTemplate that can do variable interpolation to address this problem.

- Even if you manage to address the preceding concerns, you still have an issue with attaching the custom IBehavior implementation to more than one Button component on the Page: you will end up with the same function, confirmDelete, being included more than once in the rendered template, resulting in a conflict. This can be best avoided by allowing ConfirmDeleteBehavior to generate a unique JavaScript function name at runtime.

Listing 7-36 shows the JavaScript confirmdelete.js file that has variables whose values will be determined at runtime. (jsfunc will eventually be replaced with the function name and msg will be substituted with a display message *at runtime*.)

Listing 7-36. *confirmdelete.js, Which Allows You to Configure the Function Name and the Message at Runtime*

```
function ${jsfunc}(){
  return confirm("${msg}");
}
```

Refer to Listing 7-37 for the ConfirmDeleteBehavior class. Detailed explanation is inline.

Listing 7-37. *ConfirmDeleteBehavior.java*

```
package com.apress.wicketbook.layout;

// Other imports
import wicket.behavior.AbstractBehavior;
import wicket.extensions.util.resource.TextTemplateHeaderContributor;
import wicket.markup.ComponentTag;
import wicket.model.AbstractReadOnlyModel;
import wicket.model.IModel;
import wicket.util.collections.MicroMap;

public class ConfirmDeleteBehavior extends AbstractBehavior {

  Component component;

  // Bind the JS call to the onclick event.
  public void onComponentTag(Component component, ComponentTag tag) {
    tag.put("onclick","return "+getJSFuncName()+"()");
  }

  // TextTemplateHeaderContributor evaluates the template
  // with interpolation variables based on the supplied
  // context, which is a Java map.
  // It is quite similar to VelocityContext, for example.

  IModel variables = new AbstractReadOnlyModel() {
    private Map variables;
```

```java
      public Object getObject(Component component) {
        if (variables == null) {
          this.variables = new MicroMap();
          variables.put("jsfunc", getJSFuncName());
          variables.put("msg", getJSMessage());
        }
        return variables;
      }
    };

    // This method is called after the behavior is associated
    // with the component through the Component.add(IBehavior)
    // method call. You will need to determine the component
    // markup ID later, as you will find out.

    public void bind(Component component){
      this.component = component;

      // It is absolutely essential that you output
      // component markup ID, as it will be used later
      // to determine the JavaScript function name uniquely.

      component.setOutputMarkupId(true);

      // TextTemplateHeaderContributor accepts the class
      // to be used for retrieving the classloader for
      // loading the packaged template. Since you specify
      // ConfirmDeleteBehavior as the class, you need to make
      // sure that you keep the confirmdelete.js file in the same
      // package folder structure as ConfirmDeleteBehavior.

      component.add(TextTemplateHeaderContributor.forJavaScript(getClass(),
          "confirmdelete.js", variables));
    }

    // Allow subclasses to specify the
    // custom display message.
    protected String getJSMessage(){
      return "Delete Yes/No?";
    }

    // Use the Markup ID to provide a unique name
    // for the JavaScript function.
    private final String getJSFuncName(){
      return "confirmDelete"+component.getMarkupId();
    }
}
```

Now is the time to put the ConfirmDeleteBehavior to test. Listing 7-38 shows the template that uses the button, while Figure 7-6 shows what the page looks like on the browser.

Listing 7-38. *TestDeleteButton.html, Which Uses a Button Configured with ConfirmDeleteBehavior*

```html
<html>
<body>
<span wicket:id="feedback">Feedback goes here</span>
<form wicket:id="form">
  <input type="submit" wicket:id="deleteButton1"
         value="Default Delete"/>
  <input type="submit" wicket:id="deleteButton2"
         value="Custom Delete"/>
</form>
</body>
</html>
```

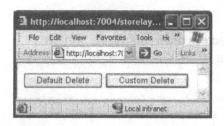

Figure 7-6. *A page that uses buttons configured with ConfirmDeleteBehavior*

Listing 7-39 presents the Page class corresponding to the template shown in Listing 7-38. Note that the deleteButton2 component specifies the message it wants displayed on the browser when you click the button.

Listing 7-39. *TestDeleteButton.java Page Class*

```java
package com.apress.wicketbook.layout;

// Other imports
import com.apress.wicketbook.layout.ConfirmDeleteBehavior;

public class TestDeleteButton extends WebPage {
  public TestDeleteButton(){
    add(new FeedbackPanel("feedback"));
    Form form = new Form("form");
    Button deleteButton1 = new Button("deleteButton1"){
      public void onSubmit(){
        info(" You clicked deleteButton1 " );
      }
```

```
  };
  deleteButton1.add(new ConfirmDeleteBehavior());
  form.add(deleteButton1);
  Button deleteButton2 = new Button("deleteButton2"){
    public void onSubmit(){
      info(" You clicked deleteButton2 " );
    }
  };
  deleteButton2.add(new ConfirmDeleteBehavior(){
    // Override the client-side JavaScript alert
    // message.
    public String getJSMessage(){
      return "You clicked Custom Delete Button!!";
    }
  });
  form.add(deleteButton2);
  add(form);
  }
}
```

Figure 7-7 shows what you will eventually see on the screen upon clicking the buttons present on the TestDeleteButton.html page.

Figure 7-7. *The pop-up boxes that show up when clicking the Default Delete and Custom Delete buttons*

Summary

In this chapter, we looked at the Wicket component hierarchy. Essentially, it consists of components that do not have a template associated with them and others that do. Wicket's Panel and Border components are examples of the latter. You learned how to use Wicket-Extensions components like DataTable, TabbedPanel, and Palette. Wicket components—custom or otherwise—can be distributed in the form of a simple jar file. But if they have references to other web-related artifacts like images, style sheets, and JavaScript files, they need to be bound to the Application object at startup so that references remain valid even in clustered deployment scenarios. Finally, you learned about the TextTemplateHeaderContributor class, which allows you to contribute contents of the given template interpolated with the provided map of variables.

■ ■ ■

CHAPTER 8

Wicket and Ajax

It probably wouldn't be too way off the mark to say that Ajax (Asynchronous JavaScript and XML) is the most talked about technology these days in the web arena. Being a web framework, Wicket's support for Ajax should therefore not come as a surprise. Ajax is essentially a combination of client-side JavaScript, CSS, HTML DOM, and browser XmlHttpRequest implementation working together to provide highly responsive web applications or rich Internet applications. Wicket supports Ajax at its core through several built-in Ajax-enabled components. So much so that you could Ajax-enable your pages without writing a single line of JavaScript processing code. In the following sections, you will try Ajax-ifying a few pages that you have already developed.

Ajax Form Validation

We looked at Wicket's server-side validation support in Chapter 2. On form submit, the server-side validation kicks in as Wicket traverses through all the Form components, executing the attached validators on component input and in the process accumulating error messages if any. The FeedbackPanel, if attached, displays the messages previously accumulated.

Let's revisit the UserProfilePage server-side validation that you put in place in Chapter 2. On validation failure, the FeedbackPanel renders each error message within the HTML <li> element. For a change, you will try a different way of error reporting. You will enclose the components that need to be validated within Wicket's wicket.markup.html.form.validation. FormComponentFeedbackBorder this time around, as shown in Listing 8-1. This Border component renders a little red asterisk beside the component that fails validation. For more details on Wicket Border components in general, refer to Chapter 4.

Listing 8-1. *UserProfilePage Modified to Accomodate the FormComponentFeedbackBorder Component*

```
package com.apress.wicketbook.ajax;

import wicket.markup.html.form.validation.FormComponentFeedbackBorder;

public class UserProfilePage extends WebPage{
```

```
public UserProfilePage(){
  //..
  final FeedbackPanel panel = new FeedbackPanel("feedback");

  TextField userNameComp = new TextField("name");
  TextField pinComp = new TextField("pin");
  TextField phoneComp = new TextField("phoneNumber");
  //..

  final FormComponentFeedbackBorder nameBorder = addWithBorder(form,
      userNameComp, "nameBorder");
  final FormComponentFeedbackBorder pinBorder = addWithBorder(form,
      pinComp, "pinBorder");
  final FormComponentFeedbackBorder phoneBorder = addWithBorder(form,
      phoneComp, "phoneBorder");

  //..
}
// A helper to add Border to the FormComponent
Border addWithBorder(Form form,FormComponent component,String borderId){
   FormComponentFeedbackBorder border = new FormComponentFeedbackBorder(borderId);
   border.add(component);
   form.add(border);
   return border;
}
```

This would mandate some changes to the template as well, as shown in Listing 8-2.

Listing 8-2. *UserProfilePage.html Modified to Accomodate Placeholder for FormComponentFeedbackBorder*

```
<!-- Rest of the page stays the same -->
<!-- Only the following components now have a span for the surrounding border -->

User Name <span wicket:id="nameBorder">
  <input type="text" wicket:id="name"/></span><br/>
Pin <span wicket:id="pinBorder"><input type="text" wicket:id="pin"/>
</span><br/>
Phone <span wicket:id="phoneBorder"><input type="text"
wicket:id="phoneNumber"/></span>
```

Figure 8-1 shows what happens on leaving the User Name field blank, entering a value of **-1** for Pin, and clicking the Save button.

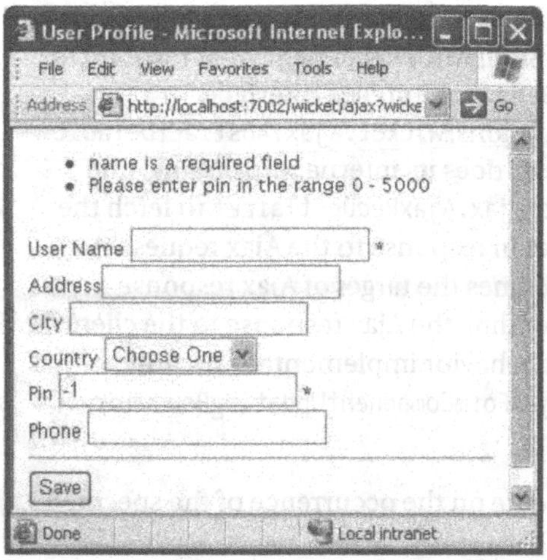

Figure 8-1. *Validation feedback through the FormComponentFeedbackBorder component*

Reporting validation errors after HTML form submit is good enough. One issue with this approach is that the user gets the feedback only after clicking the Save button.

A better user experience would mean providing feedback without resorting to a browser refresh—the way it works in desktop applications. Ajax enables just that by allowing you to query server-side validators that in turn are triggered by client-side JavaScript events. This doesn't require a browser refresh either. The browser's implementation of XmlHttpRequestObject allows you to communicate with the server asynchronously through standard URLs. It also gives you access to the response sent by the server in the form of plain text or XML. The client-side JavaScript then needs to make sense of the response sent back by the server and use HTML DOM APIs to manipulate the page content dynamically. You could, for example, provide feedback after the user has entered a value for the HTML form element and has moved the focus to another field. It essentially boils down to providing feedback on the onblur JavaScript event of the element. On the onblur event, you need to fire an Ajax request that passes in the user input, validate the input and construct the response on the server, pass it back to the browser, and finally re-render the component with the new content. Since this chapter is specifically about how Wicket and Ajax work together, for more information on Ajax, you could consult *Foundations of Ajax* by Ryan Asleson and Nathaniel T. Schutta (Apress, 2005). Before we delve further into Wicket's support for Ajax, let's discuss another concept that's central to Wicket's Ajax support—*behaviors*.

Behaviors in Wicket

Wicket encompasses a concept of behaviors that is represented by the wicket.behavior. IBehavior interface. Components can exhibit different behaviors, and they can be associated with the component at runtime by simply calling wicket.Component.add(IBehavior). Among other things, a behavior also gets an opportunity to modify the component tag attributes through the IBehavior.onComponentTag() method. wicket.behavior.AttributeBehavior, which you used in Chapter 3 to add CSS style attributes to HTML elements, in fact does just that. You could term the ability to respond to an Ajax request as a behavior exhibited by the component, and as you might have guessed, Wicket models it as one. Wicket is about components responding to browser events through listeners. Similarly, Wicket behaviors respond to browser Ajax requests through the `wicket.behavior.IBehaviorListener` interface.

As is the case with most Wicket listener implementations, `wicket.ajax.AbstractDefault` `AjaxBehavior` implements `IBehaviorListener.onRequest`, does its internal processing, and finally calls `AjaxBehavior.respond()`, passing in `wicket.ajax.AjaxRequestTarget` to fetch the actual content that needs to be sent back to the browser in response to the Ajax request. A component added to the `AjaxRequestTarget` object becomes the target of Ajax response. `AjaxRequestTarget` takes on the onus of creating and sending the Ajax response to the client. Wicket ships with quite a few commonly required Ajax behavior implementations, and `AjaxFormComponentUpdatingBehavior` is one of them. `AjaxFormComponentUpdatingBehavior`, when added to a component, takes care of the following:

- It generates the JavaScript call that needs to execute on the occurrence of the specified client-side JavaScript event (e.g., onblur).

- It also ties the event-handling routine for the appropriate event on the corresponding client-side HTML element (attaching the JavaScript call generated in the preceding step to the JavaScript event onblur, for example). Note that this occurs when the components are rendered for the first time.

- On the Wicket side (server side) of things, when the Ajax call is actually triggered from the browser as a result of some user action, it updates and validates the component against the input that was passed in through the Ajax call.

- It then gives you a chance to decide the next steps by calling the onUpdate template method, passing in the `AjaxRequestTarget` object.

Components added to the `AjaxRequestTarget` become the target of Ajax response. `AjaxRequestTarget` will render only those components (also known as *partial rendering*), and the built-in JavaScript infrastructure will make sure that it re-renders the components by initializing HTML's outerHTML property. Note that you can add as many components as you like to `AjaxRequestTarget`, and Wicket will render them in response. In this case, you need to add the `FeedbackPanel` and the `FormComponentFeedbackBorder` components to the `AjaxRequestTarget` so that they can provide the correct feedback to the user after validation.

Wicket employs standard HTML DOM APIs to update client-side content using Ajax response from the server. In order to identify the HTML elements correctly, Wicket relies on the HTML element id attribute being correctly populated for all those elements that are the targets of Ajax response. You are not required to provide unique IDs for the elements yourself—this could be error prone. Wicket will take care of this as long as you specify the following on the component during instantiation:

```
component.setOutputMarkupId(true);
```

Components that are targets of Ajax response need to emit the id attribute when rendering for the first time (see Listing 8-3). This is because the built-in JavaScript code looks up the element by its id during Ajax re-render. It's obvious that the look up would fail in the absence of this attribute. This setting is mandatory, and Wicket will throw exceptions at runtime if the setting is not in place already.

Listing 8-3. *UserProfilePage with Ajax-ified Validation*

```
package com.apress.wicketbook.ajax;

import wicket.markup.html.form.validation.FormComponentFeedbackBorder;

public class UserProfilePage extends WebPage{
public UserProfilePage(){
  //..
  feedback.setOutputMarkupId(true);
  addAjaxBehaviorToComponent(userNameComp,nameBorder,feedback);
  addAjaxBehaviorToComponent(pinComp,pinBorder,feedback);
  addAjaxBehaviorToComponent(phoneComp,phoneBorder,feedback);
  //..
}


// Component whose input needs to be validated should be
// configured with AjaxFormComponentUpdatingBehavior.

 void addAjaxBehaviorToComponent(FormComponent formComponent,
  final FormComponentFeedbackBorder border,final FeedbackPanel feedback){
    formComponent.add(new AjaxFormComponentUpdatingBehavior("onblur"){
      // You want the FeedbackPanel and the FormComponentFeedbackBorder
      // to update themselves based on the Ajax validation result.
      // Accordingly, you need to add them to the AjaxRequestTarget.
      @Override
      protected void onUpdate(AjaxRequestTarget target) {
        target.addComponent(feedback);
        target.addComponent(border);
      }
    }
  );
}


Border addWithBorder(Form form,FormComponent component,String borderId){
  FormComponentFeedbackBorder border = new FormComponentFeedbackBorder(borderId);
  // Get the border components to emit value for id.
  border.setOutputMarkupId(true);
  border.add(component);
  form.add(border);
  return border;
}
}
```

Leave the name field blank and press Tab, which should result in something like what you see in Figure 8-2 being displayed on the browser.

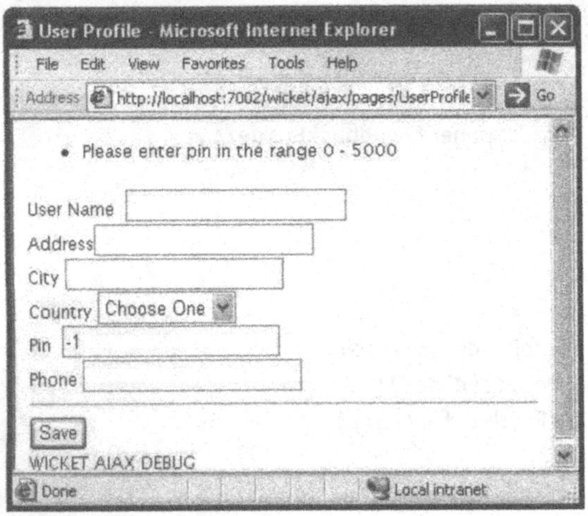

Figure 8-2. *Form field validation through Ajax*

Click the "WICKET AJAX DEBUG" link to pop up a window that displays the actual Ajax response that was received from the server. This is extremely useful when working in debug mode. If an Exception occurs during partial render, the debug window would display that Exception. You can switch off the Ajax debug mode as shown in Listing 8-4.

Listing 8-4. *Changing Ajax Debug Settings in the WebApplication Class*

```
pubic class BookStoreApplication extends WebApplication{
    //..
    public void init(){
      getAjaxSettings().setAjaxDebugModeEnabled(false);
    }
    //..
}
```

Actually, if the deployment is set to "production," the Ajax debug window will not show up.

If you test the Ajax-ified UserProfilePage, you will notice that the Feedback component display is not in sync with the validation state of the Form component. We will address this issue next.

Keeping the FeedbackPanel and Ajax Validation in Sync

Feedback messages are cleaned up upon a new request (an Ajax request in this case). So adding the FeedbackPanel as an Ajax target as shown earlier will not work, as the panel lacks an insight into the other component's input at that point in time. Wicket needs to be aware of inputs of all the Form components to be able to provide the correct feedback. The best solution to this problem is to use Wicket's wicket.ajax.form.AjaxFormValidatingBehavior class, which makes working with such things a breeze. It takes care of the following:

- Adding AjaxFormValidatingBehavior to all the container Form components when asked to (you will see how in a while)

- Submitting the HTML form in its entirety with all its contents (elements identified through *wicket:id*) as an Ajax request on a specified client-side JavaScript event (onblur, onkeyup, etc.)

- Adding all the Feedback components (those that implement Wicket's IFeedback interface) to the AjaxRequestTarget on submit

The following line of code is all that you need to add:

```
AjaxFormValidatingBehavior.addToAllFormComponents(form, "onkeyup",
        wicket.util.time.Duration.seconds(3));
```

Note that Wicket's Duration class provides a nice, readable way of specifying time instead of passing in the number of milliseconds as is the norm with Java APIs. Actually, the preceding call does a little more than what we just discussed. Instead of waiting for the user to move the focus to another field, you provide feedback while the user is typing with a configured delay (3 seconds in this case). It is not desirable to have an Ajax call made every time the user types, so this feature allows you to throttle that call to a desirable delay, such as once every 3 seconds This gives you a near real-time ability to provide feedback without overloading the server.

Remove all references to AjaxFormComponentUpdatingBehavior in the code though. Since the entire form is submitted as a part of an Ajax request (also known as *form serialization*) and validated, the Feedback component will have complete information on the validation state of all the components and hence will always reflect the correct picture. Actually, with the preceding changes, you will notice that you have only managed to render the FeedbackPanel correctly. You must be wondering how the FeedbackPanel managed to update itself on Ajax request—actually AjaxFormValidatingBehavior makes sure that it adds all implementations of Wicket's IFeedback interface (FeedbackPanel is one example) within the supplied Form component to the AjaxRequestTarget. FormComponentFeedbackBorder still has a problem in that it is not ready for Ajax-ification yet. So you will roll out your own.

Building a Custom FormComponentFeedbackBorder That Works Well with Ajax

The template shown in Listing 8-5 is similar to that of Wicket's FormComponentFeedbackBorder component. But there is a significant difference—FormComponentFeedbackBorder renders a little red asterisk beside the component only when the validation fails. So when the page is displayed for the first time, the span marked errorIndicator will not render on the browser as there are no validation failures. But then the current Wicket-Ajax setup expects the component to exist beforehand so that it can replace its outerHTML later during a subsequent Ajax call. You will fix this issue in your component by rendering the errorIndicator span *unconditionally* but at the same time making sure that the rendering of the little red asterisk is evaluated at runtime.

Listing 8-5. *A Custom FormComponentFeedbackBorder That Works Well with Ajax*

```
<html xmlns:wicket>
<body>
   <wicket:border>
      <!-- errorText component will be rendered conditionally -->
      <wicket:body/><span wicket:id = "errorIndicator">
<span wicket:id="errorText"></span></span>
   </wicket:border>
</body>
</html>
```

Listing 8-6 shows the corresponding Border class.

Listing 8-6. *The Corresponding Java Component Class*

```
Package com.apress.wicketbook.ajax;

import wicket.AttributeModifier;
import wicket.feedback.ContainerFeedbackMessageFilter;
import wicket.feedback.IFeedback;
import wicket.feedback.IFeedbackMessageFilter;
import wicket.markup.html.WebMarkupContainer;
import wicket.markup.html.basic.Label;
import wicket.markup.html.border.Border;
import wicket.model.IModel;
import wicket.model.Model;

/**
 * A border component similar to FormComponentFeedbackBorder
 * except that the errorIndicator span is displayed at all times so that
 * it is always available. The error text (*) and the error style
 * are rendered only when there is an error associated with the component.
 */

public class AjaxResponsiveFormComponentFeedbackBorder extends Border implements
        IFeedback {
    private boolean visible;

    /**
     * Error indicator that will be shown whenever there is an error-level
     * message for the collecting component.
     */
    private final class ErrorIndicator extends WebMarkupContainer {
```

```
    public ErrorIndicator(String id) {
      super(id);
      add(new ErrorTextLabel("errorText", new Model("*")));
      add(new ErrorStyleAttributeModifier("style", true,
        new Model("color:red;")));


    }


    // An error style whose visiblity is determined by the presence
    // of feedback error messages.

    class ErrorStyleAttributeModifier extends AttributeModifier {
        public ErrorStyleAttributeModifier(String attribute,
          boolean addAttributeIfNotPresent, IModel replaceModel) {
          super(attribute, addAttributeIfNotPresent, replaceModel);
        }

        public boolean isVisible() {
          return visible;
        }
    }

    // An error text label whose visibility is determined by the presence
    // of feedback error messages.

    class ErrorTextLabel extends Label {

        public ErrorTextLabel(String id, IModel model) {
          super(id, model);
        }

        public boolean isVisible() {
          return visible;
        }
    }


}

public AjaxResponsiveFormComponentFeedbackBorder(final String id) {
  super(id);
  add(new ErrorIndicator("errorIndicator"));
}
```

```
    // The ContainerFeedbackMessageFilter is used to filter out
    // feedback messages belonging to this component.
    protected IFeedbackMessageFilter getMessagesFilter() {
      return new ContainerFeedbackMessageFilter(this);
    }

    /* This method will be called on the component during
    * Ajax render so that it gets a chance to determine the
    * presence of error messages.
    */

    public void updateFeedback() {
      visible = getPage().getFeedbackMessages().messages(
        getMessagesFilter()).size() != 0;
    }
}
```

Let's use AjaxResponsiveFormComponentFeedbackBorder in place of FormComponent→
FeedbackBorder in this example. This should ensure that the Ajax validation goes through
smoothly.

You started out with the mission of enabling Ajax on some of the pages that you developed earlier. The TabbedPanel that you used in your bookstore application also has an Ajax
counterpart: wicket.extensions.ajax.markup.html.tabs.AjaxTabbedPanel. You will see how
you can put this component to use next.

Using Wicket's AjaxTabbedPanel for the Bookstore Panel

AjaxTabbedPanel, just like its non-Ajax counterpart TabbedPanel, uses links on the tabs. But
the Ajax-ified version updates the display panel in place instead. The Link components are
in fact of the type wicket.ajax.markup.html.AjaxFallbackLink. So if you have the "WICKET
AJAX DEBUG" link enabled, you will notice that every time you click a link, the Ajax response
contains the markup for the entire Panel that needs to be replaced or rendered. Then, as
usual, the JavaScript routine replaces the existing markup with the new one based on the id
attribute.

This time around, you won't package AjaxTabbedPanel as a reusable component along
with the CSS and images though, as you learned how to do in Chapter 7. Instead, you will copy
the style sheet and images to the web application's context root directory and access them
directly from within your page.

Updating the HTML Title Element Through Ajax

Wicket-Ajax updates the HTML element based on the value of the attribute id. It essentially
sets the outerHTML property of the element to the Ajax response received from the server. In
this case, you are faced with updating the page title based on the selected panel. You can add

the Label component to the AjaxRequestTarget. But unfortunately, HTML DOM does not support updating the <title> element based on the id attribute nor does the <title> element have a property by the name outerHTML. Essentially, Wicket-Ajax's way of updating the HTML element is not of any help in this specific case. Luckily, AjaxRequestTarget.addJavascript allows you to add arbitrary JavaScript code that will be sent as an Ajax response to the server. The JavaScript code will then be executed on the client. Browsers allow you to change the page title through the document.title call. You shall add the same to the AjaxRequestTarget on the server side (see Listing 8-7).

Listing 8-7. *BookShopTabbedPanelPage Modified to Use AjaxTabbedPanel*

```
package com.apress.wicketbook.ajax;

import wicket.extensions.ajax.markup.html.tabs.AjaxTabbedPanel;

public class BookShopTabbedPanelPage extends WebPage {

  // Code content same as com.apress.wicketbook.extensions.BookShopTabbedPanelPage

  protected void configureTabs() {
    // Code content same as
    // com.apress.wicketbook.extensions.BookShopTabbedPanelPage

    panel = new MyAjaxTabbedPanel("tabs", tabs);
  }

  class MyAjaxTabbedPanel extends AjaxTabbedPanel{
    public MyAjaxTabbedPanel(String id, List tabs) {
      super(id, tabs);
    }

    /* @see AjaxTabbedPanel.onAjaxUpdate(AjaxRequestTarget target) */

    protected void onAjaxUpdate(AjaxRequestTarget target){
        // This call will be executed on the client side. It will alter the page
        // title depending upon the link that is clicked.
        target.addJavascript("document.title='"
                  +label.getModelObjectAsString()+"'");
    }
  }
}
```

Wicket's Ajax support has been designed in such a way that more often that not, Ajax-ifying a Wicket page is just about either adding a predefined Ajax behavior to the existing components or replacing a non-Ajax component with its Ajax equivalent. Let's move on and look at something very interesting: Wicket's support for Ajax autocompletion.

Ajax Autocompletion

Autocompletion involves the program predicting a word or phrase that the user wants to type in without the user actually typing it in completely. How Wicket nicely hides this behind an interface is something that we will discuss next. Let's have a page with a text input field as shown in Listing 8-8. You'll maintain an in-memory list of email addresses and provide an autocompletion feature for completing such an address when the user starts typing in one.

Listing 8-8. *AutoCompleteEmail—A Template with a Text Field That Provides Autocompletion*

```html
<html>
<head>
<style>

div.wicket-aa {
  font-family: "Lucida Grande","Lucida Sans Unicode",Tahoma,Verdana;
  font-size: 12px;
  background-color: white;
  border-width: 1px;
  border-color: #cccccc;
  border-style: solid;
  padding: 2px;
  margin: 1px 0 0 0;
  text-align:left;
}
div.wicket-aa ul { list-style:none; padding: 2px; margin:0; }
div.wicket-aa ul li.selected { background-color: #FFFF00; padding: 2px: margin:0; }

</style>
</head>
<body>
    <form wicket:id="form">
        Email : <input type="text" wicket:id="email" size="40"/>
    </form>
</body>
</html>
```

Autocompletion could also be defined as behavior exhibited by a TextField component and is in fact modeled as one—AutoCompleteBehavior. The string input that you actually type in is sent in an asynchronous fashion to the server, and the response is rendered without a browser refresh using Ajax. As you would expect, AutoCompleteBehavior is a wicket.behavior. AbstractAjaxBehavior subclass. You are just expected to implement the following method and return the matching results:

```
Iterator AutoCompleteBehavior.getChoices(String input);
```

You will use a class to represent an email address since it will allow you to associate other attributes with an email ID (see Listing 8-9).

Listing 8-9. *A Class That Represents an Email Address*

```
// A class that represents the email address.
// You return a list of email String objects in AutoCompleteBehavior.getChoices( ).

class Email {
 String email;
 Email(String email) {
   this.email = email;
 }
 // StringAutoCompleteRenderer calls this when rendering.
 public String toString(){
   return email;
 }
}
```

Listing 8-10 presents the page that uses a TextField component configured with AutoCompleteBehavior.

Listing 8-10. *Text Field Configured with AutoCompleteBehavior*

```
import wicket.extensions.ajax.markup.html.autocomplete.AutoCompleteBehavior;
import wicket.extensions.ajax.markup.html.autocomplete.StringAutoCompleteRenderer;

public class AutoCompleteEmail extends WebPage {

 // An in-memory list of email addresses

 private List emailAddresses = Arrays.asList(new Email[] {
  new Email("aaron@some-company.com"),
  new Email("amit@developers.net"),
  new Email("akshay@dev.com"),
  new Email("bob@developers.net"),
  new Email("abc@hello.com"),
  new Email("best@developer.com"),
  new Email("craig@yourcompany.com"),
  new Email("chris@broadnetworks.com")});

 public AutoCompleteEmail() {

  Form form = new Form("form");
  TextField txtEmail = new TextField("email", new Model());

  /* Adding autocomplete behavior to the TextField component.
   *
   */
```

```
txtEmail.add(new AutoCompleteBehavior(
        new StringAutoCompleteRenderer()) {

/** Return the results that match the input supplied by the user.
 * In a real-world application, you might run a search against the database.
 * In this case, you shall use an in-memory representation. Just check if
 * the email starts with the input that was typed in and return it.
 */

  @Override
  protected Iterator getChoices(String input) {
   List completions = new ArrayList();
   Iterator iter = emailAddresses.iterator();
   while (iter.hasNext()) {
    String email = ((Email) iter.next()).email;
    if (email.startsWith(input)) {
     completions.add(email);
    }
   }
   return completions.iterator();
  }
 });

 form.add(txtEmail);
 add(form);
 }
}
```

This autocomplete behavior appears as shown in Figure 8-3.

Figure 8-3. *Email address autocompletion at work*

To test this, type **a** in the text field, and you should see all the email addresses that start with the letter *a* getting listed.

Providing Custom IAutoCompleteRenderer Implementations

In some cases, you might want to change the way information is rendered on autocompletion. The previous example used Wicket's StringAutoAssistRenderer class, which just renders the string representation (toString()) of the object. Wicket has always been about bringing OO to Java web development, and therefore it shouldn't come as a surprise that it abstracts the rendering behavior behind an IAutoCompleteRenderer interface. It also provides an AbstractAutoCompleteRenderer class that does most of the work (like generating the HTML/JavaScript that is required to provide the autocompletion effect) while allowing you to specify your own rendering mechanism.

Here, you'll cook up a use case that allows you to experiment with this feature. It's quite likely that a user might maintain two sets of email addresses—personal and official. There might be cases where said user might want to send certain emails to the personal ID while addressing others to the official ID. Listing 8-11 shows how you can provide that information as well in the text field.

Listing 8-11. *AutoCompleteEmail.html—A Page to Demonstrate a Custom IAutoCompleteRenderer Implementation*

```html
<html>
<head>
<style>

div.wicket-aa {
  font-family: "Lucida Grande","Lucida Sans Unicode",Tahoma,Verdana;
  font-size: 12px;
  background-color: white;
  border-width: 1px;
  border-color: #cccccc;
  border-style: solid;
  padding: 2px;
  margin: 1px 0 0 0;
  text-align:left;
}
div.wicket-aa ul { list-style:none; padding: 2px; margin:0; }
div.wicket-aa ul li.selected { background-color: #FFFF00; padding: 2px: margin:0; }

</style>
</head>
<body>
  <form wicket:id="form">
    Email :<input type="text" wicket:id="email" size="40"/><br/>
    <!-- Add a text field that does autocompletion and provides more info -->
    Informative Email : <input type="text" wicket:id="emailInfo" size="40"/>
  </form>
</body>
</html>
```

Now modify the Email class to carry that information, as shown in Listing 8-12.

Listing 8-12. *Email Class That Distinguishes Between "Official" and "Personal" Email Addresses*

```java
class Email {
  String email;
  boolean isPersonal;
  Email(String email, boolean isPersonal) {
   this.email = email;
   this.isPersonal = isPersonal;
  }
  // Will use this to provide more info
  String getEmailInfo(){
   return isPersonal?"Personal Email":"Official Email";
  }

  public String toString(){
   return email;
  }
 }
```

And modify the Page class as you see in Listing 8-13.

Listing 8-13. *AutoCompleteEmail Page with a Custom Renderer*

```java
import java.util.ArrayList;
import java.util.Arrays;
import java.util.Iterator;
import java.util.List;
// Other imports
import wicket.Response;
import wicket.extensions.ajax.markup.html.autocomplete.AbstractAutoCompleteRenderer;
import wicket.extensions.ajax.markup.html.autocomplete.AutoCompleteTextField;
import wicket.extensions.ajax.markup.html.autocomplete.IAutoCompleteRenderer;

public class AutoCompleteEmail extends WebPage {

  private List emailAddresses = Arrays.asList(new Email[] {
      new Email("aaron@some-company.com", true),
      new Email("amit@developers.net", false),
      new Email("akshay@dev.com", false),
      new Email("bob@developers.net", false),
      new Email("abc@hello.com", true),
      new Email("best@developer.com", true),
      new Email("craig@yourcompany.com", false),
      new Email("chris@broadnetworks.com", true) });
```

```
public AutoCompleteEmail() {

  Form form = new Form("form");

  // Refer to Listing 8-9 for TextField with AutoCompleteBehavior attached.
form.add(txtEmail);

  // Define the custom renderer. In addition to the email, you also render
  // additional information.

  IAutoCompleteRenderer informativeRenderer = new AbstractAutoCompleteRenderer() {

    @Override
    protected void renderChoices(Object object, Response r) {
      String val = ((Email) object).email;
      r.write("<div style='float:left; color:red; '>");
      r.write(val);
      r.write("</div><div style='text-align:right; width:100%;'>");
      r.write("" + ((Email) object).getEmailInfo());
      r.write("</div>");
    }

    // AbstractAutoAssistRenderer calls this method to get the actual
    // value that will show up on
    // selection. StringAutoAssistRenderer, which you use for the
    // "txtEmail" component, overrides
    // this method by returning a "String"
    // representation of the object (does a toString()). Since
    // you add email instances (see getChoices() below), the "object"
    // param in this case is of type "Email".

    protected String getTextValue(Object object) {
      return ((Email) object).email;
    }

  };

  /*
   * The TextField component "txtEmail" has Ajax behavior added to it.
   * You also have the option of "committing" to an implementation up front:
   * You directly program to an Ajax-ified text field here, passing in the
   * custom renderer.
   */

  TextField txtEmailInfo = new AutoCompleteTextField("emailInfo",
      new Model(), informativeRenderer) {
```

```
      @Override
      protected Iterator getChoices(String input) {
        List completions = new ArrayList();
        Iterator iter = emailAddresses.iterator();
        while (iter.hasNext()) {
          Email emailObj = (Email) iter.next();

          // Check for the email "String" but add Email objects!

          if (emailObj.email.startsWith(input)) {
            completions.add(emailObj);
          }
        }
        return completions.iterator();
      }    };
    form.add(txtEmailInfo);
    add(form);
  }
}
```

You should see something like what appears in Figure 8-4 on the browser when you type **a**
in the second input text field.

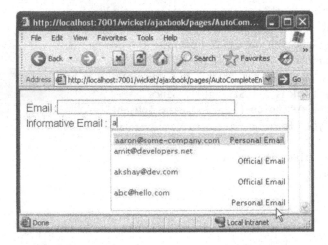

Figure 8-4. *The custom AutoComplete renderer on display*

Next you will see how you can trigger an Ajax request based on a client-side event on one
component and "Ajax-render" a different component in response.

Partially Rendering a Page in Response to an Ajax Request

Next, you will modify the UserProfilePage.html that you developed in Chapter 1 to accept the state in which the user resides. It's quite clear that you really cannot populate the state drop-down list box until the user selects the country he or she resides in. An obvious way to handle this would be to set the state drop-down content in the onSelectionChanged event of the country drop-down (see Listing 8-14).

Listing 8-14. *UserProfilePage.html Modified to Accept State-/County-Related Information*

```html
<html>
  <title>User Profile</title>
<!-- Rest of the markup same as earlier -->
<!-- Add the markup to accept state after the country drop-down -->
 Country <select wicket:id="country">
            <option>India</option>
          <option>USA</option>
          <option>UK</option>
      </select><br/>
      State/County <select wicket:id="state">
            <option>California</option>
          <option>Michigan</option>
      </select><br/>
<!-- Rest of the markup same as earlier -->
```

But now that you are armed with Ajax, you could do with a more responsive user interface. Instead of doing a server round-trip, you could refresh the state drop-down list through Ajax. This way the user will not even experience the flicker that results with a page submit and subsequent refresh. Go ahead and maintain a country-state mapping as well in the page for quick lookup, as shown in Listing 8-15.

Listing 8-15. *UserProfilePage Modified to Refresh the State Drop-Down List Through Ajax*

```java
public class UserProfilePage1 extends WebPage {

  private Map countryToStateMap = new HashMap();

  // Maintain a map of the country to its states/counties.

  private void initStates() {
    countryToStateMap.put("India", new String[] { "Maharashtra",
    "Tamilnadu", "Sikkim", "Kashmir", "Karnataka" });
    countryToStateMap.put("US", new String[] {"California","Texas",
        "Washington", "Michigan"});
    countryToStateMap.put("UK", new String[] {"Lancashire",
     "Middlesex","Yorkshire","Sussex"});
  }
```

```
public UserProfilePage() {
    // Initialize the country-state mapping -->
    initStates();
    //..

    // The state choices that need to be displayed are determined by the
    // chosen country.
    // Remember, IModel serves as an ideal data locator in this case.
    // Only at runtime do you discover the
    // states that need to be displayed in response.

    IModel statechoices = new AbstractReadOnlyModel(){

        // Wicket calls this method when it tries to look
        // for the model object for displaying the states.
        // This is the indirection introduced by the Wicket's models.

        public Object getObject(Component component){

            String[] models = (String[])
                    countryToStateMap.get(userProfile.getCountry());
            if (models == null){
                return Collections.EMPTY_LIST;
            }
            return Arrays.asList(models);
        }
    };

    final DropDownChoice stateComp = new DropDownChoice("state",statechoices);

    DropDownChoice countriesComp = new DropDownChoice("country",
            Arrays.asList(new String[] {"India", "US", "UK" })){
        protected boolean wantOnSelectionChangedNotifications(){
            // Returning true from here would result in a page submit when
            // selection changes in the drop-down. You instead want to respond
            // to an Ajax call. So return false.
            return false;
        }
    };


    // Add an Ajax component updating behavior to the country drop-down.
    // Pass in the JavaScript event ("onchange") that needs to trigger this
    // request.
```

```
countriesComp.add(new AjaxFormComponentUpdatingBehavior("onchange") {
    protected void onUpdate(AjaxRequestTarget target) {
        // Supply the component that you want to re-render.
        target.addComponent(stateComp);
    }
});

//..
form.add(stateComp);
```

```
}
```

The sample response shown in Listing 8-16 clearly tells you how Wicket wraps the Ajax response. All components that need to be re-rendered are wrapped in a <component> element along with the id attribute that identifies them. As you would have guessed, the built-in JavaScript then just looks up the HTML element corresponding to the id attribute and replaces its content (outerHTML property) with the one wrapped within the <component> tag (see Listing 8-16).

Listing 8-16. *Sample Ajax Response for Partial Rendering*

```
<?xml version="1.0" encoding="UTF-8"?>
<ajax-response>
  <component id="stateMarkup">
    <![CDATA[
        <select wicket:id="state" name="stateMarkup:state" id="state">
          <option selected="selected" value="">Choose One</option>
          <option value="0">State-1</option>
          <option value="1">State-2</option>
          <option value="2">State-3</option>
          <option value="3">State-4</option>
        </select>
    ]]>
  </component>
</ajax-response>
```

On selecting US from the Country drop-down list, you should see the State drop-down list getting populated through Ajax (see Figure 8-5).

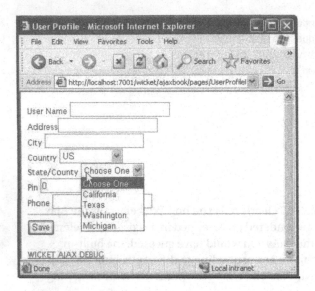

Figure 8-5. *Refreshing the state drop-down based on the selected country through Ajax*

You must have noticed in the examples that you have seen up to now that most built-in Ajax behaviors like AjaxFormComponentUpdatingBehavior allow you to specify any JavaScript event that triggers the Ajax call. One of the biggest advantages of modeling Ajax support as behaviors that can be added to components is that it results in fewer *core* classes. Supporting specialized Ajax-enabled components could have resulted in a potential class-hierarchy "explosion."

How to Let Users Know That Wicket Ajax Behavior Is at Work

Conventional web requests result in a page refresh, and typically browsers have some form of indicator to display the response status. As a result, the user is aware of the fact that the server is still in the process of rendering the response. Unfortunately, this is not the case with Ajax. Since Ajax is inherently an asynchronous communication mechanism between the browser and the server, it provides no visual feedback on the response status. Coupled with the fact that the browser does not supply any help in this regard, you see that the onus of showing the progress lies solely with the developers. Wicket recognizes this and provides a means of giving feedback as a part of the basic Ajax infrastructure through the wicket.ajax.IAjax➥IndicatorAware interface.

This interface makes it trivial to use status indicators for Ajax requests. It can be implemented by a component that has an Ajax behavior attached to it or by the Ajax behavior itself. Under such circumstances, Wicket automatically adds the JavaScript code that will show a markup element pointed to by the IAjaxIndicatorAware.getAjaxIndicatorMarkupId() markup ID attribute when the Ajax request begins, and hides it when the Ajax requests succeeds or fails.

If both a component and a behavior implement this interface, the component will take precedence. You need to add a placeholder for the "busy" indicator image first (see Listing 8-17).

Listing 8-17. *A Placeholder for the Indicator Image That Is Initially Invisible on the UserProfilePage*

```
State/County
    <select wicket:id="state">
        <option>California</option>
        <option>Michigan</option>
    </select>
    <!-- You will specify the image URL on the server side -->
    <img src="" wicket:id="indicatorImg" style="display:none"/>
    <br/>
```

The Page class accordingly requires a component to populate the value for the <img> src attribute, as shown in Listing 8-18.

Listing 8-18. *A WebmarkupContainer That Refers to the Built-in Indicator Image As a Packaged Resource*

```
import wicket.ajax.AbstractDefaultAjaxBehavior;
public class UserProfilePage1 extends WebPage {

    public UserProfilePage1(){
    //..
    final WebMarkupContainer imgContainer =new
      WebMarkupContainer("indicatorImg"){
        public void onComponentTag(ComponentTag tag){
          super.onComponentTag(tag);
      // AbstractDefaultAjaxBehavior.INDICATOR is a package reference to the
      // default indicator.gif (refer to Chapter 7 for discussion on
      // package references.
          tag.put("src",urlFor(AbstractDefaultAjaxBehavior.INDICATOR));
        }
    };
    imgContainer.setOutputMarkupId(true);
    form.add(imgContainer);
    //..
    }
}
```

If you require Ajax indicators in multiple pages, you would be required to repeat this code snippet a number of times. Wicket is all about components, so package this piece of code into something reusable (see Listing 8-19).

Listing 8-19. *An Image Indicator Component*

```
package com.apress.wicketbook.ajax;

import wicket.ajax.AbstractDefaultAjaxBehavior;
import wicket.markup.ComponentTag;
import wicket.markup.html.WebMarkupContainer;

public class AjaxIndicator extends WebMarkupContainer {

  public AjaxIndicator(String id) {
    super(id);
    setOutputMarkupId(true);
  }

  public void onComponentTag(ComponentTag tag){
    super.onComponentTag(tag);
    tag.put("src",urlFor(AbstractDefaultAjaxBehavior.INDICATOR));
  }
}
```

Now you are just required to do this:

```
public class UserProfilePage1 extends WebPage{

  public UserProfilePage1(){
    //..
    // You are just required to add the AjaxIndicator.
    final AjaxIndicator imgContainer =
        new AjaxIndicator("indicatorImg");
    form.add(imgContainer);
    //..
  }
}
```

Even though you managed to add the image component to the page, the behavior or the component is still not aware of it. Wicket's Ajax infrastructure, especially the built-in JavaScript library, can be made aware of the image by getting the component or the Ajax behavior attached to it to implement the wicket.ajax.IAjaxIndicatorAware interface (see Listing 8-20). The interface just looks for the markup ID of the image component so that, as discussed earlier, it can hide or show it during the Ajax request life cycle.

Listing 8-20. *A Behavior to Introduce an Artificial Delay in Ajax Response to See the Image Indicator at Work*

```
public class UserProfilePage extends WebPage{

    public UserProfilePage(){
        //..
        final AjaxIndicator imgContainer =
                new AjaxIndicator("indicatorImg");
        form.add(imgContainer);

        class CountryDDAjaxBehavior extends AjaxFormComponentUpdatingBehavior
            implements  IAjaxIndicatorAware{

            CountryDDAjaxBehavior(){
                super("onchange");
            }

            protected void onUpdate(AjaxRequestTarget target) {
                // Sleep for 5 seconds just to make sure that
                // the busy indicator works as it is supposed to.
                // You would obviously not want this (Thread.sleep)
                // piece of code in production.
                try{
                    Thread.sleep(5000);
                }catch (InterruptedException ignore){
                }
                // Add the Ajax target component as earlier.
                target.addComponent(stateComp);
            }
            /** Return indicator's markup ID**/

            public String getAjaxIndicatorMarkupId() {
                return imgContainer.getMarkupId();
            }
        }
    }
    //..
}


countriesComp.add(new CountryDDAjaxBehavior());
```

Figure 8-6 shows how the indicator appears on screen.

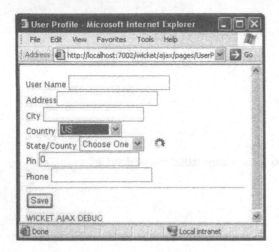

Figure 8-6. *The Ajax indicator lets users know that Ajax is at work.*

Finally, let's see how you can improve the responsiveness of the page that displays the books in the online bookstore application by using an Ajax-enabled CheckBox component.

Putting AjaxCheckBox to Work

In Chapter 3, you used check boxes to record the books chosen by the user. You even managed to retain the state of the check boxes while the user navigates across DataView pages or swaps categories. But then the action (checking a check box) always resulted in a server-side trip to store the state, which isn't too easy on the eyes. You could get the component to relay its state to the server asynchronously through Ajax. In fact, Ajax-ifying this behavior is as simple as swapping the existing Wicket CheckBox with its Ajax counterpart—wicket.ajax.markup.html. form.AjaxCheckBox.

The AjaxCheckBox component "is-a" Wicket CheckBox with AjaxFormComponentUpdating➥ Behavior attached to it for the onchange JavaScript event. The component has a template method, onUpdate(AjaxRequestTarget target), where you get to do your custom processing on an Ajax call. But the CheckBox model is automatically updated (by virtue of being configured with AjaxFormComponentUpdatingBehavior) and hence you just need to have a "no op" implementation as shown in Listing 8-21.

Listing 8-21. *BookSelectionPanel Configured with a Check Box That Updates Itself on Ajax Request*

```
package com.apress.wicketbook.ajax;
import wicket.ajax.markup.html.form.AjaxCheckBox;

public class ViewBooksPanel extends Panel {
 // Everything else remains the same.
 public class BookSelectionPanel extends Panel {
```

```
   public BookSelectionPanel(String id, Book book) {
     super(id);
     add(new AjaxCheckBox("selected", new CheckBoxModel(book.getId()))) {
       // This is the template method.
       protected void onUpdate(AjaxRequestTarget target) {

       }
     });
   }
 }
//
}
```

This concludes your adventure tour of Wicket's Ajax capabilities (for more information on built-in Ajax support, consult the Wicket Javadoc). Even though you managed to improve the responsiveness of some of the pages through Ajax, there is one disturbing pattern in the server-side code that you cannot afford to ignore: components have been coded under the assumption that all browsers have Ajax and/or JavaScript support enabled. This really might not be the case with certain browsers, thereby causing the application to malfunction. In the next section, we will discuss this extreme scenario and how Wicket allows you to tackle this problem.

Degradable Ajax

In practice, designing web applications that work only with Ajax or JavaScipt enabled on the browser is not advisable. Care needs to be taken that application pages degrade to a normal request on the nonavailability of Ajax or JavaScript support. Wicket's `wicket.ajax.markup.html.AjaxFallbackLink` component is one such example. Earlier, you ended up using the `AjaxFallbackLink` component in the example that deals with `AjaxTabbedPanel` (refer back to Listing 8-7). However, in the absence of browser support for JavaScript, `AjaxFallbackLink` calls `onAjaxUpdate`, passing in a "null" `AjaxRequestTarget` reference. So you just need to incorporate the check before adding the JavaScript code (see Listing 8-22).

Listing 8-22. *Incorporating the Check to Accommodate Degradable Ajax Behavior*

```
protected void onAjaxUpdate(AjaxRequestTarget target){
  if(target != null)
    target.addJavascript("document.title='"
         +label.getModelObjectAsString()+"'");
}
```

You can easily verify the fallback behavior by disabling JavaScript support in your browser. Upon doing that, `AjaxTabbedPanel` will gracefully degrade to a normal request, and `AjaxFallbackLinks` will continue to work as normal links.

Handling Ajax Success and Failure Events Through AjaxCallDecorator

Like any other request, Ajax request processing might result in success or failure. Based on this status, you might want to trigger certain client-side events. Wicket provides hooks to tie your custom JavaScript processing code into the built-in JavaScript infrastructure. It does this through the wicket.ajax.IAjaxCallDecorator interface. Listing 8-23 shows how the interface specification looks.

Listing 8-23. *Wicket's IAjaxCallDecorator Interface, Which Allows You to Decorate the Ajax Success and/or Failure Script*

```
package wicket.ajax;
public interface IAjaxCallDecorator extends Serializable {
  /**
  * Name of the JavaScript variable that will be true if an Ajax call was made,
  * false otherwise. This variable is available in the after script only.
  */
  public static final String WICKET_CALL_RESULT_VAR = "wcall";

  /** Decorates the script that performs the Ajax call **/
  CharSequence decorateScript(CharSequence script);

  /** Decorates the onSuccess handler script **/
  CharSequence decorateOnSuccessScript(CharSequence script);

  /** Decorates the onFailure handler script **/
  CharSequence decorateOnFailureScript(CharSequence script);

}
```

As you can see, this interface allows you to decorate a Wicket-generated JavaScript that performs Ajax callback. All Wicket Ajax behaviors extend the wicket.ajaxAbstract➥ DefaultAjaxBehavior class. This class has a hook method, getAjaxCallDecorator(), to fetch your IAjaxCallDecorator. You can override this method in your behavior class to return your IAjaxCallDecorator implementation.

Let's look at an example that demonstrates the decorator script usage. You saw in the last section that Wicket's AjaxFallbackLink degrades to a normal request in the absence of browser support for Ajax or JavaScript. Now, you'll develop a DropDownChoice component that is configured for the Ajax request by default through the onchange event. But in addition to this, you'll get the component to retry the normal request if the Ajax request fails for some reason, like the browser's XmlHttpRequest object not being available (see Listing 8-24).

Listing 8-24. *An Example to Demonstrate IAjaxCallDecorator*

```java
import java.util.List;

import wicket.WicketRuntimeException;
import wicket.ajax.AjaxRequestTarget;
import wicket.ajax.IAjaxCallDecorator;
import wicket.ajax.calldecorator.AjaxPostprocessingCallDecorator;
import wicket.ajax.form.AjaxFormComponentUpdatingBehavior;
import wicket.markup.ComponentTag;
import wicket.markup.html.form.DropDownChoice;

public class AjaxFallbackDropDown extends DropDownChoice {

  public AjaxFallbackDropDown(String id, List choices) {
    super(id, choices);
    setOutputMarkupId(true);
    add(new DropDownAjaxUpdatingBehavior());
  }

  private class DropDownAjaxUpdatingBehavior extends
      AjaxFormComponentUpdatingBehavior {
    // The original onchange script added by the
    // component. It may or may not be preset depending upon
    // the return value of wantOnSelectionChangedNotifications().

    String prevScript;

    DropDownAjaxUpdatingBehavior() {
      // Ajax call configured for onchange event.
      super("onchange");
    }

    // onUpdate call the onSelectionChanged method passing in the
    // AjaxRequestTarget.

    protected void onUpdate(AjaxRequestTarget target) {
        DropDownChoice dropDownChoice =
            (DropDownChoice)getFormComponent();

        // At the time of writing, the Wicket code
        // had the "access specifier" specified as "protected"
        // for this method. Nevertheless, you could modify the
        // source and change it to "public". The fact that
        // Wicket uses Maven for its build is of great help here.
```

```
        dropDownChoice.onSelectionChanged(target);
    }

    // Since the above method internally calls
    // onSelectionChanged, make sure that the behavior
    // is being bound to a DropDownChoice.

    protected void onBind() {
      super.onBind();
      if (!(getComponent() instanceof DropDownChoice)) {
        throw new WicketRuntimeException(
          "Behavior "
          + getClass().getName()
          + " can only be added to an isntance of a DropDownChoice");
      }
    }

    // Retrieve the original onchange script added by the component
    // if present.
    protected void onComponentTag(final ComponentTag tag) {
      if (tag.getAttributes().containsKey("onchange")) {
        this.prevScript = tag.getAttributes().get("onchange")
            .toString();
      } else {
        prevScript = null;
      }
      // Get the AjaxFormComponentUpdatingBehavior
      // to add its onchange event script.
      super.onComponentTag(tag);
    }

    protected IAjaxCallDecorator getAjaxCallDecorator() {
      return new AjaxPostprocessingCallDecorator(null) {
        // On Ajax failure, execute the original onchange script added
        // by the component. This would trigger the normal
        // request.
        public CharSequence postDecorateOnFailureScript(
            CharSequence script) {
          if (prevScript != null)
            return script + ";" + prevScript;
          else
            return script + "";
        }
      };
    }
  }
}
```

How do you make sure that the preceding code actually works in a non-Ajax setting? One option could be to use a browser with no built-in Ajax support. Note that you need JavaScript support enabled for the onchange event to trigger when the user selection changes. The easier approach to testing this component would be to programmatically throw a RuntimeException on Ajax request:

```
private class DropDownAjaxUpdatingBehavior extends
    AjaxFormComponentUpdatingBehavior {
//..
  protected void onUpdate(AjaxRequestTarget target) {
    throw new WicketRuntimeException(
      "Exception when handling DropDown Ajax request");
  }
//..
}
```

You could test this behavior by having a basic template with HTML <form> and <select> elements. In the Page class, make sure that you use AjaxFallbackDropDown in place of the DropDownChoice component and have DropDownChoice.wantOnSelectionChangeNotifications() return true.

This pretty much covers the significant features that constitute Wicket's support for Ajax at its core. Wicket integrates with several Ajax-dedicated frameworks like DOJO (http://www.dojotoolkit.org/), Script.aculo.us (http://script.aculo.us/), etc. Wicket-DOJO integration, for example, can be downloaded from http://wicket-stuff.sourceforge.net/wicket-contrib-dojo/index.html. It should be noted that projects belonging to Wicket-Contrib and Wicket-Stuff are maintained by the Wicket community and are not part of the core framework. That said, the subprojects also seem to be well supported as of now.

Summary

Ajax is about bringing the kind of responsiveness demonstrated by desktop applications to web pages.

You saw how a FormComponentFeedbackBorder renders a little red asterisk beside a component that it decorates when the latter fails the validation check. You also learned that Wicket models a component's ability to respond to Ajax requests as a behavior. Then you saw how form validation can be Ajax-ified, and you even developed a version of FormComponent▶FeedbackBorder that responds to an Ajax request in a correct fashion. You saw how to Ajax-ify a few pages that you developed earlier to explore Wicket's built-in Ajax components. AjaxFormComponentUpdatingBehavior, AjaxFormValidatingBehavior, AjaxTabbedPanel, auto-completion, and AjaxCheckBox are some of Wicket's Ajax components discussed briefly in this chapter. We briefly discussed Wicket's support for degradable Ajax components and also looked at a way to indicate the Ajax request progress indicator through Wicket's IAjaxIndicatorAware interface.

CHAPTER 9

■ ■ ■

Additional Wicket Topics

In this chapter, you will learn about Wicket's support for unit testing and later look at some of the significant changes you can expect in Wicket 2.0, which will be the next Wicket release and is currently under development.

Wicket Unit Testing

Code refactoring and *unit testing* are considered to be the two main constituents of the *test-driven development* (TDD) methodology. TDD advocates that unit tests be written before code. In this section, we will discuss unit testing support built into Wicket. Unit tests can be classified in several ways, two of which are as *in-container* tests and *out-of-container* tests. As the names indicate, the former needs the container (J2EE servlet container, for example) to be up and running for the tests to execute, while the latter imitates the behavior of the classes or the container it collaborates with. This allows you to just concentrate on unit testing the components you are interested in. The mock object framework meanwhile makes sure that the framework and surrounding environment objects that your classes collaborate with will behave as configured even when running outside a J2EE servlet container. Running tests outside a container also results in obvious productivity gains, as you aren't required to rely on frequent container restarts, and so on. Wicket's unit testing framework is based on a set of mock objects that allow you to test your Wicket-based web application outside a servlet container. You will familiarize yourself with this small subframework in the coming sections.

What Are Mock Objects?

You know that classes and objects are at the heart of any system developed using object-oriented design concepts. For the system to do anything meaningful, the objects that comprise the system need to collaborate. *Mock objects* (or *mocks* for short) are used for testing a portion of code logic in isolation from the rest of the code. In unit tests, mocks replace the objects with which your methods usually collaborate, thus offering a layer of isolation. They are empty shells that provide methods to let the tests control the behavior of all the business methods of the faked class. Your code can call methods on the mock object, which will deliver results as set up by your tests. For more discussions on mock objects, refer to http://www.mockobjects.com.

This section assumes that you have some idea of the benefits offered by TDD; the focus will solely be on arming you with the knowledge of Wicket's support for unit testing, which in turn will help you practice TDD effectively. There are several excellent texts that extol the virtues of being "test driven." To understand the philosophy of this approach, you might want to refer to Kent Beck's *Test-Driven Development: By Example* (Addison-Wesley, 2002) and *Extreme Programming Explained* (Addison-Wesley, 2004).

Unit Testing Wicket Pages Using WicketTester

JUnit is the de facto standard for writing unit tests in the Java world. Although it doesn't do a lot of heavy lifting by itself to enable you to write Wicket-specific unit tests, what it does do is provide an infrastructure and a defined test life cycle that simplifies writing tests, allows grouping of tests, and the like. More importantly, it provides an extensible framework that has led to a plethora of JUnit extension frameworks in turn. Refer to http://www.junit.org for more information on the framework.

Wicket's wicket.util.tester.WicketTester class makes testing Wicket applications really easy. It has several helper methods that allow you to simulate page rendering, click links, and check for the presence of error messages, components, etc. in the Page. It provides many of these utilities as assert*XXX*() methods that make use of JUnit's org.junit.Assert class internally to check for assertions.

WicketTester subclasses wicket.protocol.http.MockWebApplication, which in turn extends WebApplication. To see these methods in action, I'll walk you through writing unit tests for the pages that you developed earlier. The login page that you developed in the first chapter and then later improved upon in Chapter 2 is a good place to start.

Most popular IDEs (e.g., Eclipse, IntelliJ IDEA, NetBeans) come bundled with some kind of built-in support for running JUnit tests. This section does not aim to discuss JUnit in extreme detail, as other books and online articles cover it well; the goal is just to familiarize you with the unit testing support built into Wicket.

Unit Testing the Login Page

The first thing that you need to ensure is that the Login page renders fine without any errors. The method testLoginPageRender (see Listing 9-1) does exactly that. Successful execution of this test will ensure that the template and Page hierarchy matches. It's quite normal to place the JUnit tests and the classes that are being tested in the same package but under a different root folder. Maven by default expects the project Java source files under the src/java directory and the tests under the src/test directory. This ensures that test cases do not get mixed up with the actual source classes (which allows for physical separation of the two, but gives the tests package-level access to the actual source class). If you are looking for a thorough discussion on JUnit and its extensions, *JUnit Recipes* by J. B. Rainsberger (Manning Publications, 2004) could well serve as an excellent reference.

Listing 9-1. *A Test Case That Ensures the Login Page Renders Fine*

```
package com.apress.wicketbook.validation;

import wicket.util.tester.WicketTester;
// Your unit test class should extend TestCase.
import junit.framework.TestCase;
```

```
public class LoginTest extends TestCase {

  private WicketTester tester;

// If you have data that needs to be initialized before test
// execution, you should place it in this method. The JUnit
// framework will call this method just before executing the test.
// It acts like a constructor.

  public void setUp() {
    // You need an instance of WicketTester per test.
    tester = new WicketTester();
  }

  public void testLoginPageRender() {
    tester.startPage(Login.class);
    // Just to ensure that the request has not been
    // intercepted or redirected
    tester.assertRenderedPage(Login.class);

    // A page might render with an error message.
    // If the Login page does have an associated error message, the following
    // method will result in a failed assertion.
    tester.assertNoErrorMessage();
  }
}
```

For running a test under Eclipse, you are just required to select the test that you are interested in running, right-click, and select Run As ➤ JUnit Test. As you would expect, Eclipse will launch it as a JUnit test and display the results (see Figure 9-1 and Figure 9-2).

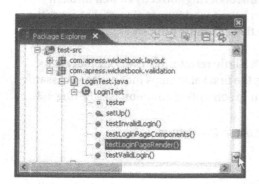

Figure 9-1. *Tests as seen in Eclipse Package Explorer*

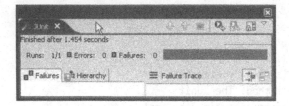

Figure 9-2. *The "famous" JUnit green bar (shown here as a gray bar on the right) that indicates successful execution of the test*

Unit tests are typically run as a part of *automated builds*. Popular build frameworks like Ant and Maven have plug-ins that allow you to automate such tasks with relative ease.

Now that the JUnit green bar flashes, make sure that the rendered page indeed has the necessary components. Again, `WicketTester` has methods that allow you to verify just that. `WicketTester.assertComponent()` needs to be supplied with the path to traverse to the component and the type of the component that it should expect to find at that location. The path to the component, as shown in Listing 9-2, should be relative to the page that contains it.

Listing 9-2. *A Test Case to Ensure the Page Has the Components You Expect*

```
class LoginTest extends TestCase{
//..
 public void testLoginPageComponents() {
  tester.startPage(Login.class);
  tester.assertNoErrorMessage();
  tester.assertComponent("loginForm:userId", TextField.class);
  tester.assertComponent("loginForm:password", TextField.class);
 }
}
```

Note that you could verify that the page labels are rendering correctly as well through `WicketTester.assertLabel()`. This would ensure you have a working set of tests that cover the login page render process. However, you have none that cover the primary login use case. Let's address that next.

But before doing so, you could probably do with a little refactoring: the code that tests that the page renders fine is common to all tests. It's the first set of steps that has to necessarily pass before you execute others. So you could move it to someplace common (see Listing 9-3).

Listing 9-3. *Moving the Commonly Occurring Code to the setUp Method*

```
public class LoginTest extends TestCase {
  private WicketTester tester;

  public void setUp() {
    tester = new WicketTester();
    tester.startPage(Login.class);
    tester.assertRenderedPage(Login.class);
    tester.assertNoErrorMessage();
```

```
}
//..
}
```

Now you can remove this repeating piece of code from all tests. This way the rest of the tests would look leaner and be succinct.

Unit Testing Wicket Pages Using FormTester

If you remember, you had designed the login use case in such a way that if you enter a user name/password combination different from "wicket"/"wicket" and then click Login, you would see the same page getting rendered again with an error message. Since WicketTester does not have any such support for submitting forms, you need to use another Wicket class that aids out-of-container testing: wicket.util.tester.FormTester. In addition to aiding with form submission, FormTester also allows you to set input values for the FormComponents contained within the Form. The "failed login" use case discussed previously could be represented as a JUnit test case, as shown in Listing 9-4.

Listing 9-4. *A Test Case That Tests the "Failed Login" Use Case*

```
import wicket.util.tester.FormTester

public class LoginTest extends TestCase {
  private WicketTester tester;

  public void testInvalidLogin() {

    // Create the form tester object, mapping to its wicket:id.
    FormTester form = tester.newFormTester("loginForm");

    // Set the parameters for each component in the form.
    // Notice that the name is relative to the form - so it's "userId",
    // not "loginForm:userId" as in assertComponent.

    form.setValue("userId", "WrongUserId");
    form.setValue("password", "WrongPassword");

    // Submit the form once the input values have been
    // filled in.
    form.submit();
    // Make sure that it does re-render the Login page
    tester.assertRenderedPage(Login.class);
    // and that an error message to that effect is displayed.
    tester.assertErrorMessages(new String[] {
        "Try wicket/wicket as the user name/password combination" });
  }
}
```

Note that when using the `FormTester` to identify the component, you are required to specify the component path relative to the `Form` and not the `Page`. It also has a setter method, `setValue()`, that allows you to input the values for the components programmatically as you would if you were inputting values through the browser.

This time around, you are expecting the login page to display the error as a result of the failed login. You can use `WicketTester.assertErrorMessages()` for this. You learned in Chapter 2 that a `Page` stores the error messages associated with all the contained components. This method compares the array of input error messages against the list of messages of type error associated with a `Page`. This test ensures that you have captured the failed login use case. Let's look at the use case that covers a successful login (see Listing 9-5).

Listing 9-5. *A Test Case to Verify the Positive Login Path*

```
public void testValidLogin() {
  // Create the form tester object, mapping to its wicket:id.
  FormTester form = tester.newFormTester("loginForm");
  form.setValue("userId", "wicket");
  form.setValue("password", "wicket");
  form.submit();
  // On a valid login, the Welcome page is rendered in response
  tester.assertRenderedPage(Welcome.class);
  // with a success message.
  tester.assertInfoMessages(new String[] {
      "You have logged in successfully" });
}
```

Note that `FormTester.assertInfoMessages()` works similarly to `assertErrorMessages()` except that the former works on messages of type info. With a little rearrangement, you can also make sure that the Welcome page renders the links to the `UserProfilePage` and `Login` pages and the welcome message label (see Listing 9-6).

Listing 9-6. *Test Case to Verify That the Links on the UserProfilePage Render Fine*

```
package com.apress.wicketbook.validation;
// Other imports
public class WelcomeTest extends TestCase {
  private WicketTester tester;

  public void setUp() {
    tester = new WicketTester();
    tester.startPage(Login.class);
    FormTester form = tester.newFormTester("loginForm");
    form.setValue("userId", getValidUser());
    form.setValue("password", getValidPassword());
    form.submit();
    tester.assertRenderedPage(Welcome.class);
  }
```

```
private String getValidUser(){
  return "wicket";
}

private String getValidPassword(){
  return "wicket";
}
// Verify that the rendered Welcome page contains the Link
// components and the welcome message.
public void testWelcomePageRender(){
  tester.assertLabel("form:message",getValidUser());
  tester.assertComponent("form:linkToUserProfile",Link.class);
  tester.assertComponent("form:linkToLogin",Link.class);
}
}
```

The Welcome page has nothing but a couple of page links, but it does provide you with an opportunity to understand how link navigability can be tested.

Testing Page Navigation

WicketTester has a method, clickLink, that emulates a click action on a link, just as the name suggests. Employ this method to ensure that the link to the UserProfilePage works, as shown in Listing 9-7.

Listing 9-7. *A Test to Ensure the Proper Functioning of Links on the UserProfilePage*

```
public void testUserProfileLink(){
  tester.assertComponent("form:linkToUserProfile",Link.class);
  // Click the UserProfilePage link.
  tester.clickLink("form:linkToUserProfile");
  // If everything is OK, you should see the page rendered.
  tester.assertRenderedPage(UserProfilePage.class);
}
```

An Issue with WicketTester Being Used As the WebApplication Subclass

Now that you've made sure that the UserProfilePage renders fine, it's also a good time to verify that the page submission works as well. Listing 9-8 shows you how.

Listing 9-8. *A Test to Ensure the UserProfilePage Submits Successfully*

```
public void testUserProfileDataSubmit() {

  FormTester form = application.newFormTester("userProfile");

  // Setting Form component values requires the component ID and
  // the value that needs to be set.
  form.setValue("name", (String) getUserProfileFormValues().get("name"));
  form.setValue("city", (String) getUserProfileFormValues().get("city"));
  form.setValue("pin", (String) getUserProfileFormValues().get("pin"));
  form.setValue("phoneNumber", (String) getUserProfileFormValues().get(
      "phoneNumber"));

  // DropDownChoice, RadioGroup components are treated a little
  // differently when setting form values.

  form.select("country", getSelectedCountryIndex());

  form.submit();
  application.assertNoErrorMessage();
}

// A DropDownChoice component needs to specify the list index
// it's interested in.

private int getSelectedCountryIndex() {
  return 1;
}

// A helper that supplies the form inputs

private Map formValues;
  if (formValues == null) {
    formValues = new HashMap();
    formValues.put("name", "Tom");
    formValues.put("city", "Dallas");
    formValues.put("country", (String) UserProfilePage.COUNTRIES
        .get(getSelectedCountryIndex()));
    formValues.put("phoneNumber", "123-456-7890");
    formValues.put("pin", "4556");
  }
  return formValues;
}
```

On running the test, you will notice that the phone number doesn't get converted correctly, thereby resulting in the unit test failure. It's not too difficult to explain this behavior though: WicketTester is an Application subclass and is also configured as the Application class for the mock environment. The custom PhoneNumberConverter is registered with the actual WebApplication subclass: ValidationApplication. Since WicketTester is not aware of this converter, it causes the test case to fail. Unfortunately, the only way to have this converter registered with WicketTester is to duplicate the existing ValidationApplication code in a class that extends WicketTester instead (see Listing 9-9).

Listing 9-9. *A WicketTester Subclass That Mimics the Original WebApplication Subclass*

```
package com.apress.wicketbook.validation;

import wicket.util.tester.WicketTester;
import com.apress.wicketbook.validation.CustomConverter;
// Other imports

public class ValidationWicketTester extends WicketTester {

  public void init() {
    super.init();
    getApplicationSettings().setConverterFactory(new IConverterFactory() {
      public IConverter newConverter(final Locale locale) {
        return new CustomConverter(locale);
      }
    });
  }
}
```

Even though this is a definite source of discomfort, you should still be able to live with it, as you would have only one Wicket WebApplication subclass per deployed application. Accordingly, you would be required to duplicate the code in a WicketTester subclass only once for unit testing purposes. It should also be heartening to know that Wicket developers are very likely to remove this limitation in the next Wicket release. Use ValidationWicketTester instead in the setUp method when instantiating the WicketTester reference, and the JUnit green bar will show up when running the test using Eclipse IDE, for example. In this test, you supplied the values to the FormComponents in the expected format and made sure that form submit goes through fine.

What you didn't bother to verify was whether the model objects are getting updated correctly. You cannot afford to ignore this because you would be using the model objects to communicate with the layers beneath the web framework. In the next section, you will learn to accomplish this as well using the FormTester component.

How to Make Sure Form Input Gets Correctly Set on the Model Objects

The server-side business components typically work with the data from Wicket's model objects. Even though you managed to test the form submit using Wicket's FormTester, you still don't have a test in place that verifies that the correct backing model object was updated as a result of form submit. Listing 9-10 shows one such unit test.

Listing 9-10. *A WicketTester Subclass That Mimics the Original WebApplication Subclass*

```
public void testUserProfileModelUpdate() {
  FormTester formTester = application.newFormTester("userProfile");

  formTester.setValue("name", (String) getUserProfileFormValues().get("name"));
  formTester.setValue("city", (String) getUserProfileFormValues().get("city"));
  formTester.setValue("pin", (String) getUserProfileFormValues().get("pin"));
  formTester.setValue("phoneNumber", (String) getUserProfileFormValues().get(
      "phoneNumber"));
  formTester.select("country", getSelectedCountryIndex());
  formTester.submit();
  application.assertNoErrorMessage();

  // Verify whether the model objects were updated in the correct fashion.

  for (Iterator iter = formValues.keySet().iterator(); iter.hasNext();) {
    String element = (String) iter.next();
    String expected = (String) getUserProfileFormValues().get(element);
    // Use the FormTester to fetch the model object.
    String actual = form.getComponent(element).getModelObjectAsString();
    assertEquals(expected, actual);
  }
}
```

Testing Wicket Behaviors

Testing behaviors that contribute to the existing markup can get tricky. For example, the com.apress.wicketbook.layout.ConfirmDeleteBehavior that you developed in the Chapter 7 adds the client-side onclick event to the button that carries this behavior. In addition to this, it also contributes the JavaScript event handler function to the <head> section of the page. Let's look at one of the ways of testing such use cases in Wicket. As a first step in that direction, you have to develop a sample page that puts these behaviors to work (see Listings 9-11 and 9-12).

Listing 9-11. *A Template with Two Submit Buttons*

```
<html>
<body>
<form wicket:id="form">
  <input type="submit" wicket:id="deleteButton1"/>
  <input type="submit" wicket:id="deleteButton2"/>
</form>
</body>
</html>
```

Listing 9-12. *The Page Class with Buttons Configured with ConfirmDeleteBehavior*

```
package com.apress.wicketbook.layout

public class ConfirmDeleteBehaviorTestPage extends WebPage {

  public ConfirmDeleteBehaviorTestPage(){
    Form form = new Form("form");
    add(form);

    form.add(new TextField("name",new PropertyModel(this,"name")));
    Button deleteButtton1 = new Button("deleteButton1");
    // Configures the button "btn" with default behavior
    deleteButton1.add(new ConfirmDeleteBehavior());
    form.add(deleteButtton1);

    Button deleteButton2 = new Button("deleteButton2");
    // Overrides the JavaScript message that will be displayed when the user
    // clicks the button
    deleteButton2.add(new ConfirmDeleteBehavior(){
      public String getJSMessage(){
        return "Delete records?";
      }
    });
    form.add(deleteButtton2);
  }
}
```

The presence of the system property wicket.replace.expected.results tells the
WicketTestCase.executeTest() method to replace the content of the expected HTML file with
the string representation of the generated Page class (see Listing 9-13). Use this property only
when running the test for the very first time. From then on, you would be using the generated
file (the one that's expected) as the reference file. The expected HTML file will be generated in
the same package as the TestCase subclass—com.apress.wicketbook.layout.ConfirmDelete►
BehaviorTest in this case. Note that in case there is a mismatch between the expected and the
actual HTML output, so the test would fail and you would get to see the actual difference in
the content of the two files that resulted in the error. Note that such tests are fragile—you need
to make sure that you regenerate ConfirmDeleteBehaviorTestPage-expected.html when you
change the layout and/or the component usage in the ConfirmDeleteBehaviorTest.

Listing 9-13. *A Test Case That Compares the Generated File Against the Expected File*

```
package com.apress.wicketbook.layout;

import wicket.WicketTestCase;

public class ConfirmDeleteBehaviorTest extends WicketTestCase {
```

```
public ConfirmDeleteBehaviorTest(String name) {
  super(name);
}

public void testDeleteBehaviorPresence() throws Exception {
  // Set the system property for the first time.
  System.setProperty("wicket.replace.expected.results", "arbitrary value");
  // executeTest is defined in WicketTestCase.
  executeTest(ConfirmDeleteBehaviorTestPage.class,
      "ConfirmDeleteBehaviorTestPage-expected.html");
}
}
```

A Sneak Peek into Wicket 2.0

Wicket developers are currently working on the 2.0 release of the product. Wicket 2.0, like any other product release, is expected to improve upon the previous versions. Significantly, Wicket adopts Java 5 at its core in its 2.0 release. There are quite a few improvements such as the *constructor refactor* and *Converter API* changes, and you get a look at them in more detail in the subsequent sections.

HOW TO OBTAIN AND BUILD WICKET 2.0

Some of the significant Wicket 2.0 features discussed in the upcoming text are based on the Wicket 2.0 Subversion repository trunk code base as of the *day* this chapter was being written. The features discussed here are not *likely* to change by the time a stable version of Wicket 2.0 is released. Wicket employs Maven 2.0 in order to build a distributable artifact. So building a Wicket release on your own just boils down to obtaining the source code from Wicket's Subversion repository and running the `mvn -Dmaven.test. skip=true install` command on the command line. Maven 2.0 is available for download here: `http://maven.apache.org/maven2`. *Wicket 2.0 requires Java 5 to be installed.*

Taking Advantage of Java 5 Features

In Java 5, a feature called *covariant returns* allows a subclass to override a superclass method and narrow the return type of the method. Although this sounds like a reasonable thing to do, Java versions prior to Java 5 don't allow you to do that. You can use this feature as shown in Listing 9-14, for example.

Listing 9-14. *Using Java 5 Covariance to Return the WebSession Subclass*

```java
import wicket.Session;
import wicket.markup.html.WebPage;

public class BasePage<T> extends WebPage<T> {

  // Illegal in Java versions < 5

  @Override
  public ValidationAppSession getSession() {
    return (ValidationAppSession)Session.get();
  }
}
```

All application pages can then extend BasePage and access the ValidationAppSession class without an explicit cast. Note that this is not possible in Wicket 1.2 for another reason besides the fact that you might be employing Java 1.4: wicket.Session.getSession() is final in Wicket 1.2. If you are in the habit of reading the session off of the ThreadLocal variable, you can have something along the lines of Listing 9-15.

Listing 9-15. *Using Java5 Covariance to Return the WebSession Subclass*

```java
public final class ValidationAppSession extends WebSession{
  public static ValidationAppSession get(){
    return (ValidationAppSession)Session.get();
  }
  //..
}
```

This is even better. You don't need the BasePage (see Listing 9-14) to narrow the return type of getSession(). Your application pages can directly read it off the ThreadLocal without doing an explicit cast.

Wicket 2.0 Constructor Refactor

Until Wicket 1.2, you were required to build the component tree on the server by adding the child component to its parent by using the Component.add() method, as shown in Listing 9-16.

Listing 9-16. *The Wicket 1.2 Way of Associating Parent and Child Components*

```java
public class UserProfilePage extends WebPage{
  public UserProfilePage(){
    Form form = new UserProfileForm("userProfileForm");
    // userName TextField is a child component of Form.
    form.add(new TextField("userName"));
    // Page ("this") is Form component's parent.
    this.add(form);
  }
}
```

This way of associating the child component with its parent has been removed in favor of passing in the parent using the component's constructor. So instead of using `Component.add()` to build the component hierarchy, you need to pass in the correct parent to reflect the hierarchy, as demonstrated in Listing 9-17.

Listing 9-17. *Specifying the Parent Component During the Construction of the Child Component, As Wicket 2.0 Requires*

```
public class UserProfilePage extends WebPage{
  public UserProfilePage(){
    // The argument "this" indicates the Page is the
    // Form's parent.
    Form form = new UserProfileForm(this,"userProfileForm");
    new TextField(form,"userName");
  }
}
```

This ensures that when you add a child component to its parent, the component tree consisting of the parent component to the enclosing Page is already set up. This allows for a few interesting capabilities:

- *Better error reporting*: In Wicket, the Page component hierarchy has to match the corresponding template hierarchy. In Wicket versions prior to 2.0, hierarchy mismatch, if any, is detected during the page render phase, which occurs after the component construction phase. But in Wicket 2.0 onward, it will be detected during component construction time , thereby resulting in the error being reported earlier. It also allows Wicket to do precise error reporting. This means that you would get an exception that points you to the line in your code that caused the mismatch.

- *Availability of template markup attributes during component construction*: Wicket 1.2 allows you to access the component markup attributes through the `Component.onComponentTag(ComponentTag tag)` callback. Alternatively, you also saw how Wicket allows you to attach behaviors to components, which in turn gives you access to the markup attributes through the `IBehavior.onComponentTag()` callback. Essentially, there was never an option to access the markup attributes during component construction in Wicket 1.2. But the constructor change incorporated as a part of Wicket 2.0 allows you to access markup attributes from within your constructor. So instead of attaching a `wicket.IBehavior` implementation as in Listing 9-18, you include the code in Listing 9-19 in the component constructor.

Listing 9-18. *The Wicket 1.2 Way of Adding/Modifying Markup Attributes*

```
aWicketComponent.add(new SimpleAttributeModifier("class","error")
```

Listing 9-19. *The Wicket 2.0 Way of Adding/Modifying Markup Attributes*

```
public class WicketComponent extends Panel{
    public WicketComponent(MarkupContainer container,String id, IModel model){
        getMarkupAttributes().put("class","error")
    }
}
```

We will further delve into this feature so that you have a good understanding of what it actually buys you in the section "Availability of Markup Attributes at the Time of Component Construction." Now is the time to actually get a feel for the Wicket 2.0 programming style. I'm sure by now you must be really curious to know how a Page developed in the next release of Wicket will look like. To demonstrate, Listing 9-20 shows how the UserProfilePage that you developed in Chapter 1 looks in a Wicket 2.0 environment.

Listing 9-20. *A Wicket 2.0–Compliant UserProfilePage Class*

```
public class UserProfilePage<T> extends BasePage<T> {

    public static final List<String> COUNTRIES = Arrays.asList(new String[] {
        "India", "US", "UK" });

    public UserProfilePage() {

        UserProfile userProfile = new UserProfile();
        CompoundPropertyModel<UserProfile> userProfileModel =
            new CompoundPropertyModel<UserProfile>(userProfile);

        // Note that the Form specifies "this" (the Page) as its Parent.
        UserProfileForm form = new UserProfileForm(this, "userProfile",
                    userProfileModel);
        new FeedbackPanel(this, "feedback");



    }

    class UserProfileForm extends Form<UserProfile> {

        public UserProfileForm(MarkupContainer parent, String id,
            IModel<UserProfile> model) {
            super(parent, id, model);
            // Form is the parent of the name TextField component.
            new TextField(this, "name").setRequired(true);
            new TextField(this, "address");
            new TextField(this, "city");
```

```
    // The DropDownChoice is configured to work with instances of String as
    // model objects.
    new DropDownChoice<String>(this, "country", COUNTRIES);
    new TextField(this, "pin", int.class).add(
      NumberValidator.range(0, 5000)).setRequired(true);
    new TextField<PhoneNumber>(this, "phoneNumber", PhoneNumber.class);
  }

  public void onSubmit() {
    info(getModelObjectAsString());
  }


 }
}
```

Notice how the components specify their parent during construction. It's also worth noting that Wicket 2.0 employs Java generics extensively in order to make the models more readable.

You already know that you can access markup attributes during component creation. In the next section, you'll see an example that demonstrates the flexibility that this feature offers.

Availability of Markup Attributes at the Time of Component Construction

Consider a Panel that supports a high level of configuration in its design and that expects these design-time parameters to be specified at construction time so that it can render accordingly on the browser based on the configuration parameters you supply (see Listing 9-21). Prior to Wicket 2.0, you would be required to specify these parameters through Java code. But since these parameters are specific to the presentation layer and control the visual appearance of the component, it's better that they be specified in the template rather than in the Page class. This allows the HTML designer to specify some design parameters. But it's important to remember that this feature goes against Wicket's doctrine of keeping the template information to a minimum and managing the rest through plain Java code.

Listing 9-21. *A Panel That Allows Design-Time Parameter Configuration*

```
package com.apress.wicketbook.validation;

// Usual imports
import com.apress.wicketbook.validation.DesignTimeAttributeHandler;

public class ConfigurablePanel extends Panel {

  // Configuration parameters of type int and String
  private String foo;
  private int bar;
```

```
    // A PhoneNumber as a design-time attribute really doesn't make sense
    // in the real world!
    // It is used here only to demonstrate a Wicket feature.

    private PhoneNumber phoneNumber;

    public ConfigurablePanel(MarkupContainer parent,String id,
            IModel model){
      super(parent,id,model);

      // Look up the attributes and configure the Panel.
      setFoo(getMarkupAttributes().get("wicket_rocks:foo"));
      setBar(Integer.parseInt(getMarkupAttributes().get("wicket_rocks:bar")));
      setPhoneNumber(new PhoneNumberConverter().convertToObject(
        getMarkupAttributes().get("wicket_rocks:phoneNumber")));
    }

  public int getBar() {
    return bar;
  }

  public void setBar(int bar) {
    this.bar = bar;
  }

  public String getFoo() {
    return foo;
  }

  public void setFoo(String foo) {
    this.foo = foo;
  }

  public PhoneNumber getPhoneNumber() {
    return phoneNumber;
  }

  public void setPhoneNumber(PhoneNumber phoneNumber) {
    this.phoneNumber = phoneNumber;
  }
}
```

Listing 9-22 demonstrates the way you would specify the configuration parameter in the template.

Listing 9-22. *A Page That Uses and Configures the Configurable Panel at Design Time*

```
<html>
<form wicket:id="form">
  <span wicket:id="configurablePanel" wicket_rocks:foo="Wicket"
      wicket_rocks:bar="2" wicket_rocks:phoneNumber="123-122-1233">
  </span>
</form>
</html>
```

When constructing the Page, you need to make sure that you map all wicket_rocks:*xxx* attribute values to the ones specified in the Page class. If you require a similar ability for another component of yours, you would again be required to repeat the code that extracts the attributes and calls the setters. So let's try to bundle this behavior into something reusable. What you need is a utility that extracts all markup attributes from the template for a given component and, after making sure that those attributes are applicable to the component, invoke the corresponding setters on the component. You add a wicket_rocks prefix just to differentiate the attributes you are interested in from the normal ones (*wicket:id* for example), something similar to a namespace in XML. For configuring the values on the component, you can use Wicket's wicket.util.lang.PropertyResolver class. This class will take care of initializing the design-time parameters as long as it's supplied with an object (the component itself), an expression (the component attribute) to look for, and the corresponding value (specified in the template as markup attributes) that needs to be set (see Listing 9-23).

Listing 9-23. *A DesignTimeAttributeHandler Class to Extract and Configure Design-Time Attributes Automatically*

```
package com.apress.wicketbook.validation;

import wicket.Component;
import wicket.Session;
import wicket.WicketRuntimeException;
import wicket.util.lang.PropertyResolver;
import wicket.util.lang.PropertyResolverConverter;
import wicket.util.value.IValueMap;

public class DesignTimeAttributeHandler implements Serializable {

  /**
   * The attribute separator that separates the prefix and the
   * attribute name, e.g., wicket_rocks:foo="12" where "wicket_rocks" is the prefix,
   * "foo" is the attribute name, and ":" is the separator.
   */

  public static String ATTRIBUTE_SEPARATOR = ":";
    /*
     * @param attributePrefix
     *    The application-specific namespace to distinguish
     *    design-time parameters.
```

```
 * @param component
 *     The component whose design-time parameters
 *     need to be set.
 */

public static void handle(String attributePrefix,Component component){

    // Extract markup attributes from the template for a given component.
    IValueMap markupAttributesMap = component.getMarkupAttributes();

    PropertyResolverConverter prc = new PropertyResolverConverter(
        Session.get(), Session.get().getLocale());

    // Iterate through all the attributes and process only those that the
    // component might be interested in.

    for (Iterator iter = markupAttributesMap.keySet().iterator();
        iter.hasNext();) {

      String expression = (String) iter.next();
      String[] splitExpression = expression.split(ATTRIBUTE_SEPARATOR);

      // Ensure that the attribute prefix specified in the template is the same
      // as the one passed to this class.

      if (splitExpression == null ||
          splitExpression.length != 2 ||
          !(attributePrefix.equals(splitExpression[0]))){
        continue;
      }

      String value = markupAttributesMap.getString(expression);
      // The attribute value
      String actualExpression = splitExpression[1];
      try {
        // Invoke Wicket's built-in class to set the values.
        PropertyResolver.setValue(actualExpression, component,
            value, prc);
      } catch (WicketRuntimeException ignore) {
        // If the attribute name is specified incorrectly, signal it as a
        // warning.
        component.warn(ignore.getMessage());
      }
    }

  }
}
```

It's worth noting that PropertyResolver takes care of the required conversion as well when setting the values on the component. When adding the Panel to the Page hierarchy, make sure that you supply the attribute prefix—wicket_rocks in this case (see Listing 9-24).

Listing 9-24. *Specifying the Template Attribute Prefix When Creating the Component*

```
class MyPage extends Page{
   public MyPage(){
     Form form = new Form(this,"form");
     new ConfigurablePanel(form,id,new Model(),"wicket_rocks");
   }
}
```

You need to modify the Panel for accommodating the DesignTimeAttributeHandler as shown in Listing 9-25.

Listing 9-25. *Removing the Explicit Calls to the Setters and Instead Using the DesignTimeAttributeHandler Class*

```
public class ConfigurablePanel extends Panel {

  // Rest of the content is the same.
  public ConfigurablePanel(MarkupContainer parent,String id,
          IModel model){
     super(parent,id,model);

     /* You don't need these now!

     setFoo(getMarkupAttributes().get("wicket_rocks:foo"));
     setBar(Integer.parseInt(getMarkupAttributes().get("wicket_rocks:bar")));
     setPhoneNumber(new PhoneNumberConverter().convertToObject(
        getMarkupAttributes().get("wicket_rocks:phoneNumber")));

     */

  }

  public ConfigurablePanel(MarkupContainer parent,String id,
        IModel model,String designtimeAttributePrefix){
     this(parent,id,model);
     // Get DesignTimeAttributeHandler to set all the attributes.
     DesignTimeAttributeHandler.handle(designtimeAttributePrefix,this);
  }
  // Rest of the content is the same.
}
```

Hopefully the preceding sections have given you a good insight into the things that are coming in Wicket 2.0. However, any discussion on Wicket 2.0 features would be incomplete without looking at the revamped Converter API specifications. You will learn about the new converter design in the next section.

Wicket 2.0 Converter Specification

In Chapter 2, you looked at a custom converter for converting an HTTP string to a phone number class representation and vice versa. Then you also registered the converter with Wicket through the WebApplication subclass. But the process turned out to be quite tedious, as Wicket's 1.2 converter design isn't really that intuitive. As we discussed in Chapter 2, a converter's responsibility is to act as a translation layer between HTTP request string parameters and your model class. The Wicket 2.0 Converter API specification gets it right through the IConverter interface, which looks like what you see in Listing 9-26.

Listing 9-26. *Wicket 2.0 IConverter Interface Specification*

```
public interface IConverter extends Serializable{
  /**
   * Converts the given string value to class c.
   * @param value - The string value to convert.
   * @param locale - The locale used to convert the value.
   * @return - The converted value.
   */
  Object convertToObject(String value, Locale locale);

  /**
   * Converts the given value to a string.
   * @param value - The value to convert.
   * @param locale - Current locale.
   * @return - The converted string value.
   */
  String convertToString(Object value, Locale locale);
}
```

The IConverter intent is quite clear now: it includes a method to convert the supplied HTTP string parameter to the appropriate model class and another one to perform the conversion the other way around. Of course, nothing is better than looking at an example that demonstrates the design change. Try adapting the existing PhoneNumberConverter to the new interface, as shown in Listing 9-27. Note that Wicket's AbstractConverter acts as the base class for all converters and implements the IConverter interface.

Listing 9-27. *Adapting PhoneNumberConverter to Wicket 2.0*

```
import java.util.Locale;
import java.util.regex.Pattern;
import wicket.util.convert.converters.AbstractConverter;
import com.apress.wicketbook.common.PhoneNumber;

public class PhoneNumberConverter extends AbstractConverter {
```

```java
static Pattern pattern = Pattern.compile("\\d{3}-\\d{3}-\\d{4}");

private String stripExtraChars(String input) {
  return input.replaceAll("[^0-9]", "");
}
/**
 * @see wicket.util.convert.IConverter# convertToObject(String value,
 *      Locale locale)
 */

public Object convertToObject(String value, Locale locale) {
  // Before converting the value, make sure that it matches the pattern.
  if (!pattern.matcher((String) value).matches()) {
    throw newConversionException("Supplied value " + value
        + " does not match the pattern " + pattern.toString(),
        value, locale);
  }

  String numericString = stripExtraChars((String) value);
  String areaCode = numericString.substring(0, 3);
  String prefix = numericString.substring(3, 6);
  String number = numericString.substring(6);
  PhoneNumber phoneNumber = new PhoneNumber(areaCode, prefix, number);
  return phoneNumber;

}

@Override
protected Class getTargetType() {
  return PhoneNumber.class;
}

/**
 * @see wicket.util.convert.IConverter#convertToString(Object value,
 *      Locale locale)
 */

@Override
public String convertToString(Object value, Locale locale) {
  if (value == null) {
    return null;
  }
  PhoneNumber phoneNumber = (PhoneNumber) value;
  return phoneNumber.getPrefix() + "-" + phoneNumber.getAreaCode() + "-"
      + phoneNumber.getNumber();
}
}
```

Now the only thing that remains is registering this converter with Wicket. A safe way to do this would be to wrap the existing IConverterLocatorFactory so that you don't end up over-writing the previously existing converters inadvertently. An IConverterLocatorFactory is a factory that creates and configures instances of IConverter. So let's define our Custom→ ConverterLocatorFactory, which wraps the IConverterLocatorFactory (a typo seems to have crept into the Converter-related class names in the current Wicket 2.0 code base and is likely to be fixed in the subsequent release) supplied to it, as shown in Listing 9-28.

Listing 9-28. *A Custom IConverterLocatorFactory That Wraps the Existing Implementation*

```
import wicket.ICoverterLocator;
import wicket.util.convert.ICoverterLocatorFactory;

public class CustomConverterLocatorFactory implements ICoverterLocatorFactory {
  // Previously existing ICoverterLocatorFactory
  ICoverterLocatorFactory old;

  public CustomConverterLocatorFactory(ICoverterLocatorFactory old){
    this.old = old;
  }

  /**
   * @see wicket.util.convert.ICoverterLocatorFactory#newConverterSupplier()
   */
  // IConverterLocator is discussed in the text that follows.
  public ICoverterLocator newConverterSupplier() {
    return new CustomConverterLocator(old.newConverterSupplier());
  }
}
```

An IConverterLocator could be thought of as a repository of converters for supported types. Essentially the onus of returning the correct wicket.IConverter for a supplied type rests with the IConverterLocator implementation. Wicket will call upon this class to fetch the IConverter to do the conversion from the string-based HTTP request parameters to the underlying model type and vice versa when rendering a component on the browser. In the implementation shown in Listing 9-29, you check whether the custom converter can handle the type conversion and delegate it to the "wrapped" IConverter otherwise.

Listing 9-29. *A Custom IConverterLocator That Wraps the Previously Existing ConverterLocator*

```
import wicket.util.convert.IConverter;
import wicket.ICoverterLocator;
// Other imports
public class CustomConverterLocator implements ICoverterLocator {

  /** Maps classes to ITypeConverters. */
  private final Map<Class, IConverter> classToConverter =
          new HashMap<Class, IConverter>();
```

```
/** Previously existing IConverterLocator **/
ICoverterLocator old;

public CustomConverterLocator(ICoverterLocator old) {
  this.old = old;
  // Set up the custom converter.
  set(PhoneNumber.class, new PhoneNumberConverter());
}

// Check if you can handle the conversion, else delegate it to the
// wrapped IConverterLocator instance.
public IConverter getConverter(Class type) {
  if (classToConverter.containsKey(type)) {
    return classToConverter.get(type);
  } else {
    return old.getConverter(type);
  }
}

protected void set(Class type, IConverter converter) {
  classToConverter.put(type, converter);
}
}
```

There is one final configuration setting that is required—registering CustomConverter➥
LocatorFactory with Wicket's Application class, and Listing 9-30 shows how it's done.

Listing 9-30. *Registering the New IConverterLocatorFactory with WebApplication*

```
import wicket.util.convert.ICoverterLocatorFactory;

public class ValidationApplication extends WebApplication {

  public void init() {
    super.init();

    // Retrieve the existing IConverterLocatorFactory
    ICoverterLocatorFactory old = getApplicationSettings()
      .getConverterSupplierFactory();
    // and register the custom implementation, passing in the
    // previously existing implementation.
    getApplicationSettings().setConverterSupplierFactory(
        new CustomConverterLocatorFactory(old));
  }
  //..
}
```

Changes to the Model API for Added Flexibility

In Wicket 1.2, the IModel.setObject() and IModel.getObject() methods have the component instance passed in as an argument. Most newcomers to Wicket find it to be a little strange to override this method in their model implementation. Wicket 2.0 removes this additional component argument, making it easier to understand when overriding these methods. So make sure that you modify the method signatures accordingly when overriding these methods in your custom model class (see Listing 9-31).

Listing 9-31. *Differences in the Signature of Wicket 1.2 and 2.0 Model Classes*

```
// Wicket 1.2 MyCustomModel
import wicket.model.Model;
Class MyCustomModel extends Model{
  public Object getObject(Component component){
    return  <Some_Model_Object>;
  }
}

// Wicket 2.0 MyCustomModel
import wicket.model.Model;
Class MyCustomModel extends Model{
  public Object getObject(){
    return  <Some_Model_Object>;
  }
}
```

Summary

Wicket supports out-of-the-container testing by supplying a set of framework-specific mock objects. WicketTester and FormTester are the classes you need to be looking at when writing unit tests for Wicket Pages and components (Panels). WicketTester has assert*XXX*() methods that allow you to verify the presence of components, error messages, page navigation through links, and so on. FormTester is of great help when dealing with FormComponents values, simulating form submit action and later verifying that the backing model objects got updated in the desired manner. We also discussed the drawbacks of the current Wicket unit testing framework. You were then introduced to some of the features of Wicket 2.0, such as constructor changes, access to markup attributes at the time of component construction, revamped converter design, and changes introduced in Wicket 2.0's Model API.

Index

You Need the Companion eBook

Your purchase of this book entitles you to buy the companion PDF-version eBook for only $10. Take the weightless companion with you anywhere.

We believe this Apress title will prove so indispensable that you'll want to carry it with you everywhere, which is why we are offering the companion eBook (in PDF format) for $10 to customers who purchase this book now. Convenient and fully searchable, the PDF version of any content-rich, page-heavy Apress book makes a valuable addition to your programming library. You can easily find and copy code—or perform examples by quickly toggling between instructions and the application. Even simultaneously tackling a donut, diet soda, and complex code becomes simplified with hands-free eBooks!

Once you purchase your book, getting the $10 companion eBook is simple:

❶ Visit **www.apress.com/promo/tendollars/**.

❷ Complete a basic registration form to receive a randomly generated question about this title.

❸ Answer the question correctly in 60 seconds, and you will receive a promotional code to redeem for the $10.00 eBook.

2560 Ninth Street • Suite 219 • Berkeley, CA 94710

eBookshop

Printed in the United States
By Bookmasters